RIMBAUD

Rimbaud

VISIONS AND HABITATIONS

Edward J. Ahearn

University of California Press
Berkeley · Los Angeles · London

This book has been published with the help of a subvention from Brown University, for which the author is grateful.

University of California Press
Berkeley and Los Angeles, California

University of California Press, Ltd.
London, England

© 1983 by
The Regents of the University of California

Library of Congress Cataloging in Publication Data
Ahearn, Edward J.
    Rimbaud, visions and habitations.
    Includes bibliographical references and index.
    1. Rimbaud, Arthur, 1854–1891—Criticism and
interpretation. I. Title.
PQ2387.R5Z53   841'.8   82-2776
ISBN 0-520-04591-2   AACR2

Printed in the United States of America

1 2 3 4 5 6 7 8 9

pour Michèle

Contents

Acknowledgments

Evidently this study has personal and professional importance for me, and I want to thank those who have given me support in my training and work on it: my parents, Harry and Gertrude Ahearn; my children, Sally and Ed; teachers, critics and friends, including Edmund Tolk, Brother Basilides Andrew O'Connor, F.S.C., Peter Demetz, Lowry Nelson, Thomas Greene, Kenneth Cornell, Cleanth Brooks, René Etiemble, Marcel Ruff, C. A. Hackett, W. M. Frohock, Richard Laden, Mary Ann Caws, Renée Riese Hubert, Robert Greer Cohn, Nathaniel Wing, Anna Balakian, and particularly René Wellek and Henri Peyre; former and current Brown University colleagues, especially Juan López-Morillas, Albert Cook, and George Morgan; David Pines and the Center for Advanced Study at the University of Illinois, Brown University, the Danforth Foundation, and the National Endowment for the Humanities, the last providing fellowship support that allowed me to complete this project; Pamela Stacey Renna and Caryl Morris, who assisted me with research on Rimbaud and French Symbolism; and indeed all the students in the departments of

French Studies and Comparative Literature, and the Human Studies program at Brown University, who helped me (within the framework of an innovative curriculum) to refine my views on Rimbaud, other writers, literary theory, and aspects of other disciplines. Nor do I want to forget those, regretfully no longer with us, who influenced and encouraged my work—the late Harry Blair, Rosalie Colie, and Reinhard Kuhn. I also must thank *La Revue de Littérature Comparée,* in which portions of chapter 3 originally appeared, and Roland Fischer and the American Association for the Advancement of Science for authorization to reproduce a diagram from his article "Cartography of Inner Space." (The figure first appeared in "A Cartography of the Ecstatic and Meditative States," *Science* 174 [1971], 897–904, copyright 1971 by the American Association for the Advancement of Science.) More than anything, however, I express my gratitude to Ann and Arnold Weinstein and to my wife, Michèle Respaut, with whom I want most of all to share this book.

Introduction

This study is comparative, thematically organized, and frankly humanistic. It aims at an understanding of Rimbaud's overall production in a wide-ranging and at the same time pointedly significant literary and intellectual context. It differs somewhat from formalist and post-structuralist emphases in recent criticism, with their versions of Rimbaud's work as defying traditional notions of structure and reference, as decentered and "unreadable"[1]—interpretations that contain much insight but that now need to be integrated into a comprehensive, insistently human perspective.

For Rimbaud is crucial to any estimate of the poetic act in our world. He has had and continues to have an extraordinary impact because his work bears powerfully on such concerns as the growth of the person; the desire for integral satisfaction; the connections among mind, language, and external reality; the imaginative individual in confrontation with modern society. For these kinds of issues to emerge fully, the thematic vitality of his work needs both to be reasserted and to be seen in an expansive and pertinent framework.

Despite the limitations of thematic studies with which we are now familiar, theme remains important because we *do* respond to content as generating form, articulating sensibility, and overflowing the text into our lives. To say this is not to minimize the importance of form, even the kind of form that subverts received notions of self, discourse, and meaning. It is to say, on the contrary, that form must be attended to because it resonates with significance, to argue that great literature opens our eyes to the troubling intensity of existence in the world not only of language but also of the psyche, of nature, and of history.

This series of terms implies the divisions of this book and, at the same time, suggests how unarbitrary they are. Arrived at through close study of Rimbaud, they seem to me right—representing his expression of fundamental experiences and concerns within a definable historical and intellectual setting. This is to say again that the thematic organization of this study is inseparable from its comparative method. Clearly, publications addressed exclusively to the analysis of one author have value. But at some point it becomes desirable to consider a major writer in ways that are both integrative and discriminating. We need to grasp underlying patterns amid the detail of a poet's entire production. But to gauge his or her significance, we also need an appreciation of individuality and value in relation to the productions of other relevant writers and intellectual figures.

Rimbaud, who has been given little comparative attention, stands up well to it.[2] He is a writer of rare intensity, whose importance nevertheless emerges effectively when his work is placed beside romantic and post-romantic poetry and related literary and intellectual materials. Precisely how I see him in relation to such writers, traditions, and ideas emerges in detail in the body of this study. Let me here summarize what I take to be the most significant emphases and analogues for the study of Rimbaud.

Chapter 1, "Childhood and the Origins of Poetry," pursues the persistence of childhood, origins, memory, continuity and rupture, innocence and vulnerability, erotic energy and surreal vision that makes of Rimbaud the inheritor and perhaps purest exemplar of the romantic poetry of childhood. Analysis of his work in relation to that poetry, especially in Blake, Hölderlin, and Wordsworth, as well as to the psychological tradition (in particular Freud, whose ideas dovetail closely with both thematic and formal features of such writing), allows us to assess the centrality of childhood in Rimbaud in terms that advance us beyond the considerable body of critical writing on this theme. For the intertwining of childhood and poetry concerns not only vision but also the temporal process, not only memory but loss. The comparison with romantic poetry and Freud thus uncovers a pervasive and *informing* element in Rimbaud's work. It accounts for a special blend of preternatural vision, persistence, loss, and discontinuous form—features visible from the earliest texts, through *Une Saison en enfer,* and on into a major series of *Illuminations,* which we can therefore see as characterized by a coherence of structure that has not been sufficiently remarked.

Chapter 2, "Ecstatic Realizations," investigates the bizarre expressions of frenzy, vision, sexual power, and savage dispersal in *Illuminations* such as "Barbare," "Solde," "Parade," and others. These poems are extreme versions of tendencies that permeate Rimbaud's writing; in the context of Freud and romantic poetry they appear as realizations of the absolute desire that is one aspect of the childlike. But in connection with a related current, that of visionary-ecstatic literature from Coleridge to Yeats and especially in Blake and Nietzsche, these texts assume another significance. Modern versions of an age-old aspiration to "altered states of consciousness," they are accompanied by numerous allusions to ecstatic traditions, grow from a visionary poetic with comparable associations, and are marked by thematics, imagery, and structural features that are similarly explainable. Nietzsche and Blake, and behind them the altered modes of experience they wanted to attain, thus give us renewed insight into the strange exaltation, typical formal elements, and *unity as a group* of these unique yet archetypal poems. Here again is thematic and formal coherence—as well as the possibility of understanding Rimbaud's deconstructed writing as a reenactment of an ancient rebellion against the constrictions of the rational and the real.

Between "Child" and "Ecstasy" there are important connections; but also between nature and city, which as symbol, context, and reality figure importantly under each of those first two headings. Chapter 3, "Visions and Habitations: Nature, City, and Society," treats these elements in Rimbaud against the background of nineteenth-century poetry and also of a poetic epistemology, a theory of creative perception, that draws on romantics such as Coleridge as well as on Marx and Engels. Nature and city are realms where we live and act, and also realities that we perceive, in part creating them through our perception. Such a perspective—man as fabricating reality through consciousness and action in history—allows for a significantly different emphasis in reading supposedly nonreferential *Illuminations* from "Fleurs" to "Promontoire." These poems *are* emphatically artificial, but they do open onto the realms of experience in the natural and man-made worlds. Indeed Rimbaud's nature poetry is one of the most beautiful produced in the wake of romantic literature. And throughout his writing we can trace the subtle but unmistakable links between consciousness, natural reality, the city, and the problems of man's existence in history and society. This approach, based on romantic concerns and Marx's thinking, is to my mind true to the reality of Rimbaud's writing, and chapter 3 contributes to the elaboration of a well-argued Marxist interpretation of Rimbaud, which has been slow to appear.[3]

Rimbaud's poetry of child and person, ecstatic gratification, nature, city, society, and history, in a comparative perspective: this summary states the contents of this book, as well as suggesting what I take to be the qualities of the most useful criticism—integrative and (to the extent of one's capacities) interdisciplinary, insisting on human significance, recognizing the interpenetration of language, psyche, and world.

Study of this sort is difficult, which in part explains the inordinate amount of time taken to complete this book. One must read in several domains, assess contexts, analogies, and contrasts with some delicacy, and then devise a form for presenting them without submerging the central figure. I have approached this task not only by using the unifying thematic emphases already described but also by dividing the three chapters into sections (as it happens, five in each chapter). In chapters 1 and 2 the opening sections treat numerous works by Rimbaud in a comparative setting, then the last sections bring that expanded understanding to bear on a detailed analysis of a series of *Illuminations,* followed by a concluding assessment. The material from other writers, presented in as concise a form as possible, supplemented by dense, unifying notes through which the reader may want to forage, thus consistently enriches our understanding of Rimbaud's work. Chapter 3, drawing on much that has gone before, requires less comparative preparation. Still the third section of that chapter systematically pursues Rimbaud's city poems, while the fourth opens beyond them to themes of society and history. The last section provides a unifying epilogue not only for the chapter but for the book as a whole.

Note on Sources and Translations

All quotations of Rimbaud are from *Œuvres,* ed. Suzanne Bernard, 2d ed., rev. (Paris: Garnier, 1960). For the sake of convenience I list here editions of other authors frequently cited:

Baudelaire, Charles. *Œuvres.* Bibliothèque de la Pléiade. Ed. Y.-G. Le Dantec. Paris: Gallimard, 1954.

Blake, William. *Complete Writings.* Ed. Geoffrey Keynes. London: Oxford University Press, 1972.

Freud, Sigmund. *The Standard Edition of the Complete Psychological Works of Sigmund Freud.* 24 vols. Ed. James Strachey. London: Hogarth Press, 1953–1974.

Hölderlin, Friedrich. *Sämtliche Werke.* 7 vols. Ed. Friedrich Beissner. Stuttgart: J. G. Cottasche, 1946–1977.

Hugo, Victor. *Œuvres poétiques complètes.* Ed. Francis Bouvet. Paris: Pauvert, 1961.

Nietzsche, Friedrich. *Werke.* 3 vols. and index vol. Ed. Karl Schlechta. Munich: Carl Hanser, 1954–1965.

Wordsworth, William. *The Poetical Works of William Words-*

worth. 5 vols. Ed. Ernest de Selincourt and Helen Darbishire. Oxford: Clarendon Press, 1941–1949.

Wordsworth, William. *The Prelude or Growth of a Poet's Mind.* 2d ed. rev. Ed. Ernest de Selincourt and Helen Darbishire. Oxford: Clarendon Press, 1959. Cited in the 1850 text unless otherwise noted.

Yeats, W. B. *The Collected Poems of W. B. Yeats.* New York: Macmillan, 1954.

All references in the notes are to these editions, and are reduced to essential information: titles, and volume and page numbers when necessary. Occasionally, for the sake of simplicity, book and line numbers of Wordsworth's *Prelude* and chapter or plate and line numbers of longer works by Blake are inserted parenthetically in the text rather than in notes.

Consonant with my presentation of a comparative perspective on Rimbaud as a writer of importance for Western literature in general, foreign language quotations are accompanied by translations. My practice is as follows. All citations of Rimbaud and citations of other poetry and prose when the original language is relevant to the discussion are given in the original; other prose passages are translated or paraphrased. Translations of foreign language quotations are provided in the text, except for passages repeated within a few pages, cognate with English, or directly explicated in my commentary. Similarly, in the interest of more streamlined sentences, foreign language titles are not translated. Translations of writers other than Rimbaud are mine, with a few exceptions indicated in the notes; those of Rimbaud are also mine, although I have consulted with profit the numerous and widely available English versions of his work: *Rimbaud: Complete Works, Selected Letters,* tr. Wallace Fowlie (Chicago: University of

Chicago Press, 1966); *Illuminations,* tr. Bertrand Mathieu (Brockport, N.Y.: Boa Editions, 1979); *Arthur Rimbaud: A Season in Hell, The Illuminations,* tr. Enid Rhodes Peschel (Oxford: Oxford University Press, 1973); *Arthur Rimbaud: Complete Works,* tr. Paul Schmidt (N.Y.: Harper & Row, 1976); *A Season in Hell and The Drunken Boat,* and *Prose Poems from the Illuminations,* tr. Louise Varèse (N.Y.: New Directions, 1945 and 1946, respectively). Finally, although some editions give Rimbaud's prose poems the title *Les Illuminations,* I follow Bernard's practice in not including the article. I frequently refer to *Une Saison en enfer* simply as *Saison,* and occasionally abbreviate other titles as well.

ONE

Childhood and the Origins of Poetry

The memories of childhood have no order, and
no end.
  Dylan Thomas

J'ai été comme un enfant
Et comme un homme
J'ai conjugué passionnément
Le verbe être et ma jeunesse
Avec le désir d'être homme
  Paul Eluard

Striking indeed is the romantic-modern preoccupation with the child. From Rousseau to the great poets of the nineteenth century, from major novelists (Dickens, Kafka, Grass) to the leading figures of psychology, the child has dominated literature and thought in unparalleled fashion. Perhaps, as Peter Coveney suggests, the disintegrating world order signaled by the French Revolution made reflection on the origins and continuity of the life of the individual a necessity. Certainly, too, Jung and Kerényi and Bachelard have shown us that the mysterious and mythic existence of the child constitutes a link between mankind and an ever-rarer awareness of Being. And, as Freud and the poets even more have revealed, the child is at the origin of any reflection about the vicissitudes of the self—the complicated pattern of possession and loss, of rupture and continuity that structures our view of reality as well as our adherence to a vision that refuses to be limited by its constraints.[1]

The writers to whom I shall allude are all important in these contexts, and each illuminates the case of Rimbaud—but none is more crucial than he. An exemplary but also unique temperament, he lived out, in personal and familial conflict, the most trying experiences of the child becoming man; he consecrated his youth to a poetry that largely grew out of such experiences; his themes and his overwhelmingly beautiful poetic expression constitute one of the single greatest realizations of the poetry of childhood, adolescence, and youth—more directly powerful even than the work of Blake or Wordsworth or Hölderlin. So much in Rimbaud's child poetry is lived intensely from within; it *embodies* in compelling form those fundamental human concerns—origins, being, ecstasy, vision, vulnerability, loss, violence, continuity, hope.

Origins

Origins, the pure and ultimate beginning, an aspiration to know the moment when we first came into existence—this primordial concern is given insistent meaning in the poetry of the romantic tradition. It is a mysterious quest ("Ein Räthsel ist Reinentsprungenes," according to Hölderlin's "Der Rhein"—the purely arisen is a riddle). And it is seen in Wordsworth's *Prelude* as ultimately unattainable. "Hard task," he says, "to analyze the mind," in which

> each most obvious and particular thought,
> Not in a mystical and idle sense,
> But in the words of Reason deeply weighed,
> Hath no beginning.
>
>   *(II, 228–232)*

Much later Freud asserted the persistence of childhood in dream, fantasy, neurosis—a persistence rarely (if at all) grasped directly, but rather displaced, repressed, projected on "screen memories," remembered in the form of constructions. This ungraspable persistence allows no clear perception of individual origin; but somehow that very imprecision is associated by writers such as Wordsworth and Coleridge with an awareness of the "unity of all" (*Prelude,* II, 221)—with a dim sense that beyond our limited being there stretches some far greater reality, so antecedent to our temporal perceptions as to seem timeless, without beginning. Gaston Bachelard puts it well: "Our reveries which turn toward the reveries of our childhood make us know a being that pre-exists our own, an entire perspective of *antecedence of being.*" The search for the origin of personal existence leads to a glimpse of a more deeply grounded life, to an intuition of Being.[2]

Noted in the early literature of psychology, this oceanic sense of being is visible in the water imagery of poets such as Wordsworth and Hölderlin in, for example, the recurrent motif of life as a river, rising from and returning to the ocean of Being. *The Prelude* is filled with such references to the origin of the mind, and the motif is at the heart of the "Lines" on Fox's death, in which death is seen as a return to Nature's "dark abyss" and in which water and sound imagery take us beyond stock allegory and powerfully evoke the fundamental reality that underlies all manifestations of life.[3] Hölderlin's "Der Mensch" and "Der Archipelagus" represent the beginnings of life and civilization as a flowering of islands from the depth of the sea, whereas "Der Rhein" uses the course of the river to figure the evolution of human life, again in a way that effectively communicates an impulsion to unity with the elemental reality of the world. Personified as a demigod, the Rhine is forced to go to the sea, despite its initial urge, characteristic of child poetry, to return to the origin. But the river never forgets the source in childhood and youth, "den Ursprung / Und die reine Stimme der Jugend" (the origin and pure voice of youth), just as in a more personal poem, "Stutgard," the poet cannot embrace the human community without first evoking the emergence of his own existence: "Heilig ist mir der Ort, an beiden Ufern, der Fels auch, / Der mit Garten und Haus grün aus den Wellen sich hebt" (Holy to me is the place, on both banks—the cliff also—which with green garden and house rises out of the waves).

Here, as in Wordsworth, is expressed a reverence for the place, the spot from which human life, habitation, and consciousness of nature well up from the fundamental waters. And when Wordsworth tries to return to his origin, his closest approximation is a different but equally elemental remembrance, of himself as "a five years' Child, / A naked Boy," bathing and plunging day-long in a stream or sporting, "A naked Savage, in the thunder shower" (*Prelude*, I, 291 ff., 1805–1806 ed.). Vigor and naked immersion in the flow of nature: such motifs, close to Rimbaud's depiction of the child, are developed in *The Prelude* by a succession of later memories involving bathing, drinking, sports, reflection in water, and absorption of the child into the environing natural scene. For the poet in later life, too, the effort to return through memory to the childhood experience is associated with a current of water imagery—the "waters, rolling from their mountain-springs / With a soft inland murmur" of "Tintern Abbey," a poem of personal memory; and the mythic evocation of the child's proximity to the sacred reality of Being in "Ode: Intimations of Immortality":

> Hence in a season of calm weather
> Though inland far we be,
> Our Souls have sight of that immortal sea
> Which brought us hither,
> Can in a moment travel thither,
> And see the Children sport upon the shore,
> And hear the mighty waters rolling evermore.

These texts of Wordsworth and Hölderlin are the proper context in which to set such poems as "Après le déluge," "Enfance," "Larme," and "Mémoire." "Après le déluge" is a parable of the growth of human society, as well as of the poet's situation and of the need for a revolutionary poetic act. But it is first and foremost a conjuring of the pure beginning or of the *idea* of such a beginning:

Aussitôt que l'idée du Déluge se fut rassise,
Un lièvre s'arrêta dans les sainfoins et les clochettes
mouvantes et dit sa prière à l'arc-en-ciel à travers la toile
de l'araignée.
Oh! les pierres précieuses qui se cachaient,—les fleurs
qui regardaient déjà.

As soon as the idea of the Flood had subsided,
A hare stopped in the clover and the swaying flower
bells and said its prayer to the rainbow through the
spider's web.
Oh! the precious stones that were hiding,—the flowers
that were looking about already.

Here the primal waters are evoked, in their astonishingly purifying virtue, but at the same time as immediately, and already, subsided, lost to consciousness, about
to be overcome by the filth and destructiveness of human
society (cities, slaughtered animals, sexual conflict, mur-
der, religion, commerce organizing and subduing the far
reaches of nature, a pervasive and crippling monotony).
Yet they are called upon again at the end of the poem, in
which we realize that the poetic act Rimbaud desires must
somehow recreate, bring back to consciousness, this ungraspable source—reason enough to assert the importance
of the romantic poetry of origins in his undertaking. And
the primary values are also the romantic ones: purity, the
innocence of the animal and vegetable orders, a veritable
natural piety, united, as in Wordsworth's "My heart leaps
up," with the sky through the spider web and the rainbow, that biblical symbol of unity.

The only appropriate human inhabitants of this realm
are children. In mourning, perhaps because their parents
died in the flood, but more fundamentally to betoken their

isolation from adults, they contemplate "marvellous images" as water still cascades down: "Dans la grande maison de vitres encore ruisselante les enfants en deuil regardèrent les merveilleuses images" (In the big glass house still streaming with water the children in mourning looked at the marvellous images). This sentence transforms human habitations through the sibilant liquidity of water and language ("ruisselante") and simultaneously underlines the child's capacity for vision ("vitres," "regardèrent," "merveilleuses images"). Then suddenly: "Une porte claqua,— et sur la place du hameau, l'enfant tourna ses bras, compris des girouettes et des coqs des clochers de partout, sous l'éclatante giboulée" (A door slammed,—and in the village square, the child spun his arms, understood by vanes and steeple cocks everywhere, under the glittering downpour). With a rapidity involving a certain discontinuity of action or perception, these lines create the "cosmic child" of Kerényi, Jung, and Bachelard: orphaned, freed from adults, like Wordsworth's child immersed in the streaming and gusting life of nature, spinning about in the wind, in complicity with the world ("compris"), self-absorbed but in contact, through Rimbaud's language, with an elemental dynamism, luminosity, and liquidity ("sous l'éclatante giboulée").

Similar notions are embodied in part I of "Enfance," notably in the second paragraph, which presents the child's origin, its fusion with nature and its emergence from the liquid world:

> A la lisière de la forêt—les fleurs de rêve tintent, éclatent, éclairent,—la fille à lèvre d'orange, les genoux croisés dans le clair déluge qui sourd des prés, nudité qu'ombrent, traversent et habillent les arcs-en-ciel, la flore, la mer.

At the edge of the forest—the flowers of dream ring,
burst, illuminate,—the girl of orange lip, knees crossed
in the clear deluge that gushes from the meadows, na-
kedness shadowed, traversed and clothed by rainbows,
flora, the sea.

The first paragraph of "Enfance" stresses the intensity of
the child's existence, "insolent," almost savage, as well as
its isolation from grown-ups; this paragraph emphasizes
rather the child as a virtual emanation of nature. A primal
rather than personal memory, this passage describes a very
early stage of childhood, in which the sexual distinction is
apparent, but other aspects of personal consciousness are
not.

Visionary in Wordsworthian terms, what is glimpsed
here is certainly also the realm of the oceanic ego-state, as
we are led to see by the structure of the single sentence
without a main verb: first the frame of vision against the
mysterious depth of the forest ("A la lisière"), then the
dreamlike atmosphere and the preternaturally visible child,
seated in the clear torrent (purity, permeability, transparence, dynamism), which in turn emerges from the natural
scene ("qui sourd des prés"). The girl seems to have been
produced by the landscape: all the verbs describe activity
by elements of nature, as the sentence captures the moment at which the natural gives rise to the human in the
form of a child. So intimate is her link with the natural
world that she is not simply naked, but exists as an elemental "nudité," shadowed, traversed, clothed by the
same pure aspects of nature that appear in "Après le
déluge"—here, in Rimbaud's magical phrase, "les arcs-
en-ciel, la flore, la mer."

This fusion of child and nature at the origin of life is
mythic; it is by definition a persistence of an absence, of

something that cannot be grasped. The course of "Après le déluge" and "Enfance," and of all Rimbaud's child poetry, as of romantic child poetry before him, testifies to this experience of loss, which indeed provides the dynamic structuring principle of this literature. In the third and fourth sections of this chapter I will verify this proposition in detail in the work of Rimbaud and others; for now it suffices to recall the importance of the theme of origins, the pervasive water imagery, and the paradox of loss and persistence throughout Wordsworth and Hölderlin as relevant for Rimbaud.

A well-known text such as "Mémoire," for example, takes on added meaning in this context. It obviously concerns the functioning of memory itself and involves the elements of association, displacement, discontinuity, and latent sexuality that Freud later stressed in the operations of the psyche. From that process there emerges a sexual and familial allegory, in part projected onto the world of nature, in part imaging the trauma of conflict and loss in Rimbaud's own family. These features of the poem are familiar, and do not require discussion here.

But the poem is also a drama of movement away from the immediacy of the origin. It begins, "L'eau claire; comme le sel des larmes d'enfance" (Clear water; like the salt of childhood tears), before evoking women's bodies. The loss of the origin is more elemental than the familial and sexual tensions that succeed it. An equivalence is made between sparkling liquidity and a childhood tinged with sadness, a sadness rendered desolate at the end by age, immobility, and impotence, the loss of transparency and freshness. Here Rimbaud offers an image of the poet late in life that is far more negative than that of the leech-gatherer in Wordsworth's "Resolution and Independence": "un vieux, dragueur, dans sa barque immobile, peine" (an

old man, dredger, in his motionless boat, struggles);
"Jouet de cet œil d'eau morne, je n'y puis prendre, / . . .
ni l'une / ni l'autre fleur" (Plaything of this mournful eye
of water, I can pluck neither the one nor the other flower);
"Mon canot, toujours fixe; et sa chaîne tirée / Au fond de
cet œil d'eau sans bords,—à quelle boue?" (My boat, still
stationary; and its chain drawn in the depth of this rimless
eye of water,—to what mud?).[4]

Another of the *Derniers Vers,* "Larme," also concerns the
child's elusive link with the world of nature, this time
with a different emotional tonality—a retrospective and
puzzled sadness that finally yields a certain assertion of
value and accomplishment. The speaker imagines his
former state, when he was older than the girl of "Enfance"
but nonetheless still a child, such as in the act of writing
he no longer is. This separation from a former self is
revealed by his questioning attitude as well as by the
muted, almost oppressive scene that he describes:

> Que pouvais-je boire dans cette jeune Oise,
> Ormeaux sans voix, gazon sans fleurs, ciel couvert.
> Que tirais-je à la gourde de colocase?

> What could I have been drinking in that young Oise,
> Voiceless elms, flowerless grass, overcast sky.
> What did I draw from the gourd of the colocynth?

This world was, nonetheless, that of the elemental child,
removed from human contact and even from the more humanized aspects of nature. Far from birds, flocks, village
girls, he would have been a "mauvaise enseigne d'auberge,"
hardly a good inducement to hospitality and society. In his
solitude he experienced an intimate closeness to nature that
is now evoked despite the distance of time:

> Je buvais, accroupi dans quelque bruyère
> Entourée de tendres bois de noisetiers,
> Par un brouillard d'après-midi tiède et vert.

> I drank, crouched in some heather
> Surrounded by tender hazel woods
> In a soft green afternoon fog.

The nearness of the natural scene is conveyed by the imagery and sound texture of "entourée," "tendres," "brouillard," "tiède"; and the child's existence in it, not quite as complete as that of the girl in "Enfance" (there is after all a self-conscious "je" speaking), is nonetheless expressed by similar motifs: his physical attitude ("accroupi"), and that fundamental act of contact with the world—"je buvais."

Then, in this narration ("puis"—the mark in so many Rimbaud poems of rupture as well as of temporal progression), important transformations occurred, embodied in images of change in nature, travel, sexual awakening, and frustration:

> Puis l'orage changea le ciel, jusqu'au soir.
> Ce furent des pays noirs, des lacs, des perches,
> Des colonnades sous la nuit bleue, des gares.

> L'eau des bois se perdait sur des sables vierges.

> Then the storm changed the sky, until evening.
> There were black countries, lakes, slender poles,
> Colonnades under the blue sky, stations.

> The water from the woods was being lost on virgin sands.

Of course, much of this scene is visible in the water itself, for in part "Larme" pursues the suggestions created by the changing images in the stream. As in "Mémoire," and like Wordsworth in *The Prelude,* Rimbaud is "incumbent o'er the surface of past time" (IV, 272), through memory interrogating the lost life in nature. And, though separated from his childhood, the poet asserts that like the fisher of gold or of shells, who seeks something precious in the depths of the sea, he *has* in fact drunk from nature: "Or! tel qu'un pêcheur d'or ou de coquillages, / Dire que je n'ai pas eu souci de boire!" (So! like a fisher for gold or shells, to say that I had no thought of drinking!).

Taken together, "Après le déluge," "Enfance," "Mémoire," and "Larme" testify eloquently to Rimbaud's preoccupation with the child as embodying a link with the origin of being, a link that endures, that is rendered present in these texts, yet one that is also, and inevitably, lost. Hence the emotional resonance of this poetry. Transfigured by beauty, but shadowed by desolation, the child's experience is asserted to be of continuing value, even if that value can only be formulated in what appear to be negative terms: "Or! tel qu'un pêcheur d'or ou de coquillages, / Dire que je n'ai pas eu souci de boire!"

Innocence and Experience

This fundamental ambiguity of the child as loss and persistence can be pursued under the category of *innocence,* a term having special meaning in Blake, but of general significance in the romantic tradition. Guiltlessness, intactness, self-possession, Freud's "primary narcissism," vulnerability to experience, closeness to death but also to poetry—all these elements are comprised in the child's innocence. In Rimbaud, whose unhappy childhood contrasts with the accents of joy that run through the poetry of Wordsworth and Hugo, these elements of innocence attain a poignant intensity.

Moral innocence—the purity of the child as opposed to the compromises, evil intent, and duplicity of adults—is a pervasive theme in romantic literature, from Rousseau's *Emile,* Blake's *Songs of Innocence and Experience,* Hölderlin's *Hyperion* and "Da ich ein Knabe war," to a series of often sentimentalized, sometimes moving texts by Hugo, in which the child's presence irradiates the existence of adults, bringing them joy, inspiring them morally and, in particular, enlightening the poet. The theme remains powerful far into the nineteenth and twentieth centuries, in the works of writers as different as Dostoyevsky and Prévert. And the purity of the child that Wordsworth wants to preserve in "Tintern Abbey" is recognizable still in Yeats's poems of "radical innocence," "A Prayer for My Daughter" and "Among School Children."[5]

Hugo's emotionalism, Wordsworth's faith in nature, Yeats's belief that "custom," goodness, generosity, and a sense of the body's and the person's organic growth can protect against the storms of life and teach us that our being is "self-delighting"—each of these differs from what we find in Rimbaud and yet is relevant to him, like fragments of a pure and gemlike existence to which he may be seen to aspire. There is much anger and guilt and self-condemnation in his work. But in "Matinée d'ivresse" and "Génie" he reaches for a state transcending traditional ethical distinctions. And in the *Saison* we see him searching for a tradition or culture in which to anchor his sense of his own innocence:

> La dernière innocence et la dernière timidité
> [The last innocence and the last timidity]
>   . . .

ô ma charité merveilleuse! ici-bas, pourtant!
[O my marvellous charity! here below, however!]

. . .

Apprécions sans vertige l'étendue de mon innocence.
[Let us appreciate without vertigo the extent of my innocence.]

. . .

Farce continuelle! Mon innocence me ferait pleurer. La
vie est la farce à mener par tous.
[Continual farce! My innocence would make me cry. Life
is a farce everybody has to lead.]

("*Mauvais Sang*")

Je suis esclave de mon baptême. Parents, vous avez fait mon
malheur et vous avez fait le vôtre. Pauvre innocent!
[I am enslaved to my baptism. Parents, you have caused my
unhappiness and you have caused your own. Poor innocent!]

("*Nuit de l'enfer*")

Ah! cette vie de mon enfance, . . . plus désintéressé que
le meilleur des mendiants, . . . quelle sottise c'était.
[Ah! that life of my childhood, . . . more disinterested
than the best of beggars, . . . what stupidity it was.]

. . .

cette pureté des races antiques!
[that purity of ancient races!]

. . .

O pureté! pureté!
[O purity! purity!]

("*L'Impossible*")

In this most compelling of personal reflections are so
many anguished, and sometimes self-ironic, signs of a continuing sense of childhood and of individual innocence, in
search of familial, societal, and cultural approval, but not

finding it. In Rimbaud's poetry the search yields neither the admiration of adults as in Hugo, nor an organic sense of culture as in Yeats, nor nature and the companionship of even a single sister as in Wordsworth's "Tintern Abbey," nor the comprehension of the poet-figure for the child. How different indeed are the texts by Wordsworth, Hugo, and Yeats in which the older poet implicitly or directly reasserts his own childhood in the comprehension of the life of his or another's children. For Rimbaud, on the contrary, innocence carries not joy but hurt, frustration, outrage.

Innocence is related to another significant aspect of the child in romantic poetry, one discussed by Freud: the child's intactness, its not having been sullied or shattered by life—more fundamentally its joyous totality of being. Jung sees the child as the symbol of the *"synthesis of the self,"* and in this he follows Freud, whose essay "On Narcissism" presents the child as fascinating to us because it is self-sufficient, inaccessible, its "own ideal." According to Freud we are envious of children because we have lost this primary narcissism, which may explain not only our overestimation of our children and love partners but also the attraction that child poetry holds for us.[6]

In fact the child's happy self-possession is a recurrent poetic theme. Its existence as a godlike being, the freedom that exists only in the child, comes, according to Hölderlin's *Hyperion,* from its unreflecting identification with its own being: "Es ist ganz, was es ist, und darum ist es so schön" (It is wholly what it is, and from that comes its beauty). Similarly Hugo, who calls the child "le seul être encor vierge et complet" (the only being still virgin and complete), thus uniting innocence and intactness. So also Yeats, whose "Prayer for my Daughter" and "Among School Children" are filled with images of natural joy and organic continuity (bird, tree, child, music, dance), and some of whose other poems represent what he calls unity of being by the figure of the half-crazed child, dancing in unreachable ecstasy.

But it is Wordsworth who perhaps saw most clearly this intriguing facet of the child's existence. In "Characteristics of a Child Three Years Old" he describes his daughter as a "happy Creature of herself / . . . all-sufficient," to whom solitude is "blithe society," who "fills the air / With gladness and involuntary songs." In "To H[artley] C[oleridge], Six Year Old," the "happy child" is seen as "exquisitely wild," pursuing his own unfathomable thought and language, fitting to "unutterable thought / The breeze-like motion and the self-born carol." "Lucy Gray" and the Lucy poems, among others, emphasize the child's solitude. "To a Highland Girl" and "The Solitary Reaper" develop the theme of the incomprehensible foreign language incarnating the self-absorbed and inaccessible life of the child or young girl, whereas the first portion of "Ruth" (before Ruth's unhappiness and madness) stresses the child's self-enjoyment. "Herself her own delight," the child Ruth was an unconscious, natural creature, like "The Green Linnet," about which Wordsworth uses similar language: "Behold him perched in ecstasies"; "Thyself thy own enjoyment."

Rimbaud's poetry is rarely if ever happy or delicate in the way that some of Wordsworth's texts are; rather the theme of the child's intactness has a strident urgency in his work, as exemplified by the intensity of the child, beyond the reach of adults, in the opening paragraph of "Enfance." *Une Saison en enfer* records the outcries of a person in the process of losing, or rather becoming aware that he has lost, that state of unconsciously unified energy: "Les criminels dégoûtent comme des châtrés: moi, je suis intact, et ça m'est égal" ("Mauvais Sang": Criminals are disgusting, like the castrated: as for me, I'm intact, and I couldn't care less); "N'eus-je pas *une fois* une jeunesse aimable, héroïque, fabuleuse, à écrire sur des feuilles d'or,—trop de chance! Par quel crime, par quelle erreur, ai-je mérité ma faiblesse actuelle?" ("Matin": Didn't *once* I have a lovely youth, heroic, fabulous, worth writing on leaves of gold—too much luck! By what crime, by what error, have I merited my present weakness?).

But the last sentence of the work also records the determination to recapture this unity of being: "et il me sera loisible de *posséder la vérité dans une âme et un corps*" (it will be permissible for me to *possess truth in one soul and one body*). "Loisible": the discovery of the conditions under which this goal is right and possible; "posséder": not a glimpse but absolute and lasting experience; and "la vérité" (truth, defined in "Conte" as the realization of essential desire) as unified in one's personal soul and body—these are projections of the child's narcissistic ego-state, inevitably lost by the adult, into a program for the future. Freud said it well: the development of the ego consists in the departure from primary narcissism and results in a vigorous effort to recover it. The fascination with the child's integrity of being, the painful loss of that state, attempts to rediscover or recreate it—as in child poetry generally—these provide the impelling energy of much of Rimbaud's development.

An aspect of the primary narcissism stressed by Freud, and paradoxically related to innocence, is the child's physical energy and intense erotic life. Coveney notes Freud's insistence on the sexuality of the young child, who comes as close as possible to embodying the pure pleasure principle, whose own body is the source of the greatest enjoyment, who is "polymorphously perverse," whose bisexuality may be at the root of later "perversions," whose narcissism may emerge as a form of homosexuality. All these emphases in Freud seem to counter the romantic image of the child but recall aspects of Rimbaud's poetry. And it is true, despite, for example, the animal vigor that Wordsworth attributes to the child, that in the child poetry of Wordsworth, Hölderlin, and Hugo a truly Freudian amnesia concerning infantile sexuality is the rule. Blake, however, is a notable exception and in this is quite close to Rimbaud. Consider, for example, this evocation of the vigorous and innocent sexuality of the child:

> Infancy! fearless, lustful, happy, nestling for delight
> In laps of pleasure: Innocence! honest, open, seeking
> The vigorous joys of morning light; open to virgin bliss.
> Who taught thee modesty, subtil modesty, child of night &
>   sleep?

Here Blake *equates* the child's sexuality with innocence. Backed by such passages, Norman O. Brown argues that, rightly understood, Freud's doctrine of infantile sexuality is in fact a reformulation of the child's innocence, that it is a vision of the guiltless joy to which the child is naturally heir before repressive tendencies set in.[7] In this perspective Rimbaud, whose attention to the erotic in the child certainly contrasts with the work of some romantic poets, can nonetheless be seen as related to the poetic tradition that stresses the child's self-enjoyment. In fact, Rimbaud's contribution is preciously realistic—for he shows us the child's and the adolescent's sexuality, suggests their capacity for ecstasy, and at the same time depicts the constraints which inhibit that capacity and before which the child is vulnerable.

The sense of inhibition and vulnerability is indeed strong. Expressions of loss are numerous: in the speaker's

reaction to his present state of weakness in "Matin" of the
Saison, in the adult's alienation from "l'enfance étrange et
[les] affections énormes" in "Guerre," and in his bitterness in "Jeunesse" at having lost the marvellous body of
childhood. But the child's exuberant sensuality retains its
force in Rimbaud's work, although perceived as lost, as
in these texts, or in the process of being destroyed, as in
the priest's perversion of the girl in "Les Premières Communions" (Rimbaud there calls Christ the eternal thief of
energy). It may be projected into a mythical past, as in
the early "Soleil et chair," which abounds in superbly
erotic satyrs and Venuses, or as in the more compelling
"H," whose "gestes atroces," "mécanique érotique," "dynamique amoureuse," "ardente hygiène des races," "passion," "terrible frisson des amours novices sur le sol sanglant" (atrocious gestures, erotic mechanism, amorous
dynamic, ardent hygiene of races, passion, terrible shudder of new loves on the bloody ground) are explicitly
related to childhood: "sous la surveillance d'une enfance"
(under guardianship by a childhood).

Here erotic experience comes shockingly to consciousness in connection with the child, and the concluding
riddle formula, "trouvez Hortense" (find Hortense), makes
it a realizable goal, not a lost past experience. This attitude is characteristic of Rimbaud, who even in defeat in
"Le Bateau ivre," looks *forward* to recapturing an elemental
vigor: "Est-ce en ces nuits sans fonds que tu dors et
t'exiles, / Million d'oiseaux d'or, ô future Vigueur?" (Is it
in these bottomless nights that you sleep and are exiled, O
million golden birds, O future Vigor?). How therefore not
to see in the child's original sexuality the motive force of
Rimbaud's ecstatic poetry, his search for "la santé essentielle," "un nouveau corps amoureux," "notre très pur
amour," "Jeunesse de cet être-ci: moi!", "jouissance de

notre santé, élan de nos facultés" (essential health, a new erotic body, our very pure love, Youth of this being: me!, rapture of our health, surge of our faculties)?[8]

But this attempt, though growing from the child's experience, is better studied in those ecstatic texts. The child and adolescent poems themselves are on the whole more realistic, more concerned with representing in concrete detail the imposition of the reality principle on the child's joy. Thus a number of verse poems concern adolescent sexuality. "A la musique," "Première Soirée," "Les Reparties de Nina," and "Roman" contain imaginings of encounters with girls, expressions of desire, evocations of the pleasures of love, and forebodings of rejection. "Sensation" and "Rêvé pour l'hiver" project erotic desire onto nature and travel, whereas "Au Cabaret-Vert" and "La Maline" record the satisfactions of real escape, one component of which is the agreeably buxom servant girl. "Vénus anadyomène," in contrast, expresses a violently negative attitude toward women, balancing the overestimation of them in "Soleil et chair" and "L'Etoile a pleuré rose." But it is in "Les Poètes de sept ans" and "Les Sœurs de charité" that the child's and the adolescent's narcissism and sexuality are most convincingly shown in opposition to disappointing aspects of reality—and also as at the root of Rimbaud's vocation for poetry.

These poems reveal a lucid sense of narcissistic and erotic elements, reconstructed and projected by the sixteen-year-old poet in images of himself at the ages of seven and twenty. In the one poem we see the youth—eyes gleaming, brown skinned, "le beau corps de vingt ans qui devrait aller nu" (the beautiful twenty-year-old body that should go naked); in the other, the seven-year-old, rubbing his groin, shocking his mother by his activities with the neighborhood children who smell of excrement, skir-

mishing with the daughter of the neighboring working
family:

> . . . il lui mordait les fesses,
> Car elle ne portait jamais de pantalons;
> —Et, par elle meurtri des poings et des talons,
> Remportait les saveurs de sa peau dans sa chambre.

> . . . he would bite her cheeks,
> Because she never wore underwear;
> —And, beaten by her fists and heels,
> Would take the savor of her skin back to his room.

These texts thus give us idealized and realistic versions
of sexual innocence: the young poet-figure is virginally
beautiful in "Les Sœurs de charité," intensely sexual in
"Les Poètes de sept ans." In both he runs up against the
constraints of reality: the ugliness of the world, which
provokes a deep and eternal wound in the poetic parable
of "Les Sœurs de charité," and the mother, with all that
she represents of the truly narrow and destructive in religion, family, society, in the autobiographical "Les Poètes
de sept ans." And both poems are true to Freud's assertion that primary narcissism and infantile sexuality are
major sources of artistic activity when they are sublimated
or channeled into the "reserve" realm of fantasy in the
wake of the onslaught of the reality principle. In "Les
Sœurs de charité" the shock of reality leads to a succession of displacements and sublimations. When woman
does not satisfy him, the poet's energy goes to nature,
political activity, intellectual effort: "la Muse verte et la
Justice ardente," "la science aux bras almes," "la nature
en fleur," "la noire alchimie et les saintes études." At the
end, only death ("O Mort mystérieuse, ô sœur de

charité") seems to remain. "Les Poètes de sept ans," less
drastic, concludes with images of solitude and voyage
after a series of motifs in which sexual energy is trans-
posed into nature and other imaginative domains:

> . . . les deux poings
> A l'aine, et dans ses yeux fermés [il] voyait des points.
> [. . . both hands
> At his groin, and in his closed eyes he would see points.]
> . . .
> A sept ans, il faisait des romans, sur la vie
> Du grand désert, où luit la Liberté ravie
> [At seven, he composed novels on the life
> Of the great desert, where ravished Liberty gleams]
> . . .
> Il s'aidait
> De journaux illustrés où, rouge, il regardait
> Des Espagnoles rire et des Italiennes.
> [He helped himself
> with illustrated papers in which, blushing red, he looked
> at laughing Spanish and Italian women.]
> . . .
> Il rêvait la prairie amoureuse . . .
> . . . pubescences d'or
> [He dreamed of the amorous prairie
> . . . pubescences of gold]

In these two poems, therefore, innocence and creativity
are linked to infantile and adolescent sexuality in ways that
illustrate Blakean and Freudian propositions. But the
dominant note is of the resistance of the real, before which
the child-adolescent-artist remains vulnerable. "Les Sœurs
de charité" and "Les Poètes de sept ans" therefore accentuate a further meaning of the child's innocence—its submission to reality, its potential for suffering and deformation.
Everything that I have said about Rimbaud implies this

vulnerability in the face of life, this sense of the inevitability of suffering:

> La dernière innocence et la dernière timidité. . . . Ne
> pas porter au monde mes dégoûts et mes trahisons.
>   Allons! La marche, le fardeau, le désert, l'ennui et la
> colère.
>
> (*"Mauvais Sang"*)

> The last innocence and the last timidity. . . . Not to
> carry to the world my disgusts and my betrayals.
>   Let's go! The march, the burden, the desert, the bore-
> dom and the anger.

Consciousness of such harsh necessity, and a corresponding sadness, are widespread in the literature preceding Rimbaud—in Hölderlin's lament in *Hyperion* that men drive the child from his paradise before nature does, in the structure of loss in "Da ich ein Knabe war" and "Hyperions Schiksaalslied," and in similar expressions of that theme in the second *Empedokles* dramatic fragment; in Coleridge's melancholy in beholding the face of a beautiful child; in Wordsworth's feeling that Hartley Coleridge is like a delicate dewdrop, easily soiled, easily slipping "out of life"; in Hugo's evocations of sleeping children, watched over by angels and the anxious poet who realize the impending awakening to reality of which the children are still unaware. Such feelings doubtless contribute as well to the use of motifs of pre-existence and disinheritance from Wordsworth's "Immortality Ode" to Baudelaire's "Bénédiction" and Hugo's *L'Art d'être grand-père*. Freud said that our extraordinary worry about children, especially our own, involves in part a projection onto them of our own narcissism, an assertion that goes far in explaining these elements of sadness and concern in nineteenth-century child poetry.[9] Even more so in Rimbaud we feel this concern for *himself,* despite the third-person speaker, generalizing titles, and dramatized situations of poems like "Les Poètes de sept ans" and "Les Effarés." His work at times seems an almost unmediated expression of the child in the very process of being subjected to Experience.

Among the evils of Experience are, first, the parents—supposedly most loving but at the same time the agents by whom the child is domesticated to adult existence. Their ultimate betrayal is their disappearance or death, which accounts for the numerous figures of lost, abandoned, and orphaned children that we encounter in the work of Blake, Wordsworth, and Hugo. One of the earliest texts that we possess by Rimbaud, "Les Etrennes des orphelins," treats this theme with a sentimentality that could be easily read as self-pitying. A somewhat later text, "Les Effarés," presents a nearly mythic dramatization of psychological and cosmic abandonment. The benign father figure, the baker, is presented amidst images of heat, food, and sexual accomplishment: "Ils voient le fort bras blanc qui tourne / La pâte grise et qui l'enfourne / Dans un trou clair" (They see the strong white arm that turns the gray dough and thrusts it into the clear hole of the oven). But he is unattainable by the children, who are lost in the cold outside, desperate and "blottis . . . / Au souffle du soupirail rouge / Chaud comme un sein" (snuggling in the breath of the red vent warm as a breast). Moreover, this allegory of separation from the parents is enlarged in the poem, made to represent a global loss, a universal feeling of exile. For the baker's fire is said to "souffle[r] la vie" (breathe out life) and is described as "ces lumières / Du ciel rouvert" (this light from heaven opened again).

The parents, of course, do not have to be dead or

absent to be the child's primary antagonist. Rimbaud was a victim of an absent parent and a repressive one, and has left us the poems to document both, "Mémoire" but especially "Les Poètes de sept ans." The latter of these repays further attention, as an exemplification of the child's unhappiness, against which the whole tradition of romantic poetry protested. To grasp this theme we will need to consider issues not only of parenthood but also of religion and education.[10]

We have seen that the mother in the poem is truly a figure of oppressive parenthood. She does not *see* her child, neither his enforced hypocrisies nor his awareness of her own hypocrisy: "Elle avait le bleu regard,—qui ment!" (She had that blue gaze,—that lies!). Scandalized by his sexuality, she seems a realistically drawn version of those figures in Blake who constrain their children, an agent of the system of religious and societal repression that Blake perceived in the "mind-forg'd manacles" of "London" and the "Priests in black gowns . . . bind-ing . . . my joys & desires" of "The Garden of Love," and that Hugo attacked in *L'Art d'être grand-père* and "L'Ane." In "Les Premières Communions" Rimbaud just as aggressively exposes the way in which the priest de-stroys the innocence of children, whereas in "Nuit de l'enfer" of the *Saison* he reveals how profoundly he himself was marked by religion: "C'est l'exécution du catéchisme. Je suis esclave de mon baptême. Parents, vous avez fait mon malheur et vous avez fait le vôtre" (This is the execution of the catechism. I am enslaved to my baptism. Parents, you have caused my unhappiness and you have caused your own). And in "Les Poètes de sept ans" the antireligious theme is equally important, for the child rejects God in favor of men and is fearful of the joyless discipline associated with religion:

Il craignait les blafards dimanches de décembre,
Où, pommadé, sur un guéridon d'acajou,
Il lisait une Bible à la tranche vert-chou.

He feared the livid December Sundays,
When, with pommaded hair, on a mahogany table,
He would read the cabbage-colored pages of a Bible.

But on a related issue, that of education, "Les Poètes de
sept ans" perhaps most urgently calls for comparison with
the romantic tradition of child poetry. From Rousseau and
Wordsworth to Yeats and Prévert, there is a sustained
criticism of education as consistently harming children.
Blake and Prévert represented education as a way of de-
stroying buds and caging birds; Hölderlin and Hugo saw
it as occurring too soon, prematurely depriving us of our
childhood; and Rousseau, Wordsworth, and Coleridge depicted it as unnatural, excessively rationalistic, producing
enfeeblement and boredom through constraint. Yeats wor-
ried about the danger of the body being "bruised to pleasure soul," while earlier Rousseau and Wordsworth had
been appalled by the self-displaying, conceited monsters
that education can create. Wordsworth perhaps speaks best
for them all, he who passionately desired "knowledge not
purchased by the loss of power!" (*Prelude*, V, 425).

But among all these writers, how many recount the
experiences of the child itself as effectively as Rimbaud in
"Les Poètes de sept ans"?

Et la Mère, fermant le livre du devoir,
S'en allait satisfaite et très fière, sans voir,
Dans les yeux bleus et sous le front plein d'éminences,
L'âme de son enfant livrée aux répugnances.

Tout le jour il suait d'obéissance; très
Intelligent; pourtant des tics noirs, quelques traits,
Semblaient prouver en lui d'âcres hypocrisies.

And the Mother, closing the homework book,
Would go away satisfied and very proud, without seeing,
In the blue eyes and under the brow filled with eminences,
The soul of her child given over to repugnances.

All day he sweated obedience; very
Intelligent; still some black ticks, some traits,
Seemed to witness sour hypocrisies in him.

"Very intelligent"—but under what pressure, and at what cost: given over to repugnance, sweating from obedience, his anguish expressed in nervous ticks, his candor turned into hypocrisy. This is the Rimbaud who achieved superlatively in school until the explosion came, the child whom Georges Izambard later described in this way: "a timid child, a bit stiff, well behaved and almost sweet, with clean nails, spotless notebooks, astonishingly correct homework, ideally scholastic classnotes, in short, one of those little exemplary and impeccable monsters, perfectly embodying the academic first-prize animal."[11] Izambard claims to have seen Rimbaud from the vantage of the kindly teacher—although we must not forget Rimbaud's ambivalence toward him in the first of the *voyant* letters. But Rimbaud's poem shows us the young poet more directly. He *was* the innocent and vulnerable romantic child, containing the seeds of great beauty and joy, but deformed by parents, religion, and education.

In authors like Blake and Hugo such a vision of the unhappy child is the starting point for a thoroughgoing critique of an oppressive society, and in chapter 3 I discuss similar themes in Rimbaud. In the texts presently under consideration, however, what strikes us most is the note of personal suffering, the experience of the child and adolescent expressing his sense of having been brutalized.

This suffering explains the virulence of Rimbaud's attacks against adult figures of authority in "Les Assis," "Les Douaniers," and "Accroupissements"—poems marked by anger, ridicule, the imagery of excrement and unnatural love. Hatred of such intensity does not evolve without negative effects on the psyche, as is shown in "Honte," in which the speaker accepts the image of himself as an "enfant gêneur" (bothersome child), full of ruses and treachery, literally stinking up everything. This text is filled with death imagery directed against the speaker by himself, but concludes with a desperate appeal for prayer—poignant inner poetry, expressive indeed of the plight of the "enfant gêneur." In "Les Chercheuses de poux" the movement is more positive: from the torment and indolence of the child, through the erotically tinged ministrations of the two women in delousing him, to a sensuous experience of release, almost of innocent happiness:

> Voilà que monte en lui le vin de la Paresse,
> Soupir d'harmonica qui pourrait délirer;
> L'enfant se sent, selon la lenteur des caresses,
> Sourdre et mourir sans cesse un désir de pleurer.

> And there rises in him the wine of Laziness,
> Harmonica sigh close to delirium;
> The child feels in himself, in tune with the slowness of the
>   caresses,
> A desire to cry ceaselessly surge and die.

Together these texts are remarkable in showing the violent feelings of the child in the face of the adult world, in revealing the sense of degradation to which he is prey and from which he needs to be saved. Even in a poem whose political implications are inescapable, "Le Dormeur du val," this emphasis on the suffering child remains important. The last line coldly asserts what we have gradually realized, that the soldier has been killed in battle. But there is no explicit criticism of war, nor even any expression of the soldier's (or child's) view—which at once explains the poem's effectiveness and its slight tendency to sentimentality. For what does strike us is its reassertion of the primordial image of the child in nature—its evocation, through light and liquid imagery, of the natural world and of the child-soldier's immersion in it: "un petit val qui mousse de rayons"; "la nuque baignant dans le frais cresson bleu" (a little valley foaming with rays; his nape bathing in the fresh blue watercress). The soldier's death is thus presented not as a military or political event but as an elementary impropriety in the order of things, a betrayal of health, nature, childhood and parenthood:

> Souriant comme
> Sourirait un enfant malade, il fait un somme:
> Nature, berce-le chaudement: il a froid.

> Smiling as
> A sick child would smile, he is napping:
> Nature, rock him warmly: he is cold.

A far more powerful poem, "Le Cœur volé," involves military figures but uses them to much more movingly assert a horrible loss of purity. It is an intensely personal text, not only in its use of the first person but also in the

way Rimbaud described it when he sent it to Izambard in
the first *lettre du voyant.* In seeming mockery, he asks if the
poem is satire, or poetry, then asserts that it is at bottom a
work of fantasy. Supposedly not serious, therefore—but at
the same time, while mocking Izambard, Rimbaud wants
to avoid his censure: "Mais, je vous en supplie, ne soulig-
nez ni du crayon, ni trop de la pensée" (But, I beg you,
don't underline in pencil, nor too much in thought either).
Indeed, behind the mystifying formulas of the letter and
the almost buffoonish qualities of the poem itself,[12] there
is an overt appeal by the suffering adolescent child, first to
Izambard, then, through the poem, to us: "Ça ne veut pas
rien dire" (This doesn't mean nothing).

As we read the poem, then, we are mystified and moved.
We comprehend all too well and are troubled by the atmosphere of imprecision (Are these men soldiers or sailors?), by
the overtones of sexual humiliation, and by the literally
realized *haut-le-cœur* (stomach heave) that W. M. Frohock
and Yves Bonnefoy perceive. The speaker imagines his heart
lying on the poop of a ship, "drooling" in the tobacco juice
and soup that the soldier-sailors have spat on it. That these
motifs imply the homosexual group rape of Rimbaud that
Colonel Godchot imagined is possible and unverifiable. But
some event or feeling of equal horror is certainly there, for
in its vague and brutal sexuality the poem conveys a sense of
an irremediable degradation. This degradation is communicated through imagery of liquids that have lost their purity
and become viscous and repulsive:

> Mon triste cœur bave à la poupe,
> Mon cœur couvert de caporal:
> Ils y lancent des jets de soupe,
> Mon triste cœur bave à la poupe.

> My sad heart drools on the poop,
> My heart covered with caporal:
> On it they spew streams of soup,
> My sad heart drools on the poop.

Intimately soiled, the speaker is ridiculed ("Sous les quolibets de la troupe / Qui pousse un rire général"), threatened in his sexuality ("Ithyphalliques"), corrupted ("Leurs quolibets l'ont dépravé!"). There is an appeal for purification: "O flots abracadabrantesques, / Prenez mon cœur, qu'il soit lavé!" (O abracadabrantesque waves, take my heart, let it be washed!). But at the end there remains a sense of disorientation, of the speaker's complete inability to cope with what has happened to him: "Quand ils auront tari leurs chiques / Comment agir, ô cœur volé?" (When they've used up their quid, how to act, O stolen heart?). This text is rooted in the personal history of Rimbaud and in the political events of his time, inviting reflection on the relationships between societal, military, and sexual oppression; yet the text remains more primary than all that, communicating an ultimate violation of the self, the destruction of the integrity of the child's being that is the meaning of innocence.

Pushed this far, suffering innocence comes close to death. The final vulnerability is naturally that of mortality, especially the child's, as Freud understood when he described the projection of narcissism onto the child as an attempt by the ego to shore up its weakest point, its fear of death. However, the death of the child, which haunts some romantic poets, is connected not only with its fragility but also with its intactness: if growing up is to lose childhood's self-possession, isn't death in some sense a protection of, a natural outcome of that innocence?

The first of these themes, the obsession with the child's vulnerability to death, is best illustrated in Hugo, in the massive personal sorrow of *Les Contemplations* and in other texts in which he laments the fact that children have "je ne sais quelle soif de mourir le matin" (an unfathomable thirst to die in the morning). Several of Wordsworth's poems involve a similar fear of death for the child, quite often by drowning. But the other dimension of the child's death, as fulfillment of its being, is perhaps stronger in Wordsworth—witness "The Danish Boy" ("Like a dead Boy he is serene"), the Lucy poems, and others concerning nature's "inmates," who seem fused with the natural world and who can retain that state only in death. In the famous passage about the boy of Winander in Book V of *The Prelude,* Wordsworth uses echo and reflection motifs to describe the boy's absorption in nature, which is followed, naturally and inevitably it seems, by his death. In one manuscript Wordsworth wrote the passage in the first person, a sign indeed that the child's unconscious immersion in nature, perhaps accomplished fully only in death and lost to the older poet, remained a compelling impulse in his developing poetry.[13]

A certain attraction to death and deathlike states or motifs, as related to the innocence of the child, is discernible in Blake's Thel, a pre-existent soul who declines to be born, refuses to confront the violation of life, and whose state is represented by images of childlike and natural purity (infant smiles, dreams, sleep, the rainbow, reflection of clouds in water) and by innocent and nearly insentient creatures (lilies, lambs, clouds, clods, worms). Related images of unconscious and fragile innocence appear in child poetry by Wordsworth, Hölderlin, and Hugo. There is probably some connection between such elements and the imagery of dream, nest, and birds in "Les Etrennes des orphelins"; the child-water-nature-death motifs in "Le Dormeur du val"; and Rimbaud's melodramatic and cliché-ridden "Ophélie," in which flower, nest, reflection, and drowning motifs illustrate a version of the child's death in nature: "ton cœur écoutait le chant de la Nature"; "la voix des mers folles . . . / Brisait ton sein d'enfant" (your heart listened to the song of Nature; the voice of mad seas broke your child's breast). In later works related imagery, stripped of its sentimentality and beautifully controlled, expresses a quite literal death wish; consider "Bannières de mai," "Le loup criait," and especially "Comédie de la soif": "J'aime autant . . . / Pourrir dans l'étang"; "fondre où fond ce nuage sans guide"; "Expirer en ces violettes humides / Dont les aurores chargent ces forêts" (I like as much to rot in the pond; to melt where this guideless cloud melts; Expire in these damp violets left by dawn in these forests). Similarly, we read of the speaker's exhausted state in "Délires II": "j'enviais la félicité des bêtes,—les chenilles, qui représentent l'innocence des limbes, les taupes, le sommeil de la virginité!" (I was envious of the felicity of animals,—caterpillars, which represent the innocence of limbo, moles, the sleep of virginity!).

But if the child's innocence, its intactness and its purity, involves a fragility that brings with it the threat of death, the movement of *Une Saison en enfer,* as of romantic child poetry in general (Blake, Wordsworth, Hugo, less consistently Hölderlin), involves a present attempt to overcome that threat: "Non! non! à présent je me révolte contre la mort!" ("L'Eclair": No! No! at present I am rebelling against death!). This is the sign of a persistence, of an attempt to overcome the weakness of the child. Beyond the search for the origin, beyond the child's innocence as self-possessed joy and vulnerability, there is the movement forward—indeed the preservation of childhood as the source and matter of the poetic project itself.

Poetry, Vision, Time

The bond between childhood and poetry is indeed pervasive, in Rimbaud as in the romantic tradition. We need to examine the significance of that bond, from early texts through the *Saison,* and also of recurrent themes and structures in the child poetry and Freud's work before we can most profitably undertake systematic treatment of the child poems in the *Illuminations.*

First then, two verse poems that, along with "Les Poètes de sept ans" and "Les Sœurs de charité," show how important is the connection between child and poet throughout the first phase of Rimbaud's production. "Ma Bohème," quite early, describes a successful experience of the young poet as he confronts the universe through a spontaneous, fantastic humor—indeed it is one of Rimbaud's happiest poems. Characteristically, it develops themes of departure and travel, as well as of nature, poetry, and love: "J'allais sous le ciel, Muse! et j'étais ton féal; / Oh! là! là! que d'amours splendides j'ai rêvées!" (I moved under the sky, Muse! and was your vassal; Oh! Oh! Oh! what splendid loves I dreamed!). The self-amused tone (this is already a retrospective poem) is heightened when the poet speaks of his indigent devotion to his vocation: "Mon paletot aussi devenait idéal"; "Mon unique culotte avait un large trou" (My coat, too, was becoming ideal; My only pants had a big hole). The second of these sentences exorcises the threats of orphanhood and sexuality associated with the children's *culottes* in "Les Effarés" and "Les Poètes de sept ans." For at the center of "Ma Bohème" there is again a

child-poet, who overcomes the danger of parental abandonment and attains a satisfying contact with the world:

> —Petit-Poucet rêveur, j'égrenais dans ma course
> Des rimes. Mon auberge était à la Grande-Ourse.
> —Mes étoiles au ciel avaient un doux frou-frou
>
> Et je les écoutais, assis au bord des routes,
> Ces bons soirs de septembre où je sentais des gouttes
> De rosée à mon front, comme un vin de vigueur.

> —Dreamy Tom Thumb, I sowed rhymes
> As I went along. My inn was at the Big Dipper.
> —My stars in the sky made a soft rustling sound
>
> And I listened to them, sitting on roadsides,
> Those good September evenings when I felt drops
> Of dew on my brow, like a wine of vigor.

With great confidence this passage conveys an intimate
and affectionate apprehension of the universe ("doux frou-
frou"), deriving the energies of the child from the "vin de
vigueur" of nature itself. So self-assured is the speaker, in
fact, that he concludes on a note of fantasy:

> . . . rimant au milieu des ombres fantastiques,
> Comme des lyres, je tirais les élastiques
> De mes souliers blessés, un pied près de mon cœur!

> . . . rhyming amid fantastic shadows,
> Like lyres, I plucked the elastics
> Of my wounded shoes, one foot near to my heart!

These lines recall the poem's subtitle, "Fantaisie," which
again emphasizes the victory over potential dread. (Rim-

baud later uses the same word to describe "Le Cœur volé"
to Izambard.) And this victory is impressive, the product
of a liberating imagination, capable of linking lyres and
shoelaces, of balancing humor and commitment, suffering
("blessés") with self-affection ("un pied près de mon
cœur"). "Mon cœur": the last words of the poem—is this
Rimbaud's most convincing statement of innocence?

"Le Bateau ivre" is more excited and more somber, and
in some respects almost inexhaustibly rich. I want to emphasize only its connections with the issues I have been
treating.[14] Its starting point is childlike, a dream of red-
skins, noise, color, violence, and liberation:

> Je ne me sentis plus guidé par les haleurs:
> Des Peaux-Rouges criards les avaient pris pour cibles,
> Les ayant cloués nus aux poteaux de couleurs.

> I no longer felt guided by the haulers:
> Screaming Redskins had taken them for targets,
> Having nailed them naked to colored stakes.

Moreover, comparisons with the child are used to express
the nature of the experiences that follow this liberation:
"plus sourd que les cerveaux d'enfants" (more heedless than
childrens' brains); "Plus douce qu'aux enfants la chair des
pommes sures, / L'eau verte pénétra ma coque de sapin"
(Sweeter than the flesh of sour apples to children, the
green water penetrated my hull of fir). The last lines intro-
duce another re-enactment of the oceanic child state:

> Et dès lors, je me suis baigné dans le Poème
> De la Mer, infusé d'astres, et lactescent,
> Dévorant les azurs verts; où, flottaison blême
> Et ravie, un noyé pensif parfois descend;

Où, teignant tout à coup les bleuités, délires
Et rhythmes lents sous les rutilements du jour,
Plus fortes que l'alcool, plus vastes que nos lyres,
Fermentent les rousseurs amères de l'amour!

And from then on, I bathed in the Poem
Of the Sea, infused with stars, and lactescent,
Devouring the green azure; where, livid and ravished
Flotsam, a pensive drowned man sometimes sinks;

Where, suddenly dyeing the blueness, deliriums
And slow rhythms under the gleams of daylight,
Stronger than alcohol, vaster than our lyres,
The bitter reds of love ferment!

The being of the world, characteristically expressed through bathing and reflection imagery (rendered almost infantile by "lactescent"), reconciling death with an elemental erotic power—this experience engenders the visions that are then recounted. These visions represent "ce que l'homme a cru voir" (what man believed he saw), and "homme" may be thought to contrast with "enfant." The importance of the childlike is especially evident at the moment of diminishing impetus, unsuccessful communication, signaled by the conditional: "J'aurais voulu montrer aux enfants" (I would have wanted to show to children). The true audience for the child-boat-poet's tale is made up of children; perception of the vision is therefore a function of becoming, or remaining, childlike.

But the vision does break down, and the adult structures and purposes initially rejected by the boat crowd in again at the end ("Je regrette l'Europe aux anciens parapets"), this time with accents of despair and imprisonment:

Je ne puis plus, baigné de vos langueurs, ô lames,
Enlever leur sillage aux porteurs de cotons,
Ni traverser l'orgueil des drapeaux et des flammes,
Ni nager sous les yeux horribles des pontons.

I can no longer, bathed in your languors, O waves,
Sail in the wash of the cotton transports,
Nor cross the pride of flags and flames,
Nor swim under the horrible eyes of prison ships.

Despite the continuing appeal of the exiled but still future "Vigueur" of the world, the child-boat-speaker's experience by the end becomes strongly negative. The death-wish re-emerges: "O que ma quille éclate! O que j'aille à la mer!" (O let my keel burst! O let me go to the sea!)—only to be gathered up in an image of the being who is at the origin of it all:

Si je désire une eau d'Europe, c'est la flache
Noire et froide où vers le crépuscule embaumé
Un enfant accroupi plein de tristesses, lâche
Un bateau frêle comme un papillon de mai.

If I desire a water of Europe, it's the puddle,
Black and cold, where toward the sweet-smelling dusk
A crouching child full of sadness releases
A boat frail as a butterfly in May.

The sad child, crouching over the water like the child in "Larme," the water now black and cold as at the end of "Mémoire": the poem ends with a return to this lonely figure, with a shrinking of the oceanic and visionary to the proportions of disabused experience, despondent memory, the horror and constraints of the real world.

"Ma Bohème" and "Le Bateau ivre" thus give joyful
and despondent testimony to the centrality of the child in
Rimbaud's notion of poetry. They also relate to significant features of the tradition in which I am situating
him: the child's preternaturally intense vision; structures
of consciousness and expression emphasizing temporality,
rupture, continuity, memory, progression; the attempt,
faithful to the child's fantastically vivid experience, to
transcend the limits of adult awareness.

The insistence on childhood as the source of creativity is
a universal theme, recognizable in Hölderlin's *Empedokles,*
in Blake's belief that the "vast Majority" of children are
"on the side of Imagination or Spiritual Sensation," in
Hugo's treatment of Palestrina in "Que la musique date du
seizième siècle," in Baudelaire's "Bénédiction," "Le Voyage," and "Les Vocations." Baudelaire summarizes and expresses the best in this tradition when he asserts: "genius is
only *childhood rediscovered*"—and when he adds, "at will,
childhood endowed now, to express itself, with virile organs, and with analytic intelligence."[15]

It is also Baudelaire who acutely locates the link between child and artist in the heightened vision of the
child, which is lost to most adults, is rediscovered perhaps in states of convalescence and intoxication, and is
the proper characteristic of art. This "faculty of seeing" is
marked by extremely vivid perception, as these formulas
indicate: "the faculty of being vividly interested in
things"; "such vividly colored impressions"; "the child
sees everything in *newness;* he is always *drunk*"; "the
child's joy in absorbing form and color." Similarly, Hugo
imagines an extraordinary openness to perception in the
child Palestrina, and in the "Immortality Ode" Wordsworth gives classic expression to the theme, speaking of
"celestial light," "the glory and the freshness of a

dream," "visionary gleam," "the hour / Of splendour in the grass, of glory in the flower."

Second, as especially the phrases from Wordsworth suggest, the child's intensely sensuous vision has something preternatural about it; it transcends normal, adult consciousness of nature, even of the real. This divergence from the natural is made into a systematic challenge by Baudelaire, who sees the child's vision as "much more colored, washed clean, and gleaming than real life," and who emphasizes in children and "primitives" the taste for the artificial, the marvellous, the theatrical, the ideal, the immaterial, the highly imaginative. Indeed, some of Baudelaire's formulations on the "surnaturel" indicate how directly relevant is this conception of the child's preternaturally sensuous vision to Rimbaud's poetry, and not only to "Enfance" (as we shall see when we discuss the *Illuminations* later in this chapter). Thus: "un intérêt surnaturel qui donne à chaque objet un sens plus profond . . . les sens plus attentifs perçoivent des sensations plus retentissantes, . . . où les sons tintent musicalement, où les couleurs parlent, où les parfums racontent des mondes d'idées" (a supernatural interest that gives to each object a deeper sense; the more attentive senses perceive more resounding sensations, in which sounds ring musically, colors speak, and perfumes recount worlds of ideas). Glimpsed momentarily in ordinary experience, perhaps pursued through drugs, infusing the work of artists like Delacroix, such perception belonged initially to the child. Child poetry in Wordsworth, Hugo, Baudelaire, and Rimbaud is an attempt to recapture a perception that did exist and can persist, if not for long in life, then at least in art.

Thus the child's superbly heightened consciousness is inextricably associated with, perhaps even glimpsed through, the experience of loss. This experience of loss is represented by a complex of motifs (pre-existence, fall, sleep, custom and boredom, theater, visionary and ordinary light) in writers from Wordsworth to Rimbaud; encountered in poems like "Après le déluge," "Larme," and "Mémoire"; and it is responsible for the characteristic *temporal* structure of romantic child poetry. We see an acute consciousness of progression, rupture, continuity; an awareness of the present self, tenuously but nostalgically related to the dim forms of its past existence, yet also attempting to prepare to live in the future; a simultaneous sense of glory and exile, of fading and of confidence in the lost, disinherited child from whom the poet will emerge. These features play a role in the work of Hugo and Baudelaire, go far to explain the themes of loss, memory, and emptiness throughout Hölderlin's writing, and illuminate as well the dialectical interactions of contraries through which Blake *refuses* to equate imagination with memory— his faith, that is, in the ever-vigorous energies of child, artist, history. But it is especially in Freud and Wordsworth that we find a description of discontinuous but progressive temporality that is sufficiently complex to advance our understanding of Rimbaud.

Jacques Derrida, for example, emphasizes that Freud's conception of the functioning of the psychic apparatus is essentially intermittent, with energy alternately projected and withdrawn, with consciousness arising instead of permanent memory traces, with a discontinuous experience of time generated by this activity of recurrent blocking off. Freud's simple formulation in "Creative Writers and Day-Dreaming" of a three-point temporal mode of experience is quite close to our childhood poetry: the present impression, the link with infantile fantasy, the desire for future fulfillment; it can, in fact, be applied to the subtleties of form of that poetry. For Freud, memory (but memory as displaced reconstruction of an absent past, memory as imagination, and at bottom revealing a lost, repressed content of child-hood)—memory is *the* principle of our psychic lives, through which present and future selves may be structured. Childhood, discontinuity, the linking of present with un-conscious past and potential future, self-structuring by the ego—all these elements are involved in Freud's concept of memory and are relevant to Rimbaud's writing.

In addition, Norman O. Brown and Herbert Marcuse, two other commentators of Freud, emphasize, respectively, the danger of being engulfed by memory, and its potential for liberating the psyche—overcoming repression and exces-sive rationality, restoring the content of fantasy and desire, even yielding critical standards tabooed by current forms of consciousness. These conceptions are close to the range of meaning in Rimbaud's treatment of memory—witness on the one hand "Mémoire," on the other "Guerre."

Finally, Freud paid special attention to the phenomenon of repetition, finding in it at times the pleasure of redis-covering what is good and known to be so, at others the intent to confront and master unhappiness. Repetition al-ways concerns the infantile, he argues, and in therapy the object is to overcome repetition in favor of recovering the content of reconstructed memory. These formulas may go far in explaining the notable recurrence of memory and childhood themes in Rimbaud and the other poets, as well as the way in which their works enact patterns of loss and recovery, attempting to salvage from childhood the en-ergies of ongoing existence.

Wordsworth, in particular, provides a sense of the in-tricacies of childhood experience and a poetic form com-plex enough to be of use in discussing Rimbaud. We earlier noted the assertion of the child's visionary experi-ence in the "Immortality Ode," without mentioning that

Wordsworth agonizes over this experience as definitively concluded: "It is not now as it hath been of yore"; "The things which I have seen I now can see no more"; "there hath past away a glory from the earth"; "Whither is fled the visionary gleam? / Where is it now, the glory and the dream?"; "the radiance which was once so bright / [Is] now for ever taken from my sight"; "nothing can bring back the hour / Of splendour in the grass, of glory in the flower." So many repetitions of loss, which the poet is nonetheless intent on surmounting.

Hence the insertion in the middle of the poem of the stanzas on pre-existence and immortality, the experience of a mysterious continuity of being ("O joy! that in our embers / Is something that doth live"), the effort to participate in childhood and nature "in thought," the viewing of mutability and mortality with a "philosophic mind," in fact, the desire to continue despite dimunition: "We will grieve not, rather find / Strength in what remains behind." This poem illustrates Wordsworth's persistent search for continuity of being and also the difficulties of achieving it. The child may be "father of the Man," but it is not easy to retain a sense that all one's days are "Bound each to each by natural piety," Wordsworth's goal in "My heart leaps up." Nor is it always possible to make the earth the abode of childhood, "An unsubstantial, faery place," the experience afforded by the bird's song in "To the Cuckoo." "Resolution and Independence" somberly emphasizes the same difficulty, though resolving it in the awesome figure of the old man, while "Tintern Abbey" and *The Prelude* provide insights into a poetic form that attempts to be faithful to the elusive evolution of the self.

"Tintern Abbey," earlier and less tragic than the "Ode," recounts the poet's return to a cherished spot, but the poem is a formal microcosm of the entire ambiguous existence of the self in time. The element of return is stressed in the opening lines, with "again" and "once again" repeated several times and mimicked by images that "connect" landscape and sky. Correspondingly, the passage of time is repeatedly mentioned: "Five years have past; five summers, with the length / Of five long winters!" These reiterated elements enact through imagery and verbal texture the theme of the poem; they also illustrate Freud's concepts of repetition, memory, and reconstruction. That is, the return is not in any way a simple one, for in verse paragraphs two and three Wordsworth describes his "long absence" in London, during which he returned in memory to the scene that he now revisits. This spiraling process of memory involves two removes in time: his present recall at Tintern Abbey of rememberings of the spot while absent from it. This spiral leads him to recollect past mythical illuminations *now* subject to doubt: "If this / Be but a vain belief, yet, oh! how oft—," and then to describe again the absence from the scene. These twin complex processes of memory link the first visit, subsequent rememberings of it, and the present second visit. So complex, made up of doubt and assertion, is the intertwining of past and present; so necessary is the element of verbal reiteration as an enactment of past memory in the present of the poem: "yet, oh! how oft"; "How oft, in spirit, have I turned to thee"; "How often has my spirit turned to thee!"

   This gathering up enables the poet to situate himself in the present moment, aware of the tenuousness of memory yet assured of the link with his past, and also with his future:

>   And now, with gleams of half-extinguished thought,
>   With many recognitions dim and faint,
>   And somewhat of a sad perplexity,

> The picture of the mind revives again:
> While here I stand, not only with the sense
> Of present pleasure, but with pleasing thoughts
> That in this moment there is life and food
> For future years.

The realization of unity within the temporal flux is immediately followed by yet another return in memory, to the
animal vigor the younger poet possessed when he first
came to Tintern Abbey. But "that time is past," and the
poet admits himself to be "changed," unable even to
"paint / What then [he] was." Nonetheless he insists that
he has had "abundant recompense," and asserts a continuing relationship with nature as the "anchor," "nurse,"
"guide," and "guardian" of his being.

The poem could end here, but amazingly introduces
another doublet, this time a completely separate human
life, that of the poet's younger sister, whom he imagines
experiencing the same process of immersion in nature,
loss, and retention of the past through memory. In an even
more complex interplay of temporal perspectives, which
illustrates Freud's projection of primary narcissism in fear
of mortality, Wordsworth imagines Dorothy after his
death, in the act of recalling her own youth as well as his
existence, and thus seeming to perpetuate his backward-
looking glance in a movement beyond his own life into the
future. Only then does the poem draw to a close, circling
back on itself in an invocation of the scene and the action
of return with which it began:

> Nor wilt thou then forget,
> That after many wanderings, many years
> Of absence, these steep woods and lofty cliffs,
> And this green pastoral landscape, were to me
> More dear, both for themselves and for thy sake!

This extraordinary temporal dialectic is relevant to our discussion of Rimbaud's child poems, as are certain features of *The Prelude*, a large work illustrating problems of form and the origin of the poetic act itself in the contemplation of childhood. A paradoxical version of the epic—personal and autobiographical—it recounts the growth of the poet's mind from childhood on. Its structure quite literally emerges from this concern. For after searching for a suitable epic theme, then berating himself and almost unconsciously thinking back to his early years, the narrating poet realizes, all the way at the end of Book I, that he has in fact begun to write an epic on his own evolution. Reflecting on his childhood has "revived" his mind, the subject is a good one, so he choses it "at this time." The work seems to evolve naturally from the contemplation of childhood.

Yet *The Prelude*, despite its aspiration to continuity, cannot completely hide a sense of rupture. The "recollected hours" have a visionary charm (I, 631–632), but the poet is conscious of a "vacancy" between him and his past, of a physical and inner falling off, even of being two consciousnesses (II, 27–33; IV, 278). And the course of his life (education, London, France) involves such a loss of identity with his best self that he is at one point virtually unable to continue living effectively. He rediscovers his true identity only by an effort of will, by the help of sister and friends, and by a return to nature, heralded by imagery of returning Spring, the dawn of a new day—seasonal and cyclical motifs that assert continuity (XII, 31–43, 201–207).

Childhood, departure, return—a typical structure, impelled by the constant functioning of memory, and memory as in part imagination, as Wordsworth asserts in comparing the course of *The Prelude* to someone gazing into a moving stream, seeing much, *fancying more,* unable to separate what is in the water from what is reflected on its surface (IV, 256–273). This passage suggests the tenuousness of the enterprise, the element of fabrication, the attempt to make a connected narrative texture from a discontinuous experience. So many linking, narrating, philosophizing passages surround the true core of *The Prelude,* those intense "spots of time" throughout the work: the experiences of the child in Books I and II, the mountain illuminations in Books VI and XIV, and the spots of time themselves—most powerful in childhood, involving elemental emotions and scenes of "visionary dreariness." Those spots seem to reveal the mind's mastery over "outward sense," having a "renovating virtue" to nourish our minds in later life, glimpsed but quickly closing up, so that the poet must find, "as far as words can give," the energy to enshrine "the spirit of the Past / For future restoration" (XII, 208–335).

Can we compare the complex temporal patterns in Wordsworth's attempt in *The Prelude* to narrate smoothly the poet's fading experience with Rimbaud's only comparable but characteristically much shorter work, *Une Saison en enfer?* There are great differences: Rimbaud's highly elliptical prose and Wordsworth's integrative blank verse; Rimbaud's admittedly fragmented form ("ces quelques hideux feuillets de mon carnet de damné"—these few hideous pages from my notebook of the damned) and Wordsworth's use of the traditional devices of epic structure. Further, Rimbaud develops the cyclical motifs of night and day ("Nuit de l'enfer," "Matin") and the seasons ("L'Automne déjà!"—the opening words of the last section, "Adieu") to describe not the growth of a whole life but a limited and violently disruptive period of a few years. Rimbaud's work is more private than Wordsworth's, more intense, less ambitious. His youth, the incompleteness of his work, play a role here. But so does his genius:

though the *Saison* is not unrelated to preceding literary convention, its power comes from Rimbaud's refusal to impose a falsely smooth form on a disjointed experience.[16]

Although such autobiographical elements as the obsession with childhood and awareness of temporal evolution dominate and structure the *Saison,* they are present in elliptical—and tormented—ways. The narrator recalls his childhood at several points, with increasingly despairing notes. A passage already mentioned contains a series of rapid allusions to the speaker's life: "Encore tout enfant"; "Sur les routes"; "Dans les villes"; "Mais l'orgie et la camaraderie des femmes m'étaient interdites" (While still a young child; On the roads; In cities; But orgies and the camaraderie of women were forbidden to me). Thus begin the first sentences of the first four paragraphs of a section of "Mauvais Sang," and they give the bare outlines, hardly to be filled in, of the course of the poet's existence from childhood to present. References to his childhood thereafter are scattered and more negative in tone. It is evoked in a hallucinatory way in "Nuit de l'enfer," more soberly in "L'Impossible," and in both cases followed by expressions of dismay and self-criticism: "Horreur de ma bêtise"; "quelle sottise c'était" (Horror of my stupidity; what stupidity it was).

Finally, at the beginning of the next-to-last chapter, he appreciates the value of his childhood and youth but sees them as irretrievably lost:

N'eus-je pas *une fois* une jeunesse aimable, héroïque, fabuleuse, à écrire sur des feuilles d'or,—trop de chance! Par quel crime, par quelle erreur, ai-je mérité ma faiblesse actuelle? Vous qui prétendez que des bêtes poussent des sanglots de chagrin, que des malades désespèrent, que des morts rêvent mal, tâchez de raconter ma

chute et mon sommeil. Moi, je ne puis pas plus m'ex-
pliquer que le mendiant avec ses continuels *Pater* et *Ave
Maria. Je ne sais plus parler!*

   ("Matin")

Didn't *once* I have a lovely youth, heroic, fabulous, worth
writing on leaves of gold,—too much luck! By what
crime, by what error, have I merited my present weakness? You who claim that animals sob from grief, that
the sick despair, that the dead have bad dreams, try to
recount my fall and my sleep. Me, I can no more explain
myself than the beggar with his continual *Paters* and *Ave
Marias. I no longer know how to speak!*

This dispossession from one's past is the ultimate vulnerability, and Rimbaud's exaltation of youth and use of the
romantic motifs of fall and sleep place him in the tradition
of the poets discussed earlier; recall Wordsworth's "Ode":
"Our birth is but a sleep and a forgetting." The inexplica-
bleness of the loss, the sense of diminishment, its connection with the inability to communicate—all these elements
are expressed within the characteristic temporal structure
we noted in other poets, especially Wordsworth. Rimbaud
uses the *passé simple,* or simple past, designating a singular
event now entirely past: "N'eus-je pas *une fois*"; while the
present of adult experience constitutes an essential dimunition: "ma faiblesse actuelle." *"Je ne sais plus parler!"* summarizes the definitive loss of the experience and even of the
ability to express it, more tortured than in Wordsworth's
"Tintern Abbey."
   But precisely at this point, at the moment of realization
of loss (and in a movement paradoxically similar to Wordsworth's desire for "recompense" in the "Ode" and "Tintern
Abbey"), comes the assertion of a more positive note,

again expressed in temporal terms: "Pourtant, aujourd'hui, je crois avoir fini la relation de mon enfer" (However, today, I believe I have finished the recounting of my hell). This line sends us back to a similar pattern at the opening of the work, which provides a temporal framework for the evolution of the whole—the same structure of bliss, loss, and attempted recovery (despite sardonic doubt) that we have been tracing:

> Jadis, si je me souviens bien, ma vie était un festin
> [Long ago, if I remember correctly, my life was a feast]
>
> . . .
>
> Un soir, j'ai assis la Beauté sur mes genoux
> [One evening, I sat Beauty down on my lap]
>
> . . .
>
> Or, tout dernièrement . . . j'ai songé à rechercher la clef du festin ancien, où je reprendrais peut-être appétit.
> [Now, just recently, I've thought of looking again for the key to the ancient feast, where perhaps I would find appetite again.]
>
> *(Introduction)*

These are again paradigmatic structures and formulas, which we shall shortly see as informing the child poems in the *Illuminations:* first, the definitively past time ("Jadis"), whose ongoing happiness is expressed by the imperfect tense and communal imagery; then the isolated moment of temporal rupture ("Un soir"); then recent time ("Or, tout dernièrement"), and a verb of meditative activity projecting to a future still shrouded in uncertainty but holding the possibility of recovering the lost bliss ("j'ai songé"; "rechercher"; "reprendrais peut-être").

Characteristically, the narrator does not apply this three-point framework directly to his own life; rather in "Mauvais Sang" he enlarges the scope of his concern by searching for antecedents in the past life of his race, just as later, having achieved greater clarity, he relates his personal quest to the purity of ancient races ("L'Impossible"). This enlarged temporal perspective leads the speaker to a momentary insight:

> C'est cette minute d'éveil qui m'a donné la vision de la pureté!—Par l'esprit on va à Dieu!
> Déchirante infortune!
>
> ("*L'Impossible*")

> It's this minute of awakening which gave me the vision of purity!—Through the mind we go to God!
> Heart-rending misfortune!

What is "déchirant" here may be not only the religious issue, which has led to disputes among critics, but just as much the difficulty of attaining a "minute d'éveil," and indeed the momentariness of experience in general.

Other chapters of the *Saison* reinforce this view by rejecting uninterrupted narration in favor of hallucinatory exclamation ("Nuit de l'enfer") and dramatic objectification ("Délires I"). The outline of chronological progression is not lost, however. The speaker's resolution at the end of "Nuit de l'enfer" to save himself is soon followed in "Délires II" by a temporally precise recounting of the course of Rimbaud's esthetic development, described as "l'histoire d'une de mes folies" (the story of one of my follies):

> Depuis longtemps je me vantais. . . . Je rêvais. . . . J'inventai. . . . Ce fut d'abord une étude
> [For a long time I had boasted. . . . I dreamed of. . . . I invented. . . . At first it was a study]
>   . . .

Je m'habituai. . . . Puis j'expliquai. . . . Je finis par
trouver. . . . Enfin . . . je vécus, étincelle d'or de la
lumière *nature*. . . . Je devins un opéra fabuleux
[I habituated myself. . . . Then I explained. . . . At the
end I found. . . . Finally I lived, golden spark of the
light *nature*. . . . I became a fabulous opera]

. . .

Ma santé fut menacée. . . . Je dus voyager. . . . Cela
s'est passé. Je sais aujourd'hui saluer la beauté.
[My health was threatened. . . . I had to travel. . . .
That's past. Today I know how to say hello to beauty.]

Note how the verb tenses at the beginning of so many
sentences in "Délires II" reveal an acute sense of temporal
progression, an imposition of order on the past that prepares the speaker for the future.

From this point on, and bolstered by the clarity of
"L'Impossible," Rimbaud more and more turns toward the
future:

Non! non! à présent je me révolte contre la mort!
[No! No! at present I am rebelling against death!]
  (*"L'Eclair"*)

Quand irons-nous . . . saluer la naissance du travail nouveau, . . . adorer . . . Noël sur la terre!
[When will we go . . . to greet the birth of the new
work, . . . adore . . . Christmas on earth!]
  (*"Matin"*)

Moi! moi qui me suis dit mage ou ange, dispensé de
toute morale, je suis rendu au sol, avec un devoir à
chercher, et la réalité rugueuse à étreindre!

[Me! me who called myself magus or angel, exempt from all morality, I am thrown back to earth, with a duty to find, and a rough reality to embrace!]

. . .

Oui, l'heure nouvelle est au moins très sévère. . . . Il faut être absolument moderne. . . . Cependant c'est la veille. Recevons tous les influx de vigueur et de tendresse réelle. Et à l'aurore, armés d'une ardente patience, nous entrerons aux splendides villes.
[Yes, the new hour is at least very severe. . . . It is necessary to be absolutely modern. . . . However, this is the vigil. Let us receive all the influxes of vigor and of real tenderness. And at dawn, armed with ardent patience, we will enter the splendid cities.]

   ("Adieu")

The desire to overcome loss is as clear here as anywhere in Wordsworth. In fact we cannot neglect the potential for self-mystification in Rimbaud's use of traditional motifs ("Noël," "splendides villes") to project satisfaction. Nonetheless, the effort to escape the grip of the past is strong: "Il faut être absolument moderne." And throughout there is the quest for unified being, no longer in childhood, but imagined in the future: "il me sera loisible de *posséder la vérité dans une âme et un corps*" (it will be permissible for me to *possess truth in one soul and one body*).

This scanning of relevant features of the *Saison* reinforces what I have said about Rimbaud's relation to romantic child poetry and to Freud. More important, it may also present the truest reading of the work, the best way to deal with its apparent contradictions and ambiguities. The *Saison* is a powerful, strained, and energetic version of Wordsworth's "The Child is father of the Man." The speaker's childhood dominates the work, fitfully but recurrently, which corresponds to Freud's view of repetition as rediscovery of the content of the past and to Wordsworth's attempts to preserve that content through memory. The *Saison* rigorously adheres to the fragmented experience of time that implies, and in this it is close to the consciousness of loss that impels Wordsworth's poetry, even *The Prelude* with its striving for a continuous mode of presentation. More than *The Prelude*, the *Saison* is ever faithful to the "minute d'éveil," which constitutes both absolute intensity of experience and a sense of "déchirante infortune."

But the unifying and reconstructive impulse is strong as well in the *Saison*. The three-point temporal movement of the psyche visible in Freud and Wordsworth is emphasized by Rimbaud at the beginning and at the crucial turning point near the end of his work (Introduction, "Matin"). Moreover, memory in the *Saison* is ultimately constructive, extending beyond the individual to the nation and the race ("Mauvais Sang," "L'Impossible"), and is combined with self-analysis, self-objectification, and precise recounting ("Délires" I and II) to produce resolution for the present and future ("Nuit de l'enfer," "Adieu"). Finally, at its end the *Saison* enacts the victory of unifying Eros over the regression and dissolution of the death instinct ("je me révolte contre la mort"; "*la vérité dans une âme et un corps*"), and thus attempts to preserve the integral sense of self that first appeared as the infant's primary narcissism and that underlies all subsequent evolutions.

The connection between child and poet, visible in Rimbaud's poetry from "Ma Bohème" to "Les Sœurs de charité," "Les Poètes de sept ans" and "Le Bateau ivre," persists therefore as a unifying thread in Rimbaud's later prose work. But another theme treated in this chapter, the attempt to preserve the "superreal" vision of the child in

the face of rupture and loss, hardly fares well in the *Saison*.
"Le Bateau ivre," "Après le déluge," and "Enfance" relate
to the visionary child in poetry from Blake to Baudelaire;
but these poems also confront the loss of that special perception, the closing in of a threatening reality. The *Saison*
goes further, attacking the activities of the poet in the
name of a submission to a sense of the real that is as
puritanical and denuded as anything in Freud's reality
principle: "Moi! moi qui me suis dit mage ou ange,
dispensé de toute morale, je suis rendu au sol, avec un
devoir à chercher, et la réalité rugueuse à étreindre! Paysan!" ("Adieu"). Thus the work that most energetically
attempts to preserve the unity of the poet's existence does
so by discarding that part of the child-self that rebels
against the submission to the real. As we now begin our
reading of the *Illuminations,* we must not forget this aspect
of the *Saison.*[17] It is a work revealing the urge to unification from child to man to artist but also the opposition
between that self-structuring being and the implacable reality he desires to surmount.

The Illuminations: *Childhood and the Struggle with the Real*

The materials just discussed, as well as the theme of the
origin and the view of the innocent and vulnerable child
presented earlier, provide the appropriate context for the
child poems in the *Illuminations.* The bond between childhood and poetry, the heightened clarity of the child's experience, the confrontation with loss, the persistence of memory
and the counterpointing of present-past-future in complex
literary forms, the struggle against the closing in of the
"real," and the search for visionary perception—all these

elements are systematically involved in the prose poems
"Vies," "Aube," "Enfance," "Guerre," and "Jeunesse."

I begin with "Vies" because it traces the entire process,
from origin, through loss and the undertaking and com-
pletion of the poetic enterprise, to an ironic distance from
that enterprise. We can begin by noting its denseness as
well as its simultaneous emphasis on multiplicity and discontinuity: the plural title, the division into separate parts
not joined by explicit links, the use of dashes to indicate
discrete stages, the unexplained and bitter separation of
the speaker from all that preceded in his life, or rather
lives—from all that he sardonically summarizes in the
three parts of the poem.

The first part suggests one of those lives, a mythic
experience involving the familiar themes of pre-existence
and exile, vision, and memory:

> O les énormes avenues du pays saint, les terrasses du
> temple! Qu'a-t-on fait du brahmane qui m'expliqua les
> Proverbes? D'alors, de là-bas, je vois encore même les
> vieilles! Je me souviens des heures d'argent et de soleil
> vers les fleuves, la main de la campagne sur mon épaule,
> et de nos caresses debout dans les plaines poivrées.—Un
> envol de pigeons écarlates tonne autour de ma pensée.—
> Exilé ici, j'ai eu une scène où jouer les chefs-d'œuvre
> dramatiques de toutes les littératures. Je vous indiquerais
> les richesses inouïes. . . . Qu'est mon néant, auprès de la
> stupeur qui vous attend?

> O the enormous avenues of the holy country, the terraces of
> the temple! What have they done with the Brahman who
> explained the Proverbs to me? From then, from there, I still
> even see the old women! I remember the hours of silver and
> sun near the rivers, the hand of the country on my shoulder,
> and our caresses standing in the spice-scented plains.—A

flight of scarlet pigeons thunders around my thought.—
Exiled here, I have had a stage on which to play the dramatic masterpieces of all literatures. I would suggest to you
unheard-of riches. . . . What is my nothingness, compared
with the stupor that awaits you?

This Eastern paradise, antecedent to the speaker's normal or real life, reminds us of motifs in Hölderlin, Wordsworth, and "L'Impossible" of the *Saison*. It was a world of
expansiveness, aureoled with the sacred, involving a vivid
perception of nature and an erotic intimacy similar to the
projection of libido beyond the self that Marcuse sees in
nature poetry.[18] And it is presented as having been really
experienced, indeed as simply "present"—consider the exclamatory opening sentence with its lack of any verbal
element. At the same time it is lost ("Qu'a-t-on fait?");
though persisting in sight and memory ("je vois encore";
"je me souviens"), it has become definitively distant, as
the temporal and spatial oppositions emphasize ("D'alors,
de là-bas"; "—Exilé ici"). Between it and the speaker's
ordinary existence there seems to remain only a sense of
ongoing psychic life: "—Un envol de pigeons écarlates
tonne autour de ma pensée." Elusively beautiful, this sentence suggests the natural world's dynamism and presence
to sensation and consciousness—as in "Enfance" a consciousness still tinged with the heightened coloration of
the other world.

Some continuity therefore exists in this transitional stage,
but its description is quickly followed by the brutal assertion of exile: "—Exilé ici, j'ai eu une scène où jouer les
chefs-d'œuvre dramatiques de toutes les littératures." Not
only pre-existence, persistence, and loss, therefore, but immediately the artistic enterprise, presented in the ironically
hyperbolic mode that attains its apogee in the last part of

the poem. In "Vies" the elemental curve of the artist's career
is rendered furious not only by the initial experience of loss
but also by the disabused later perspective.

"Vies" therefore has none of Wordsworth's sense of "recompense" or the *Saison*'s will to health and wholeness.
The richness of the artist's many lives is a source of bitterness, not satisfaction. Thus, part II recounts the existential
life of the speaker, the life of the individual that most of us
regard as the real one—and does so again with anger and
also with considerable biographical fidelity:

> Je suis un inventeur bien autrement méritant que tous
> ceux qui m'ont précédé; un musicien même, qui ai
> trouvé quelque chose comme la clef de l'amour. A
> présent, gentilhomme d'une campagne aigre au ciel
> sobre, j'essaye de m'émouvoir au souvenir de l'enfance
> mendiante, de l'apprentissage ou de l'arrivée en sabots,
> des polémiques, des cinq ou six veuvages, et quelques
> noces où ma forte tête m'empêcha de monter au diapason
> des camarades. Je ne regrette pas ma vieille part de gaîté
> divine: l'air sobre de cette aigre campagne alimente fort
> activement mon atroce scepticisme. Mais comme ce scep-
> ticisme ne peut désormais être mis en œuvre, et que
> d'ailleurs je suis dévoué à un trouble nouveau,—j'attends
> de devenir un très méchant fou.

> I am an inventor far more deserving that all who have
> preceded me; a musician even, who has found something
> like the key of love. At present, gentleman of a bleak
> countryside with a sober sky, I try to rouse myself with the
> memory of mendicant childhood, the apprenticeship or ar-
> rival in wooden shoes, the polemics, five or six widowings,
> and a few drinking bouts where my strong head kept me
> from rising to the pitch of the comrades. I do not miss my
> old share of divine gaiety; the sober air of this bleak coun-
> tryside nourishes very actively my atrocious skepticism. But

as this skepticism can no longer be put to use, and since besides I am now devoted to a new worry,—I am waiting to become a very wicked madman.

Within the strictly personal framework of this portion of the poem, childhood, temporal evolution, memory, and the esthetic enterprise are again central. Rimbaud's poetic achievement, expressed by characteristic musical and erotic motifs, preceded by his indigent and wandering childhood, the apprenticeship in poetry he gave himself, his rustic appearance upon arriving in Paris, his disappointing emotional attachments, the disputes and carousing with Verlaine and others—all these events are evoked in a strongly temporal perspective. For the artistic career that followed upon the loss of childhood is already over, more radically even than in "Délires II," in this "à présent" of the narration. The present moment is colored by skepticism and despair, which lead in part III to utter detachment: "Je suis réellement d'outre-tombe, et pas de commissions" (I am really beyond the grave, and no commissions). This present moment implies only a future of negative possibilities: "je suis dévoué à un trouble nouveau"; "j'attends de devenir un très méchant fou."

"Vies" reveals Rimbaud's experience of self and vocation as formed by the elements of romantic child poetry: a sense of personal pre-existence, the vibrant presence of nature, a structure of persistence and loss, the immediate arising of the artistic enterprise. It also shows us the bitterness that can accompany these themes in his work. Its structural division into separate parts turns richness into a troubling discrepancy of mythic and biographical selves. The poem makes us believe in all these selves, but they all also contribute to the depth of the speaker's anger, much of which is directed at *us*: "Qu'est mon néant, auprès de la stupeur qui vous attend?" The very bitterness of the speaker's tone, which rhetorically asserts the authenticity of his several lives, also reveals the tragic sense of loss that shadows childhood and poetry in Rimbaud's writing.

"Vies" summarizes the complete curve of the artist's existence. The beginning of that curve, the child's experience of nature, is the subject of "Aube":

> J'ai embrassé l'aube d'été.
> Rien ne bougeait encore au front des palais. L'eau était morte. Les camps d'ombres ne quittaient pas la route du bois. J'ai marché, réveillant les haleines vives et tièdes, et les pierreries regardèrent, et les ailes se levèrent sans bruit.
> La première entreprise fut, dans le sentier déjà empli de frais et blêmes éclats, une fleur qui me dit son nom.
> Je ris au wasserfall blond qui s'échevela à travers les sapins: à la cime argentée je reconnus la déesse.
> Alors je levai un à un les voiles. Dans l'allée, en agitant les bras. Par la plaine, où je l'ai dénoncée au coq. A la grand'ville elle fuyait parmi les clochers et les dômes, et courant comme un mendiant sur les quais de marbre, je la chassais.
> En haut de la route, près d'un bois de lauriers, je l'ai entourée avec ses voiles amassés, et j'ai senti un peu son immense corps. L'aube et l'enfant tombèrent au bas du bois.
> Au réveil il était midi.

> I've kissed the summer dawn.
> Nothing was yet moving on the fronts of the palaces. The water was dead. The camps of shadows did not leave the woodland road. I walked, waking up the live, warm breaths, and the precious stones watched, and the wings rose up soundlessly.

The first enterprise was, in the path already filled with cool and pale glints, a flower that told me its name.

I laughed at the blond *wasserfall* that tossed its hair through the pines: at the silver summit I recognized the goddess.

Then I lifted one by one the veils. In the lane, waving my arms. In the plain, where I proclaimed her to the cock. In the city she fled among the steeples and domes, and running like a beggar on the marble quays, I pursued her.

At the top of the road, near a laurel wood, I hemmed her in with her massed veils, and sensed a little her immense body. Dawn and the child fell to the bottom of the woods.

On waking, it was noon.

Less despondent than "Vies," this text however also stresses loss, not by division into parts but by complexities of tense and person. Its opening statement, "J'ai embrassé l'aube d'été," suggests most of the significant elements of the poem: nature ("été"), childhood and beginnings ("aube"), the erotic component ("embrassé"), the past and by implication the theme of loss (the past tense), and the speaker's simple assertion of the reality of the experience (the matter-of-fact tone). The last of these gives the poem its surprising quality—its confidence in the reality of the child's encounter with a mythic being in nature.

Initially, in this retrospective narration, just before the appearance of the dawn's light, nature seemed dead: "Rien ne bougeait. . . . L'eau était morte." But the child's presence evokes a response in nature, corresponding to the increasing light, and to which he in turn reacts with emotion and recognition: "J'ai marché, réveillant les haleines . . . et les pierreries regardèrent"; "La première entreprise fut . . . une fleur qui me dit son nom"; "Je ris au wasserfall blond"; "à la cime argentée je reconnus la déesse." An adult perspective sees this as merely the progressive appearance of dawn, but the literality of the poem presents it otherwise—as the child's intuition of an animistic, sexual, divine force in nature. This vision recalls Wordsworth's and Hölderlin's sense of the numinous, their belief that children retain the mythic sense that earlier cultures had, their desire to rediscover it and communicate it to others[19]—except that "Aube" emphasizes the erotic component, as the child raises the goddess' veils, pursues her, approaches her "immense body," then falls with her into the unconsciousness of sexual union and sleep:

> En haut de la route, près d'un bois de lauriers, je l'ai entourée avec ses voiles amassés, et j'ai senti un peu son immense corps. L'aube et l'enfant tombèrent au bas du bois.
> Au réveil il était midi.

In this conclusion achievement and loss are identified. There is union with the goddess, but also unconsciousness, much as in Wordsworth's "Our birth is but a sleep and a forgetting" (the "Immortality Ode") and Rimbaud's "tâchez de raconter ma chute et mon sommeil" ("Matin": try to recount my fall and my sleep). Similarly the action at the end is the only one in which the child and the goddess participate jointly; yet it is an act that produces falling, unconsciousness, and disruption, as tense and person emphasize. Throughout, the narration is in the first person, but now a sudden alienation is revealed. The being who experienced union with the dawn is now called "l'enfant"— connected in no visible way with the *je* who has been recounting this *entreprise*. Moreover the *passé simple* of "tombèrent" mixes triumph and loss, imparting to the whole temporal structure of the poem a similar ambivalence.

As in child poetry generally and elsewhere in Rimbaud, this structure is strongly marked. We clearly see the progression of the action ("la première entreprise," "le sentier déjà empli," "alors je levai") and a corresponding spatial movement from nature through the city to an eminence associated with travel and nature ("en haut de la route"). But there is also a careful staging of a variety of past tenses to indicate initiation, progression, intensification, culmination, and loss. Thus this extraordinary narration begins in the ordinary, everyday tense, the *passé composé* (compound past), followed in paragraph two by standard use of the *passé composé* and imperfect. But with the child's discovery of an animistic reality in nature, the tense shifts to the *passé simple,* from "les pierreries regardèrent" through "je levai un à un les voiles." In the subsequent pursuit of the goddess by the child, the narration returns to *passé composé* and imperfect, presumably to convey movement, dynamism, familiarity. But these tenses also prepare a shocking contrast when the culminating act occurs: "L'aube et l'enfant tombèrent au bas du bois"—falling, forgetting, the splitting of self and distancing of the child, and the *passé simple,* here signaling a moment of absolute experience that is definitively over. Then the last sentence, like Wordsworth's fading into "the light of common day," conveys the awakening to ordinary reality—the time of the imperfect, which is impersonal, curt, and final: "Au réveil il était midi." Thus "Aube" accomplishes, by its strategies of person and tense, the revelation of the child's experience as of greatest moment but apparently belonging to another self, unconscious, concluded.

Yet, as Wordsworth repeatedly asserted, something persists—the certainty of glorious achievement, the cyclical metaphor implied in the title (which Wordsworth developed into a metaphysical allegory in the "Ode," but which is suggestively left untouched in Rimbaud's poem), the fact of the poem itself. The child's apparently ungraspable experience remains the source of the poet's creative activity, as is clear in three other *Illuminations,* "Enfance," "Guerre," and "Jeunesse."

Following immediately upon the imploring conclusion of "Après le déluge," "Enfance" makes use of the divisions into separate stages, the growth and discontinuity of the person, and the evolutionary movement from nature to city to art that we have seen in "Vies" and "Aube." In its greater detail, it provides fuller insight into the progression from child through more than one kind of imaginative activity. Thus parts I through III concern the child's exceptional existence and its development in time; part IV evokes the loss of childhood, the invented roles through which an adult speaker now tries to recreate the child's worlds, and also the *failure* of that attempt; then, from the despondency of part V, there emerge suggestions of a further poetic activity, aimed not so much at recapturing childhood as at actualizing its potential for a vision transcending the ordinary categories of the real.

Part I recapitulates the romantic child—its wildness, solitude, immersion in nature, and visionary capacity. This period of early childhood has its own temporal progression, visible in the succession of the part's three paragraphs. I earlier discussed the second paragraph and hinted at the evocation of the earliest phase of childhood in paragraph one:

> Cette idole, yeux noirs et crin jaune, sans parents ni
> cour, plus noble que la fable, mexicaine et flamande; son
> domaine, azur et verdure insolents, court sur des plages
> nommées, par des vagues sans vaisseaux, de noms
> férocement grecs, slaves, celtiques.

This idol, black eyes and yellow mane, without kin or
court, nobler than fable, Mexican and Flemish; its domain, insolent azure and verdure, runs on named
beaches, through shipless waves, with names that are
ferociously Greek, Slav, Celtic.

This portrait is close to Bachelard's *enfant cosmique* and
Jung's primordial child. Alone, without parents, companions, or traces of civilization (as just after the flood, the sea
is uncontaminated by ships); in contact with an oceanic
and elemental nature of sky, vegetation, waves; almost
disembodied yet fiercely sensual, evoked hardly as a human
face but as an abstraction of magical and animal features
("Cette idole, yeux noirs et crin jaune"): the child here is a
primitive force, worthy of adoration, a primordial divinity.
Its enormous energy seems to be communicated to nature:
"insolents," the elements of the scene are said to *run* with
the child. Too, there are suggestions of a subversion of our
notion of the real. The child is "plus noble que la fable,"
fabulous *and* acutely alive, transcending the fictional by
the ferocious vigor of its existence ("férocement") on the
particular, actually existing beaches ("des plages nom-
mées") on which it runs. Alien to the modes of experience
of the adult, the very young child embodies a more intense
reality.

From this reality there emerges in the second paragraph
a recognizable, somewhat older, child. Paragraph three
presents the consciousness of a child who is older still,
aware of being surrounded by female presences of all ages
and kinds, familiar and exotic: children, big sisters, young
mothers, superb blacks, sultanas, tyrannical princesses.
Females one and all, they recall Rimbaud's family situation
and also the enveloping feminine figures in Blake's *Songs of
Innocence and Experience* against whom the child-visionary

artist must rebel. Hence the enumeration ends on a sentimental note, "personnes doucement malheureuses" (gently
unhappy persons), followed by an ironic comment: "Quel
ennui, l'heure du 'cher corps' et 'cher cœur' " (What a
bore, the hour of the "dear body" and "dear heart").

This comment by an as-yet-unidentified speaker implies
distance in time and perspective, a discontinuity that is
also apparent in part II. There, consciousness of individuals and family, of death and the functioning of memory,
are clearly at work in the scene, and the personages are
those who well up in the mind of an older but still young
child:

> C'est elle, la petite morte, derrière les rosiers.—La jeune
> maman trépassée descend le perron.—La calèche du cou
> sin crie sur le sable.—Le petit frère (il est aux Indes!) là,
> devant le couchant, sur le pré d'œillets.—Les vieux qu'on
> a enterrés tout droits dans le rempart aux giroflées.

> It's she, the little dead girl, behind the rose bushes.—
> The dead young mamma is coming down the steps.—
> The cousin's carriage creaks on the sand.—The little
> brother (he is in India!) there, against the sunset, on the
> meadow of pinks.—The old ones buried upright in the
> rampart with the gillyflowers.

Like the girl in Wordsworth's "We Are Seven," this child
experiences death without adult finality. Indications of the
past are absorbed into a kind of notational present, in
which the unavowed functioning of memory is seen in the
interference of two events. This could be a Freudian screen
memory, fusing past and present, giving rise to no overt
statement or comment, yet filled with meaning because
bearing on the child's awareness of family, separation,

mortality: dead female relatives, again no father, absent male siblings, the elders dead and buried.

This familial emptiness is succeeded in following paragraphs by another, that of an uninhabited country property. Absence is abundantly stressed and becomes the condition of a privileged experience. The absent proprietor, empty inn, chateau for sale, windows without blinds, unused church, uninhabited keepers' lodges—all present enticing possibilities for exploration and vision. Hence "L'essaim des feuilles d'or entoure la maison du général" (The swarm of golden leaves surrounds the house of the general) suggests an enveloping contact with a dynamic nature. "On suit la route rouge pour arriver à l'auberge vide" (You follow the red road to reach the empty inn) constitutes both an invitation and an empty destination. "Les palissades sont si hautes qu'on ne voit que les cimes bruissantes. D'ailleurs il n'y a rien à voir là-dedans" (The palisades are so high that you can see only the rustling tree tops. Besides there's nothing to see inside) embodies a dialectic of lower-upper, outer-inner, vision-sound, obstacle-penetration, fullness-emptiness.

In this nothingness created by man's absence, nature reasserts itself, absorbing even the objects constructed by human beings: "Les prés remontent aux hameaux sans coqs, sans enclumes. L'écluse est levée. O les calvaires et les moulins du désert, les îles et les meules!" (The meadows rise up to the hamlets without cocks, without anvils. The sluice is raised. O the calvaries and mills of the desert, the islands and the millstones!). The waters are liberated, recreating something like the conditions at the opening of the poem and producing an exclamatory immediacy that is given without comment and for which no commentary would be adequate: "O les calvaires et les moulins du désert, les îles et les meules!"

In this setting a vision of fantastic richness once again
becomes possible to the child who, despite his youth, had
already lost it:

Des fleurs magiques bourdonnaient. Les talus le
berçaient. Des bêtes d'une élégance fabuleuse circulaient.
Les nuées s'amassaient sur la haute mer faite d'une
éternité de chaudes larmes.

Magic flowers were buzzing. The slopes cradled him.
Animals of a fabulous elegance moved about. The clouds
were massing on the high sea made of an eternity of hot
tears.

The flowers of part I, audibly present, return, and the sea
and clouds press around with a fullness of existence. If "le"
refers to the child who, by implication, has walked out to
have this vision at the abandoned property, it is suggested
that nature cradles him, which involves a return to the
condition of early childhood. Typically too, the vision
takes us beyond recognizable nature to a realm that is
magical and fabulous. But this transcendence of normal
reality is accompanied by suffering ("une éternité de
chaudes larmes") and discontinuities of time and person.
All occurs in the imperfect tense, an ongoing state but one
that—like imperfects in the *Saison* and "Aube," but for
the first time in this poem—is *narrated* as *past*. Note also
the third-person pronoun, which recalls "Après le déluge"
and "Aube" in distancing and objectifying the child, separating him from the still unacknowledged speaker of the
poem.

This ambivalence of vision and unhappiness carries over
into part III, an anaphora of seven sentences beginning

with *il y a* that conveys the immediacy of the child's world. There is a universality about this part as well—for example, in the use of *vous* throughout; it seems the epitome of the pure experiences of the child, a purity that is conceivable only after childhood is over. It involves first the acuteness of sensation and response, the directly physical impact of experience, in short the newness stressed by Baudelaire: "Au bois il y a un oiseau, son chant vous arrête et vous fait rougir" (In the woods there is a bird, its song stops you and makes you blush). Then there is the child's freedom from time ("une horloge qui ne sonne pas"—a clock that doesn't strike), and its curiosity ("une fondrière avec un nid de bêtes blanches"—a pit with a nest of white things). There is also the child's proclivity for the imaginative: cathedrals and lakes that rise and fall like backdrops, beribboned wagons, "une troupe de petits comédiens en costumes" (a troop of little costumed actors). This last theme recalls the argument in Wordsworth, Coleridge, and Baudelaire that the child's imaginative power and its interest in theater, fairy tales, and fantastic literature betoken a rebellion against constricting notions of reality. And, at the end, there is again the vulnerability to adults and to deprivation, which we have seen in so much of Rimbaud's earlier verse: "Il y a enfin, quand l'on a faim et soif, quelqu'un qui vous chasse" (There is finally, when you're hungry and thirsty, someone who chases you away).

This signals the end of childhood. Part IV is narrated by an adult who speaks in the first person. The self-forgetfulness of the child is lost, and a gap exists between the self and the sense of Being that in the romantic tradition was the patrimony of the child. This change is apparent in the series of figures with which the speaker now identifies himself:

Je suis le saint, en prière sur la terrasse,—comme les
bêtes pacifiques paissent jusqu'à la mer de Palestine.

Je suis le savant au fauteuil sombre. Les branches et la
pluie se jettent à la croisée de la bibliothèque.

Je suis le piéton de la grand'route par les bois nains; la
rumeur des écluses couvre mes pas. Je vois longtemps la
mélancolique lessive d'or du couchant.

I am the saint, in prayer on the terrace,—like the
peaceful animals grazing down to the sea in Palestine.

I am the scholar in the dark armchair. The branches
and the rain beat against the library window.

I am the wanderer of the open road through the dwarf
woods; the sound of sluices covers my steps. For a long
time I see the melancholy gold wash of the sunset.

This series of imaginative roles recapitulates much in
Rimbaud's work and has archetypal resonances for the romantic tradition of poetry. The saint in prayer, the ascetic
savant in his study, and the wanderer recall "la nature en
fleur," and "la noire alchimie et les saintes études" (nature
in flower; black alchemy and holy studies) of "Les Sœurs
de charité," the "vibrements divins des mers virides" (divine vibrations of viridian seas) and the "Paix des pâtis
semés d'animaux, paix des rides / Que l'alchimie imprime
aux grands fronts studieux" (Peace of pastures sown with
animals, peace of wrinkles that alchemy prints on great
studious brows) in "Voyelles," and the figure of the
wandering child-poet who appears in works from "Ma
Bohème" through *Une Saison en enfer.* The peaceful totality
of nature; the sea as elemental reality; the figures of the
saint, savant, wanderer—all imply a sacred undertaking,
the effort to comprehend the totality of the world and to
penetrate the absolute beyond. They remind us of the
wanderers in Hölderlin and Wordsworth, Hugo's interest

in the occult, his description of solitary shepherds in *Les Contemplations,* Yeats's wandering beggars and hermits and his evocation of the poet, alone in his tower, searching for secret knowledge in an interiorized quest for the ultimate reality.[20]

Part IV of "Enfance" is therefore archetypal in demonstrating the temporally conditioned emergence of a conscious self, a motif we observed as characteristic of child poetry. Moreover, it shows us the recurrent poetic-spiritual roles that, as the following sentence reveals, are adopted as unsuccessful replacements for the child's absorption in nature: "Je serais bien l'enfant abandonné sur la jetée partie à la haute mer, le petit valet suivant l'allée dont le front touche le ciel" (I would gladly be the child abandoned on the jetty floating out to the high seas, the little farmhand following the lane whose brow touches the sky). Saint, savant, wanderer—all are efforts to recreate the abandoned, cosmic child, vulnerable yet in literal contact with sea and sky. But the essential rupture is not to be overcome—as the conditional "je serais" emphasizes. The limpidity of childhood is gone and is replaced by a different scene, strangely beautiful, but marked by heaviness, impenetrability, distance, foreboding: "Les sentiers sont âpres. Les monticules se couvrent de genêts. L'air est immobile. Que les oiseaux et les sources sont loin! Ce ne peut être que la fin du monde, en avançant" (The paths are rough. The knolls are covered with broom. The air is immobile. How far away are the birds and the springs! This is perhaps only the end of the world, advancing).

A world has ended, in fact, with this distancing of childhood's birds and springs that recalls analogous motifs and movements in "Larme," "Mémoire," "Le Bateau ivre" and the first part of "Vies." And so part V of "Enfance" evokes another state, the sterility that follows upon the loss of childhood and the failure of attempts to recreate it. Utterly alone, the speaker imagines an underground existence that, as in "Vies," is "d'outre-tombe": "Qu'on me loue enfin ce tombeau" (Finally let me rent this tomb); it is beneath the houses, mud, and sewers of the city: "Ville monstrueuese, nuit sans fin!" (monstrous City, endless night!). This vision of alienated experience, echoing motifs in writers from Blake to Dostoyevsky, carries with it the temptation of a refusal of communication as well as another complex of characteristic images: "la lampe éclaire . . . ces journaux que je suis idiot de relire, ces livres sans intérêt" (the lamp illuminates these papers that I am stupid to reread, these books without interest); "Aux heures d'amertume je m'imagine des boules de saphir, de métal. Je suis maître du silence. Pourquoi une apparence de soupirail blêmirait-elle au coin de la voûte?" (In hours of bitterness I imagine orbs of saphire, of metal. I am master of silence. Why would an appearance of a vent grow pale in the corner of the vault?). The child's immersion in sea, sky, verdure is gone, replaced by a nonnatural notion of art and the structuring of a resistant self, in danger perhaps of arid rigidity, but open as well to future transformations.

Such transformations, at least in the realm of vision, are hinted at. The last sentence questioningly evokes either the presence or absence of light from the outside world, and it lends the close of the poem an ambivalent suggestion of an opening. The next-to-last paragraph, too, implies larger imaginative possibilities:

Moins haut, sont des égouts. Aux côtés, rien que
l'épaisseur du globe. Peut-être les gouffres d'azur, des
puits de feu. C'est peut-être sur ces plans que se rencon-
trent lunes et comètes, mers et fables.

Less high up, are sewers. To the sides, nothing but the
thickness of the globe. Perhaps the gulfs of azure, wells
of fire. It is perhaps on these levels that moons and com-
ets, seas and fables meet.

Hesitatingly, these lines imply new planes of perception
that avoid the world of men and that strike out in another
direction, toward the elemental realities of the universe:
"les gouffres d'azur, des puits de feu," "lunes et comètes,
mers"—but also "fables." At the beginning of the poem,
the "idole" of childhood is called "plus noble que la fable,"
and here at the end the speaker imagines a kind of vision
more elemental and cosmic than our normal perceptions,
and also more fabulous. Childhood is lost, the poetic roles
adopted by the speaker are no more, his enterprise is
threatened by sterility, yet the possibility of glimpsing a
fundamental reality remains. An attribute of childhood is
thus preserved.

We are ready now to consider "Guerre," which treats
with schematic economy the stages in the evolution of
child to artist that we analyzed in detail in "Enfance." It is
a poem, moreover, that is far more confident of future
success, conscious as it is of a reservoir of explosive power
remaining in the artist-speaker.[21]

As in "Vies," dashes delineate the phases of the child-
artist's evolution. The first two sentences explicitly establish the characteristic retrospective view of the speaker's
childhood: "Enfant, certains ciels ont affiné mon optique:
tous les caractères nuancèrent ma physionomie. Les
Phénomènes s'émurent" (As a child, certain skies sharpened my optic: all the characters nuanced my physiognomy. The Phenomena roused themselves). As in "Aube"
and the *Saison,* the *passé composé* and *passé simple* establish a
narration of a past time during which extraordinary events

occurred and ended. But the concision of expression and
abstract vocabulary signal the presence of a mature, analytical speaker, no longer involved in childhood, now capable of intellectual assessment and (later) of looking to
the future. Again there is the theme of the child's acuteness of vision, which is produced by the action of nature—
"certains ciels." But the painter's word "ciels" suggests a
not wholly natural perception of the world, and this un-
usualness is emphasized by the combination of abstract
words, capitalization, and verbs of motion and impact to
describe the forces that affected the child—affected him
even to the point of "nuancing" his very physiognomy.
We can again draw analogies to Wordsworth, who imagined Lucy's form and face as subtly molded by the sound of
storms and waters, whose own perception was made visionary by the movement of certain skies and blasts of wind,
and who was led by nature beyond sense to glimpses of
"unknown modes of being," unlike human beings, that
troubled the boy's mind. Wordsworth's anecdotal memories and sacred conception of nature differ from Rimbaud's
spare, almost scientific, mode in "Guerre." But both point
to the child's consciousness as transcending the ordinary
world of sense, penetrating the realm of the concrete, and
revealing immense forces that seem almost disembodied
but are nonetheless instinct with life, movement, and
power.

The second phase of "Guerre" is equally schematic and
equally faithful to the typical structures of child poetry. It
shows the experience of adulthood itself as the vulnerability to which the child has all the while been exposed:
"—A présent, l'inflexion éternelle des moments et l'infini
des mathématiques me chassent par ce monde où je subis
tous les succès civils, respecté de l'enfance étrange et des
affections énormes" (—At present, the eternal inflection of

moments and the infinity of mathematics pursue me
through this world where I submit to all the civil successes, respected by strange childhood and enormous affections). Everything is there: the typical temporal situation
of the adult poet (Wordsworth's "And now" of "Tintern
Abbey," Rimbaud's "Or, tout dernièrement" of the *Saison,*
"à présent" of "Vies"); the enforced acceptance, underlined
by the mathematical-philosophical vocabulary, of the in-
flexibility of time and space, the rigidity of existence in
"ce monde" of adult consciousness; the pain of being
pursued through life, *submitting to* the paltry successes of
grown-up experience, becoming alienated from childhood,
and adopting the required respect for the now adult
speaker. The "affections énormes" of his childhood, his
young erotic energy, seem strange and alien to the repressed consciousness of the adult speaker.

But, as opposed to the anguish expressed in "Matin"
upon confronting a similar experience of self-alienation, in
"Guerre" a powerful intelligence looks forward to a third
phase, to be constituted by an act that he is meditating:
"—Je songe à une Guerre, de droit ou de force, de logique bien imprévue," adding, "C'est aussi simple qu'une
phrase musicale" (—I am thinking of a War, of right or of
might, of a completely unforeseen logic. It's as simple as a
musical phrase). This last sentence, set off as a concluding
paragraph, could easily refer to all that precedes. The complexities of the evolution from child to artist are here
simplified into an elemental three-point curve as schematic
as Freud's proposition of narcissism, departure, and return:
"Enfant"; "A présent"; "Je songe."

But "phrase musicale" could also refer specifically to the
act of warfare that the speaker contemplates. "Je songe"—
the same verb as in the introduction to the *Saison,* a meditative activity, conveying an intimate relation to self and

positing a future act. And that act: free of the hesitancy of the *Saison* and "Enfance," it is mental ("Je songe"), artistic ("phrase musicale"), yet, like the floods of "Après le déluge," of really destructive potential ("une Guerre"). By implication, it is an act capable of substantially transforming or eliminating the conditions to which as an adult the speaker must submit. Whether this act is lawful is therefore no longer relevant ("de droit ou de force")—it will be an act "de logique bien imprévue," overthrowing the logic of existence, the rules of adult reality. As in Blake and Breton, the evolution from child to adult to artist brings with it a fundamental challenge to the principle of reality.

The last of the child poems in the *Illuminations,* "Jeunesse," gives us considerable material for trying to understand this challenge to the real. It also points us to other texts—to the "ecstasy" poems, which will be discussed in chapter 2—which aspire to possess an unrepressed, superreal condition—while at the same time it underlines all the paradoxes that this effort entails. Alternately straightforward and obscure, "Jeunesse" exhibits the repetitive concern for childhood and growth that Freud accentuated, the sense of loss and nostalgia that characterizes so much child poetry, and yet also a triumph over vulnerability and a projection toward a future esthetic experience—a projected triumph more explicit and more confident than that in most of the other texts discussed. These features are evident in the title, in the division into partly discontinuous and partly overlapping sections, in a form that obviously differs from that of Wordsworth but that is comparably complex. This overlapping complexity compels us to discuss "Jeunesse" not part by part but thematically.

First is the biographical-temporal backbone, visible in the title and in parts II and III. Part II opens with a nostalgic glance at the speaker's childhood:

Homme de constitution ordinaire, la chair n'était-elle pas
un fruit pendu dans le verger, ô journées enfantes! le
corps un trésor à prodiguer; ô aimer, le péril ou la force
de Psyché? La terre avait des versants fertiles en princes
et en artistes, et la descendance et la race nous poussaient
aux crimes et aux deuils: le monde votre fortune et votre
péril.

Man of ordinary constitution, wasn't the flesh a fruit
hung in the orchard, O childhood days! the body a trea-
sure to squander; O to love, the peril or the power of
Psyche? The earth had slopes fertile in princes and artists, and lineage and race pushed us to crimes and
mournings: the world your fortune and your peril.

We encounter again the theme of the child's glorious
bodily and sexual existence, contrasted with the diminished "constitution ordinaire" of the adult man—*homme*
being italicized to emphasize the gap between the two.
The retrospective imperfect, the imaginative possibilities
of the child ("princes," "artistes," "crimes," "deuils"), and
the fabulous richness of possibilities in its world ("le
monde votre fortune et votre péril") are all familiar notes.
The *nous* and *vous* forms, perhaps somewhat like the plural
"Vies," are probably meant to suggest the enlarged, multiple existence of the child. But—like the switches of pronouns in "Après le déluge," "Aube," and "Enfance"—they
also contrast with the *tu* of the speaker addressing himself
elsewhere in the poem, and thus insinuate a certain discontinuity. Similarly, the mythological Psyche, the literary
title ("Sonnet"), and the very overtly organized pairings in
the last sentence quoted all might be read as evoking
childhood through the distance of convention, the filter of
gathering cliché.

For the speaker is indeed removed from childhood, even perhaps from youth, certainly from the adolescence of part III (all ellipses in this passage are Rimbaud's):

> Les voix instructives exilées . . . L'ingénuité physique amèrement rassise . . . Adagio. Ah! l'égoïsme infini de l'adolescence, l'optimisme studieux: que le monde était plein de fleurs cet été! Les airs et les formes mourant . . . Un chœur, pour calmer l'impuissance et l'absence! Un chœur de verres de mélodies nocturnes . . . En effet les nerfs vont vite chasser.

> The instructive voices exiled . . . Physical ingenuousness bitterly calmed . . . Adagio. Ah! the infinite egoism of adolescence, the studious optimism: how the world was full of flowers that summer! The airs and forms dying . . . A choir, to calm impotence and absence! A choir of glasses of nocturnal melodies . . . Yes, the nerves are soon going to slip anchor.

Called "Vingt ans," this passage either dates the poem quite late in the progression of Rimbaud's poetic life or, if written before he was twenty, constitutes a projection forward, beyond the repetitive nostalgia for the past. (The poem thus reminds us of the projections into past and future in "Les Poètes de sept ans" and "le jeune homme . . . de vingt ans" of "Les Sœurs de charité" and shows how pervasive the past-future dialectic is in Rimbaud's child poetry). In any case, there is again the motif of exile, the loss of communication with unnamed voices, an even more bitter experience of physical dimunition with the loss now of adolescence as well as childhood, a pervasive feeling of nervous distraction, impotence, absence. This part of "Jeunesse" takes us further and more sadly along the scale of temporal evolution and loss than poems such as "Aube," "Enfance," or "Guerre."

But recognizing again the temporal structure of loss, we can examine the present moment at which the speaker finds himself and attempts to understand its hopeful possibilities. In the poem's discrete, overlapping structure, we find this "à présent" in part I, the second half of part II, and the opening of part IV. Part I is called "Dimanche," which recalls an earlier, seven-year-old speaker's fury on those awful Sundays, and which, more than "Sonnet" and "Vingt ans," situates the poem's opening movement in the boredom-accented reality of the present, of adult experience. Indeed, much of part I brings to mind the child's enforced submission to an oppressive reality that, as we saw earlier, destroys innocence in so many of Rimbaud's verse poems:

Les calculs de côté, l'inévitable descente du ciel, et la visite des souvenirs et la séance des rhythmes occupent la demeure, la tête et le monde de l'esprit.

—Un cheval détale sur le turf suburbain, et le long des cultures et des boisements, percé par la peste carbonique. Une misérable femme de drame, quelque part dans le monde, soupire après des abandons improbables. Les desperadoes languissent après l'orage, l'ivresse et les blessures. De petits enfants étouffent des malédictions le long des rivières.—

Reprenons l'étude au bruit de l'œuvre dévorante qui se rassemble et remonte dans les masses.

Calculations aside, the inevitable descent from heaven, and the visit of memories and the seance of rhythms occupy the dwelling, the head and the world of the mind.

—A horse riddled with carbonic plague takes off on the suburban turf and along the cultivated and wooded

plots. A miserable theater woman, somewhere in the
world, sighs for improbable surrenders. The desperadoes
languish for storm, drunkenness, and wounds. Little children stifle curses along the rivers.—

Let us take up again the study to the sound of the
devouring work that is gathering and rising among the
masses.

"Les calculs de côté": the speaker begins by taking what
my students always recognize as a "study break" from the
intellectual and esthetic "étude" that absorbs him. Instead
he thinks of the underlying experiences that all along have
motivated it—the fatality of fall and loss ("l'inévitable
descente du ciel"), the persistence of memory ("la visite
des souvenirs"). Then, in the second paragraph, he evokes
the context in which his program is pursued. And, precisely, it is the world of experience, in which the animal
and vegetable realms are organized, made artificial, cor-
roded by the smoke of the industrial city, in which the
impulse to the fantastic and dramatic is trivialized by the
conditions of reality ("misérable," "femme de drame,"
"improbables"), in which stock romantic figures of crimi-
nality "languish" for the opportunity for efficacious revolt,
in which we again see the beings who are central to this
dreary world—the unhappy children, always close to
water, alone, stifling their furious unhappiness. So many
motifs characteristic of the romantic tradition and of Rimbaud's child poetry, all rendered ineffectual by the blan-
keting force of reality, typically embodied in the city but
generalized into a picture of the banality of every facet of
existence. But the speaker of "Jeunesse" dominates this
world—so different from the suffering child's inside view
in the verse poems—and sees it in a comprehensive perspective, as "quelque part dans le monde." Thus he pre-

pares to take up his work again, this time with a view of reality that emphasizes dynamism, unification, and—ambivalently—community: "Reprenons l'étude au bruit de l'œuvre dévorante qui se rassemble et remonte dans les masses."

"Reprenons," "calculs," "étude": "Jeunesse" is the most methodical of the child poems, developing the reasoned dimension of Rimbaud's *voyance,* the method affirmed in "Matinée d'ivresse," the act only glimpsed in "Guerre." The conclusion of part II, after the intervening lines on childhood, expands on this program and its tenuous relationship with the activity that is gathering among the masses:

> Mais à présent, ce labeur comblé, toi, tes calculs, toi, tes impatiences, ne sont plus que votre danse et votre voix, non fixées et point forcées, quoique d'un double événement d'invention et de succès une raison, en l'humanité fraternelle et discrète par l'univers sans images;—la force et le droit réfléchissent la danse et la voix à présent seulement appréciées.

> But at present, this work done, you, your calculations, you, your fits of impatience, are no more than your dance and your voice, not fixed and not at all forced, although a reason for a double event of invention and success, in fraternal and discreet humanity throughout the universe devoid of images;—power and right reflect the dance and the voice only now appreciated.

This passage is obscure enough to invite the speculation that Rimbaud did not give it final revision. Maybe so, but much meaning emerges, and the confusing syntax and pronouns seem to contribute to that meaning. Here the effort

of systematic study—"calculs," "impatiences," "labeur"—
is now "comblé," fulfilled, in a present of accomplishment
and success. This passage, picking up a phrase from part I,
"la séance des rhythmes," states the utter transformation
("ne sont plus que") of laborious effort into the more spontaneous, free-flowing, creative activities of *danse* and *voix*.
If we read the switch from *toi* to *votre* as bespeaking an
enlargement of self akin to what Rimbaud suggested in his
famous "JE est un autre" (I is another) and which some of
the ecstasy poems seem to achieve, then *danse* and *voix*
would imply that the speaker has arrived at a rhythmic and
musical state of being, uninhibited and harmonious possession of self.[22] Indeed one could argue that this transformation is echoed in the difficult sentence structure, in particular the words that from the duality of invention and
successful conclusion cause to emerge a single principle of
reason, "raison" here having resonances both of methodical
human activity and also of universal energies at work in
the world.

The passage is also more explicit about the relation of
Rimbaud's project to the masses of part I: his transformed
state is neither "fixed" nor "forced" into the existence of
humanity, which may be fraternal but which also remains
distant, "discrète." The phrase "l'univers sans images" depicts the human abode in the world as a kind of scattered
emptiness; or if it refers to the poet's newly achieved state,
it implies that he has surpassed the realm of visual sense,
achieved an almost disembodied mode of existence. Finally, the newness of this state, the element of dynamic
progression, is emphasized by a second "à présent"; only
now are "la danse et la voix" appreciated, although they in
fact are the realities reflected by "la force et le droit." "La
force et le droit"—the same words employed in "Guerre,"
here apparently representing the structures that human be-

ings believe to rule their universe, but that are only a mirroring of the more elemental realities to which the poet has now acceded.

Transformation of self, accession to a musical and rhythmic mode of existence, the intuition of a "raison" transcending the categories of right and might in the human sphere—and a corresponding distancing from that sphere—these are the elements that thus far constitute the program of "Jeunesse." Following the biographical details of part III, part IV develops these elements by projecting a suprareal esthetic and personal experience in more confidently detailed terms than we have yet seen:

Tu es encore à la tentation d'Antoine. L'ébat du zèle écourté, les tics d'orgueil puéril, l'affaissement et l'effroi. Mais tu te mettras à ce travail: toutes les possibilités harmoniques et architecturales s'émouvront autour de ton siège. Des êtres parfaits, imprévus, s'offriront à tes expériences. Dans tes environs affluera rêveusement la curiosité d'anciennes foules et de luxes oisifs. Ta mémoire et tes sens ne seront que la nourriture de ton impulsion créatrice. Quant au monde, quand tu sortiras, que sera-t-il devenu? En tout cas, rien des apparences actuelles.

You are still at the temptation of Anthony. The frolic of zeal cut short, the ticks of puerile pride, sagging and fright. But you will set yourself to this work: all harmonic and architectural possibilities will be excited around your seat. Perfect beings, unforeseen, will offer themselves for your experiments. In your vicinity will flow dreamily the curiosity of ancient crowds and of idle luxuries. Your memory and your senses will be but the nourishment of your creative impulse. As for the world, when you go out, what will it have become? In any case, nothing like present appearances.

In this conclusion, the *present* is all impatience for the *future*, awareness of faults that will be overcome, confidence that the artist-saint's ascetically disciplined program will succeed. Untitled, the passage is open-ended, to the point of embodying an uncompromising surmounting by the post-Baudelairean child-artist of *reality* itself. For the speaker imagines himself *inhabiting* an imaginative world, *existing* at the center of musical and architectural *possibilities*. These motifs are recognizable as traditional symbols of the life and creations of the imagination, used in Rimbaud's city and ecstasy poems to create a fantastic transcendence of ordinary categories of experience, but they do not here imply merely the *esthetic* as normally understood. Rather these possibilities are given a dynamic, experiential existence through the suggestion of personal contact ("autour de ton siège") and the reflexive verb of excitement and movement ("s'émouvoir"—the same verb used in "Guerre" to evoke the preternatural existence in childhood of the "Phénomènes"). What was lost in the child's past is now to be regained; indeed, these possibilities will be substantial enough to give rise to experiments with unexpected and perfect beings. "Imprévus" is another word used in "Guerre," to describe the destructive and transforming act of warfare wholly surpassing the known logic of reality. Here its use with "expériences" and the suggestive "s'offriront" reminds us of the child's sexual energy and the erotic imagery in the ecstasy poems, which describe the encounter with, and even the metamorphosis into, such superior beings. Subversive of our norms of reality, the project meditated in "Jeunesse" implies as well an ecstatic self-transformation.

The distanced relationship with the world of men also reappears in a sentence that implies the transcendence of time-space that some of the city and ecstasy poems achieve:

"Dans tes environs affluera rêveusement la curiosité d'anciennes foules et de luxes oisifs." Self-indulgent in tone, reducing the immense "œuvre" of the masses in part I to a vague curiosity, this sentence presents the speaker as a self-sufficient and immensely superior figure, indifferent to all others. And he is indifferent to their world as well, to what they—and we—call reality. While in another context the sentence concerning memory, the senses, and creativity would seem traditional, here, in the concluding words of the poem, the speaker sees himself as stepping definitively out of the world. Especially the expression "apparences actuelles" suggests that experience as we know it is only a succession of appearances in time. By implication, the realm that the poet will *create* and *inhabit* will be more fully *real*.

The contours of this projected reality are most difficult to grasp, because we view reality in the very terms that Rimbaud's poem attempts to transcend. How can we understand this mental activity that will also be a world, possible, created, but also intimately experienced by its creator? The logic of such assertions is so "unexpected," so scornful of our distinctions between subjective and objective, imaginary and substantial, that we falter—as the poem intends us to falter. We can only recall Rimbaud's claim for an *objective* poetry, not at all "un effet de légende,"[23] and link him to serious attempts to modify the implacability of what we call reality in the writing of poets like Blake and Breton and such radical post-Freudians as Marcuse and N. O. Brown. Indeed, when we come to discuss the ecstasy poems and those concerning the city and nature, we shall see just how difficult it is to comprehend to what extent they may represent the real world, to what degree they are entirely inner-focused, uniquely imaginary, to what extent they aim to transcend the con-

traries of real and imaginary (at least in the consciousness
of the reader) through the power of a mental act and the
efficacy of language.

Gathering Up

Such ambitious and ambiguous poetry, extraordinary in
itself, is on the evidence of Rimbaud and the others a
culmination of the poetic fidelity to childhood. The tradition, from Wordsworth to Baudelaire and Rimbaud and
beyond, sees poetry as outgrowth, persistence, preservation of the child's vivid perceptions, which are at once
sensuously more acute and more liberated from the limits
of sense than adult vision. Thus the great poet of nature,
Wordsworth, ultimately conceives of the mind as sub-
limely superior to the world of sense, with the deepest
experiences of childhood opening onto a celestial radiance
and a mysterious abyss beyond the solidity of the normal
world. Hugo's poem on Palestrina depicts the child as
seeing through sense to the spiritual, and Blake's apocalyptic imagination glimpses a world of transcendent energy. Even Baudelaire, oppressed by the weight of time
and the sordid burden of human existence, appalled in
"Le Voyage" by the submission of the child to the im-
mortal ennui of life, nonetheless stresses in the child (and
artist) the tendency to the spiritual, immaterial, abstract,
imaginative—in sum, the revolt against nature and the
real.

Rimbaud's "Les Poètes de sept ans," "Les Sœurs de
charité," "Ma Bohème," and "Le Bateau ivre" similarly
reveal the child as source of the artist. Together with many
other verse poems they also show the struggle between an
oppressive reality and the child's innocent and narcissistic,

self-centered and incredibly beautiful vision and energy. The *Illuminations* emphasize the theme of vision even more forcefully: the presentation in "Enfance" of childhood as "nobler than fable"; the dreamlike visions of the young child and the metallic yet cosmic realm that appears to open to the poet later; the recognition that poetic roles are played to rediscover childhood; and the abstract yet living "Phénomènes" of the child's "optique," and the war that is to succeed them in "Guerre." Finally, there are the more detailed and paradoxical formulations of "Jeunesse"—the speaker's self-transformation; his projected experience of superior beings; his subversion of our concepts of *possible, present, apparent;* his confidence that he can personally step out of reality.

Everything in Rimbaud suggests that this stepping out in no way involves the traditionally spiritual positions of Wordsworth or Hugo, nor the apocalyptic certainty of Blake. Originating in the child's vision, which in texts like "Enfance" and "Aube" has the resonance and intensity of Baudelaire's *surnaturel* and Wordsworth's celestial light, Rimbaud's enterprise in its later phases is threatened by falling off into self-involved estheticism when confronting failure.[24] When successful it seems aimed at transforming what we may perceive to be real, enlarging and enriching and also unsettling our sense of what is there, even to the point of making us wonder whether it is there at all. Of course in "Enfance," "Guerre," and "Jeunesse," this subversion of the real is only projected; these poems follow the course of self-evolution from child, through loss, to an intuition of the imaginative worlds that might recapture something of the child's experience. Those worlds are the subject of chapters 2 and 3; here we have seen the origin of those worlds in the life of the suffering visionary child.

Thus the child-artist's vision is inseparable from the temporal dialectic that structures this poetry. On this point Freud and the poets contribute a fascinating depiction of certain features of the psyche's evolution: the awareness of an absent bliss, constituting an original sense of glory and vulnerability; the interweaving three-point temporal structure involving the persistence of the content of childhood; memory as displaced reconstruction; a fundamental discontinuity, yet an impulse that gathers up past and present in a movement toward the future. Wordsworth, in particular, indicates the complicated poetic structures generated by (and at the same time giving form to) this process of self-elaboration in time. And we discovered a similar complexity in Rimbaud: the elliptical but temporally precise autobiographical structures of the *Saison*, with its sense of loss, its consideration of antecedents, its self-objectification and self-analysis, its will to confront the present (and not incidentally, the real) in a movement toward future integration of self (especially "Adieu"—"*la vérité dans une âme et un corps*").

Consider, too, the mythic narration of experience and loss in "Aube"; the chronological progression of discrete phases in "Enfance," which is simplified into a confident epitome in "Guerre"; the separate, overlapping parts of "Jeunesse" and "Vies," which together show contradictory temporal positions and attitudes—the one an all-confident projection of the definitive surreal act, the other embodying a desolate state in which that act has already receded far into the past and now seems emptied of value. Among these, "Enfance" (especially parts III and V—the selfishness of adults, the alienation of the city) provides a link with the outraged sense of aggression against the child, which is expressed in the *Saison* and so many of the verse poems. In the other *Illuminations*, the temporal process itself becomes the ultimate vulnerability, the essential deprivation; witness the sense of ending and loss in "Aube," "Jeunesse," "Vies," and the consciousness of alienation from an earlier self ("respecté de l'enfance étrange et des affections énormes") of "Guerre."

A variety of forms for this repetitive interrogation of the bond between child and artist, then, and an array of temporal and attitudinal perspectives, link Rimbaud to the romantic child poets and also establish his uniqueness. Among the features Rimbaud and the romantics share are: the emphasis on origins, time, memory; the complexities of tense and person; the motifs of pre-existence-fall, vision-sleep, dawn-noon; the nostalgia for the past and the impulsion toward the future. The intensity of these temporal impulses is as strong in him as anything in Wordsworth or Hölderlin or Blake. At times Rimbaud resolutely or exuberantly moves forward (the *Saison,* "Guerre," "Jeunesse"); at times he expresses a sense of the past as so irremediably distant that it generates an emotional state different from Hölderlin's but approaching madness ("Vies"). In all these respects "Vies" and "Jeunesse" are the most exaggerated of the *Illuminations,* the most uniquely Rimbaldian in their segmented structure and their extremes of surreal confidence and meaningless loss.

They are also the most troubling of Rimbaud's child poems. Rimbaud's deflating of the solidity of the world in "Jeunesse," the speaker's assertion of a self-engendered realm, seems to evidence Freud's view of the artist as, in part at least, rejecting reality in an infantile adherence to magic thinking and language, although Freud's view of reality and imagination is too simple, too dichotomized. But the centrality of the child in Rimbaud, the magic solutions of "Après le déluge" and "Guerre," the attack on the real in "Jeunesse," and, conversely, the rejection of imagination for a most elementary notion of the real at the end of the *Saison* and apparently throughout the last part of Rimbaud's life—all show Rimbaud as equally ruled by a dichotomy of real and unreal, wanting absolutely to "changer la vie," debunking that effort in the cruellest terms. Moreover, the growing indifference to others in "Jeunesse" implies a disturbing degree of human alienation. That poem reveals a form of imaginative activity that constitutes an essential attack on humankind and its world.

"Vies" exacerbates all these elements. As discussed earlier, in that poem the speaker's past (mythic pre-existence, childhood, subsequent evolution, artistic achievements) are correctly evaluated but dismissed. Attitudes toward self and others become virulent: "Qu'est mon néant, auprès de la stupeur qui vous attend?" (What is my nothingness, compared with the stupor that awaits you?) This is a wholly negative version of the "out of this world" motif found in "Jeunesse," involving not only aggression toward others but a judgment of the speaker's own project as worthless. The conclusion of "Vies" goes even further in this respect:

> Dans un grenier où je fus enfermé à douze ans j'ai connu le monde, j'ai illustré la comédie humaine. Dans un cellier j'ai appris l'histoire. A quelque fête de nuit dans une cité du Nord, j'ai rencontré toutes les femmes des anciens peintres. Dans un vieux passage à Paris on m'a enseigné les sciences classiques. Dans une magnifique demeure cernée par l'Orient entier j'ai accompli mon immense œuvre et passé mon illustre retraite. J'ai brassé mon sang. Mon devoir m'est remis. Il ne faut même plus songer à cela. Je suis réellement d'outre-tombe, et pas de commissions.

In an attic where I was locked up at the age of twelve, I
knew the world, I illustrated the human comedy. In a
cellar I learned history. At some night festival in a
northern city, I met all the women of the old painters.
In an old lane in Paris I was taught the classical sciences.
In a magnificent residence surrounded by the entire Orient I accomplished my immense work and passed my illustrious retirement. I have brewed my blood. My duty
is finished. It is no longer even to be thought of. I am
really beyond the grave, and no commissions.

This conclusion of "Vies" employs and deflates many of
the features of romantic child poetry: the biographical outline ("douze ans," "à Paris"); the sense of antecedence and
evolution (the opposition between *passé simple* and *passé
composé* in the first sentence, the ironic "Orient entier"
later); the components of a universal visionary poetry (history, the erotic, painting, science); the temporal dialectic,
which at the end of the poem finally allows no opening to
the future ("Il ne faut même plus songer à cela"[25]). The
tone—mixing absurd hyperbole with self-irony ("Dans
une magnifique demeure"; "J'ai brassé mon sang")—corresponds to this sense of hopelessness. Though no more final
than any other text by Rimbaud, "Vies" debunks the
movement from childhood to visionary poetry. What began in purity, and at times is imagined to engender transcendent vision, is here submitted to a total critique.

Together with the other texts examined, then, "Vies"
provides something like a model of the career of the child
become poet: origins, loss, progression, the accomplishment of a transforming poetry, then radical distancing
from that achievement. In studying other aspects of that
poetic enterprise, we need to keep in mind the shadow cast
by "Vies," as well as the way in which the other childhood

poems prepare that achievement and how much of it is
summarized at the end of "Jeunesse." For perhaps even
more than in the other poets, the child's experience and
the attempt to transform reality are linked in Rimbaud.
The undertaking is hazardous, in a fundamental sense
doomed to failure, perhaps also revelatory of an alienation
produced by the child's suffering, the acute vulnerability
that we have encountered so frequently. Yet it also springs
from some deep and true experience of the child, from its
intactness, energy, vision, innocence. As we shall see in
our study of the ecstasy poems and those on nature and
city, Rimbaud seems sometimes to have accomplished in
his writing what he desired—the transfiguration of world
and self that is a re-enactment of the child's primordial
ecstasy.

TWO

Ecstatic Realizations

Energy is the only life, and is
from the Body; and Reason is the
bound or outward circumference of Energy.
Energy is Eternal Delight. . . .
Exuberance is Beauty.

William Blake

For there to be art, for there
to be any esthetic doing and seeing,
one physiological condition is
indispensable: frenzy.

Friedrich Nietzsche

What ecstatic poetry is and the importance of the ecstatic poetry produced by Rimbaud have not been generally understood. For readers reared in Western cultures, altered states of consciousness, together with their corresponding literary forms, require a special effort of comprehension, which is aided by the furnishing of an appropriate comparative context. Rimbaud's exuberant, searing, tragic poems are best understood in relation both to the nineteenth-century current of ecstatic writing (primarily Nietzsche and Blake, but also Hölderlin, Coleridge, and Yeats) and also to a variety of ecstatic traditions to which some of these writers hearkened. With such materials in mind, I shall argue that Rimbaud produced in a modern context a poetry corresponding to central elements of several ecstatic traditions, that the striking thematic and formal features of his work are thus both highly comprehensible and of great importance.

This chapter is divided into five sections. In the first, I discuss a celebratory poetry of body, world, and divinity for which especially Nietzsche, but also Blake, provide significant parallels, and which provokes the reader, proclaiming a philosophy of exuberance that borders on and prepares the ecstatic. The second section is devoted to the wide-ranging, quite various allusions to altered states throughout Rimbaud's work, which in the context provided by students of the ecstatic show Rimbaud as reproducing typical motifs, even to the point of encompassing contradictory tendencies in an ecstatic syncretism. In the third section, I identify some elements of ecstatic poetics and form as they emerge from the *lettres du voyant* and the *Saison,* again in a comparative perspective. The fourth section concerns Rimbaud's enactments or realizations of the preceding topics in a series of major *Illuminations:* "Matinée d'ivresse," "Being Beauteous," "Dévotion," "Barbare,"

"Villes I." The chapter concludes with an assessment of the limitations, failures, and successes of Rimbaud's ecstatic enterprise and poetic achievement.

Celebrations: Body, World, Divinity

Altered states of consciousness, ranging from dream, hallucination, and drug experiences to ecstasy and mystical glimpses of oneness with reality,[1] are by definition subversive of accepted notions of self, body, and external world in modern Western culture. The ecstatic poet, desirous of attaining more intense experience than such limiting conceptions allow, is therefore necessarily involved in a phase of attack and contrary celebration.

In Rimbaud's case, as in many another nineteenth-century writer, the critique is directed generally against Western rationalism (received notions of consciousness and reality) and against a repressive version of Christianity. It is true, as Nietzsche argued in *Dawn,* that Christian ascetic mysticism had produced a kind of anti-body, anti-world ecstasy, and that Rimbaud himself was attracted to similar experience in some of the *Derniers Vers* and the *Saison.* But on the whole, Rimbaud's critical effort, like Blake's and Nietzsche's, involves an attack on received Christian ethics. At a despondent, skeptical moment in the *Saison,* he laments the fact that, "depuis cette déclaration de la science, le christianisme, l'homme *se joue,* se prouve les évidences. . . . M. Prudhomme est né avec le Christ" ("L'Impossible": since that declaration of science, Christianity, mankind has been *playing and deluding itself,* proving obvious ideas to itself. . . . Monsieur Prudhomme was born with Christ). These lines reveal all his bitterness against contemporary forms of experience, thought, reli-

gion, and social interaction. But on the contrary, the poetry that I discuss in this section aims at reinvigorating
human experience. The analogies with Blake and
Nietzsche elucidate how coherent and significant this effort
is in Rimbaud, as well as furnishing an extended, philosophical context for his brief poems, which, however, are
often programmatic and provoking to reflection in their
own way. Ethics, body, world, divinity, community, and
forms of poetic realization are therefore important, first
briefly in Nietzsche and Blake,[2] then in Rimbaud, from
the early "Soleil et chair" through a group of later pieces,
culminating in the dynamic affirmations of "Génie."

The attack on Western rationalism is a commonplace of
the romantic tradition, and Blake's criticism of science,
empirical philosophy, a "Philosophy of Five Senses," as
well as Nietzsche's fulminations against excessively Apollonian philosophy from Socrates to Kant are too well known
to require repetition. More pertinent is their analysis of the
debilitating hypocrisy of received Christian ethics. In
chapter 1 we saw Blake's depiction of the repression of the
child by parental and religious figures; for example, in
"The Garden of Love" of *Experience,* in which black-clad
priests bind the speaker's "joys & desires," initiating a
pattern of repression and rebellion that persists in his
work, notably in the figure of Orc. Blake also shows us
more subtle versions of such repression, suggesting in *Experience* that pity and humility are disguised selfishness and
deceit, that denial of anger may lead to more deadly kinds
of aggression, and asserting in *The Marriage of Heaven and
Hell* that passivity, reason, prudence, and refusal of desire
are forms of weakness, "the cunning of weak and tame
minds which have power to resist energy." Against this
false notion of the good, evil is viewed positively as "the
active springing from Energy." Energy, excess, pride, lust,

wrath, naked sexuality ("the genitals Beauty") and impulse are, on the contrary, some of the positive forms of human experience.

Nietzsche's ethical attack is similar to Blake's, although frequently even more violent. His work is a sustained "auto-suppression and -transcendence of morality" (Selbst-aufhebung der Moral), attempting to go completely beyond good and evil, viewing such ethical distinctions as inevitably weakening body and soul, and attacking Judeo-Christian ethics as a "slave" morality that has conquered a stronger, "noble" tradition. He too emphasizes that self-abasement and pity can produce resentment, and shows how guilt enmeshes consciousness in a paralyzing obsession with the past, how asceticism reveals an unhealthy hatred of life and its satisfactions. Opposed to all that, there is Nietzsche's intriguing and troubling "noble" ethic of self-affirmation, strength, will, activity, with its celebration of life to the point of desiring the eternal recurrence of all, even suffering: the universe as *circulus vitiosus deus,* affirmed and joined by a self-delighting humanity.

Central to Nietzsche's project is the revalorization of the body. His perspective aims to overcome the alienation from the body that has been effected by Western philosophy and religion. He sees the Dionysian satyr chorus as embodying superb somatic and psychic health, and the Greek cultivation of male beauty as a key to the attainment of the supple and innocent body-self, mirrored in an appreciation of the surrounding world. Hence Zarathustra's attacks on the body's despisers; his preaching of the healthy ego, body, and world; his sense that the cultivation of the self involves recognition of its bodily nature: "Your body and its great reason: that does not say 'I,' but does 'I.' . . . The self also seeks with the eyes of the senses; it also listens with the ears of the spirit. . . . It

controls, and it is in control of the ego too. . . . There is
more reason in your body than in your best wisdom." For
Nietzsche, there is indeed "a mighty ruler" in the body:
"In your body he dwells; he is your body."

But the biological body, the bodily self, has a potential
for enlargement of both animal and divine kinds. For
Nietzsche the satyr chorus is an image of primal man, that
is, of the "synthesis of god and goat." Indeed, the Greek
gods in general reflect a race of noble and proud beings, in
whom man's animality experienced itself as divinized. Acceptance of animality is thus paradoxically the key to the
recognition of our own divinity, according to Nietzsche.
But Nietzsche holds this because he conceives of divinity
in opposition to the distant, Christian God; for him divinity means participation through the body in the immense
energy of the world. Hence his repeated emphasis on the
Dionysian, on profusion and squandering, on the overflowing soul of the "overman," on the "psychology of the
orgiastic as an overflowing feeling of life and strength."
Note that the orgiastic (collective frenzy) involves a group
experience of self-transformation that is, however, fundamentally asocial, in which "authentic man," cleansed of
the "illusions of culture," forgets civic rank and lives outside all social spheres. The body, animal and divine, thus
leads to the experience of ecstasy, which we consider in the
next section, as well as to the puzzling question of ecstatic
community, which we encounter throughout.

Blake's perspective is hardly pagan or biological, but
many of his ideas are close to Nietzsche's. Viewing the
traditional divinity as a projection of all that is deformed
in human psychology and social structures, he asserts that
"All deities reside in the human breast." Or, formulated
more polemically: "Thou art a Man, God is no more, /
Thine own Humanity learn to Adore." Blake expresses this

literal belief in man's capacity for divinity in his prophetic books by recounting the fall of the one great Human Divine Being into alienation and dispersion, and by intimating the transformations that would be needed for man to regain his fully integrated state.

In this complex process of renovation, the body is crucial, for it cannot be imagined as different from the soul. In *The Marriage of Heaven and Hell* the body is described as the visible portion of the soul in an age of shrunken vision, the "portion of Soul discern'd by the five Senses, the chief inlets of Soul in this age." Lest this seem to overaccentuate soul, Blake immediately re-emphasizes the body: "Energy is the only life, and is from the Body"; "Energy is Eternal Delight." The body then is participation in the energy that is the fundamental reality, a notion accompanied, as in Nietzsche, by emphasis on themes of profusion, overflowing, excess. Blake's overflowing aims at a vision that is apocalyptic rather than Dionysian, but that nonetheless produces great joy: "The whole creation will be consumed and appear infinite and holy, whereas it now appears finite & corrupt." For this, too, the body is essential: the "doors of perception" must be cleansed, which will "come to pass by an improvement of sensual enjoyment." Thus even in Blake's later apocalyptic works the body remains an important agent of regeneration. Revolution and liberation are in their initial and penultimate phases represented by the sexually violent Orc and Los's and Luvah's Dionysian revelry; the movement toward the fully divine humanity passes through the guiltless sexual sports of Beulah; and the highest state, Eternity, abounds in the most intense activity, that of the risen body as universal energy.

These materials in Blake and Nietzsche, which I can only summarize here, are directly relevant for Rimbaud. Negational ethics in the service of a view of the body as both animal and divine, and which lead to celebration of existence and universe, correspond to central features of Rimbaud's work. The tendency to ecstasy, the enigma of asocial collectivity, and the conflict of apocalyptic and Dionysian moments (transcendent and immanent poles of a single, elemental experience?) are also persistent aspects of his writing. Finally, the forms of writing by Blake and Nietzsche, while complex and greatly different, alert us to aspects of Rimbaud's work: denunciation of ruling mentalities, proclamations of new philosophies, and forms capable of enacting the newly discovered (or rediscovered) sense of vitality.

Many of these aspects are already apparent in the early "Soleil et chair," a highly derivative but, considering the poet's age and circumstances, also provocative poem. Typically, it bemoans rationalism, the influence of Christianity, the closing off of the senses, and the degradation of the body:

> [L'Homme] dit: Je sais les choses,
> Et va, les yeux fermés et les oreilles closes.
> [Man says: I comprehend things,
> And he goes off, his eyes closed and his ears closed.
> · · ·
> l'autre Dieu nous attelle à sa croix
> [the other God harnesses us to his cross]
> · · ·
> l'Homme est triste et laid
> [Man is sad and ugly]
> · · ·
> Il a des vêtements, parce qu'il n'est plus chaste,
> · · ·
> Et qu'il a rabougri . . .
> Son corps Olympien aux servitudes sales!
> [He wears clothes, because he is no longer chaste,
> · · ·

> And because he has stunted . . .
> His Olympian body in filthy servitude!]
>
>   . . .
>
> Notre pâle raison nous cache l'infini!
> [Our pale reason hides the infinite from us!]

In cliché form, these lines rehearse the attack on Christian, rationalist, anti-body thought. More interestingly, such themes are related to another well-known motif, the lament for lost pagan health and the desire to recover it, which for the materials under discussion here provides an informing structure roughly equivalent to the myth of childhood on the personal level. Hence the opening portion of the poem stresses nostalgia and loss, in connection particularly with the body:

> —O Vénus, ô Déesse!
> Je regrette les temps de l'antique jeunesse,
> Des satyres lascifs, des faunes animaux,
> ....
> Je regrette les temps où la sève du monde,
> L'eau du fleuve, le sang rose des arbres verts
> Dans les veines de Pan mettaient un univers!
>
> —O Venus, O Goddess!
> I miss the time of antique youth,
> Of lascivious satyrs, of animal fauns,
> ....
> I miss the time when the world's sap,
> The river's water, the rose blood of green trees
> In the veins of Pan created a universe!

Among the echoes of romantic and Parnassian authors, Rimbaud's characteristic intensity appears in this evocation of the vitality of the body, a splendid fusion of animality and divinity. The parallelism of sap, water, and blood, enforcing a view of the universe as existing within the figure of Pan, hardly breaks new poetic ground. But the similarity to Nietzsche's view of man as animal and divine and to Blake's myths of the reintegration of universal reality within a giant mankind is noteworthy. Such motifs persist in Rimbaud's poetry, and understandably so, since "Soleil et chair" is the first of a succession of texts that tend more and more to transcend nostalgia in favor of a structure of projected realization of man's divinity:

> Si les temps revenaient, les temps qui sont venus!
> —Car l'Homme a fini!
> [If the days were to come back, the days that have come!
> —For Man has finished!]
>
> . . .
>
> Il ressuscitera, libre de tous ses Dieux
> [He will revive, free of all his Gods]
>
> . . .
>
> . . . le dieu qui vit, sous son argile charnelle,
> Montera, montera, brûlera sous son front!
> [. . . the god who lives, under his fleshy clay,
> Will rise, rise, burn under his brow!]
>
> . . .
>
> O! L'Homme a relevé sa tête libre et fière!
> Et le rayon soudain de la beauté première
> Fait palpiter le dieu dans l'autel de la chair!
> [O! Man has raised again his head free and proud!
> And the sudden ray of the first beauty
> Makes the god tremble in the altar of the flesh!]
>
> . . .
>
> O splendeur de la chair! ô splendeur idéale!
> [O splendor of flesh! O ideal splendor!]

Progressively these lines from the last two parts of "Soleil et chair" evoke the desire for regeneration and then its actualization. This act involves a liberation from tradi-

tional gods and, in contrast, an experience of man's own
divinity, which is felt as innate, interior, in the body. The
mixture of physical and idealizing vocabulary is a bit awk-
ward but suggests a first attempt to convey the body's
capacity for divinization.

In short, "Soleil et chair" appears as an initial effort to
criticize man's repressed state and to enact poetically a
version of a revitalized existence—an enterprise that continues to inform Rimbaud's work, as these expressions
from three of the *Illuminations* attest:

> On nous a promis d'enterrer dans l'ombre l'arbre du bien
> et du mal, de déporter les honnêtetés tyranniques, afin
> que nous amenions notre très pur amour.
> [They promised us to bury in shadow the tree of good
> and evil, to deport tyrannical proprieties, so that we may
> bring forward our very pure love.]
>
> *("Matinée d'ivresse")*

> Il est l'amour, mesure parfaite et réinventée, raison mer-
> veilleuse et imprévue
> [He is love, measure perfect and reinvented, marvellous
> and unforeseen reason]
>
> *("Génie")*

> J'avais en effet, en toute sincérité d'esprit, pris
> l'engagement de le rendre à son état primitif de fils du
> Soleil,—et nous errions, . . . moi pressé de trouver le
> lieu et la formule.
> [I had indeed, in all sincerity of spirit, undertaken to
> return him to his primitive state of son of the Sun,—and
> we wandered, . . . with me pressed to find the place and
> the formula.]
>
> *("Vagabonds")*

Similarly, in "Angoisse" the poet expresses his desire to overcome his "inhabilité fatale" (fatal incapacity) and to achieve the "restitution . . . de la franchise première" (restitution of the first franchise), that is, to experience a transformed existence: "O palmes! diamant!—Amour, force!—plus haut que toutes joies et gloires!—de toutes façons, partout,—démon, dieu,—Jeunesse de cet être-ci: moi!" (O palms! diamond!—Love, power!—higher than all joys and glories!—in every way, everywhere,—demon, god,—Youth of this being: me!).

Together, these phrases suggest the magnitude of the project that is begun in "Soleil et chair." In addition to the antiethical, pagan, and erotic motifs, we see a musical analogy that suggests enlarged and harmonious existence, the recurrent notion of a rediscovery of a lost state, the expression in "Angoisse" of an intensified experience of the self as well as its potential for a kind of demonic divinization, a systematic search to realize this state ("moi pressé de trouver le lieu et la formule"), and the threat of failure that, apparently more menacingly than for Blake and Nietzsche, continues to undermine his undertaking ("notre inhabilité fatale").

"Soleil et chair" thus points to central aspects of Rimbaud's later work. To further illustrate these we now turn to similar thematic elements in texts representing several stages of his production and embodying as well typical forms—what we may call provocations, programmatic proclamations, engenderings, and realizations or enactments.

Take together, for example, the *Illuminations* "H" and "Antique," the earlier verse poem "Tête de faune," and the first text in the unpublished and obscene "Les Stupra." All these texts involve Rimbaud's pagan myth; the theme of the body as animal, sexual, quasi-divine; and techniques of provocation and actualization. The outrageous emphasis in "H" on violation—"monstruosités," "gestes atroces," "solitude" and "méchanique érotique," "lassitude" and "dynamique amoureuse"—has set critics to chattering of masturbation, pederasty, and prostitution. And the poem indeed does concern an unleashing of multiple forms of sexuality. "Les Stupra," private poems in more ways than one, are perhaps more provoking still, in their emphasis on penis and anus, blood and excrement, as well as in their homosexual theme:

> Les anciens animaux saillissaient, même en course,
> Avec des glands bardés de sang et d'excrément.
> Nos pères étalaient leur membre fièrement.

> Ancient animals spurted, even as they ran,
> With glans larded with blood and excrement.
> Our fathers displayed their members proudly.

Both "Les Stupra" and "H" shockingly call attention to the body—to its full sexual potential and to its animality. Note also that in both the pagan myth of "Soleil et chair" continues to function. "Les anciens animaux" is a lament for a lost state of animal-human vigor, which has now given way to "une heure stérile" (a sterile hour). But if that text is pessimistic, "H" is hardly so. It first harks back to earlier epochs of vigorous health: "Sous la surveillance d'une enfance elle a été, à des époques nombreuses, l'ardente hygiène des races" (Under guardianship by a childhood, she has been, in numerous epochs, the ardent hygiene of races). And by its riddle conclusion ("trouvez Hortense"—find Hortense) it implies that the speaker possesses the secret to revitalized experience and provokes the reader to attempt to discover this secret for himself.

Provocation thus becomes invitation, and the notions of private poem, initiation, secret, and realization are all enlarged, with "Les Stupra" taking their place in a series of disturbing, inviting communications.

The prose poem "Antique," a later version of "Tête de faune," illustrates the end of the thematic and formal continuum opposite to "Les anciens animaux." For in conveying an accessible vision of one of the mythic creatures first seen in "Soleil et chair," it moves away from mere animality and toward a sense of a larger, quasi-divine being whom it evokes not through provocation but through serene and confident enactment. To read "Antique" together with "Tête de faune" emphasizes the completeness of this enactment:

Antique

Gracieux fils de Pan! Autour de ton front couronné de
fleurettes et de baies tes yeux, des boules précieuses,
remuent. Tachées de lies brunes, tes joues se creusent.
Tes crocs luisent. Ta poitrine ressemble à une cithare, des
tintements circulent dans tes bras blonds. Ton cœur bat
dans ce ventre où dort le double sexe. Promène-toi, la
nuit, en mouvant doucement cette cuisse, cette seconde
cuisse et cette jambe de gauche.

Antique

Gracious son of Pan! About your brow crowned with
flowerets and berries your eyes, precious orbs, move.
Stained with brown lees, your cheeks become hollow.
Your fangs gleam. Your chest resembles a zither, tin-
klings circulate in your blond arms. Your heart beats in
that stomach where the double sex sleeps. Walk, at
night, gently moving that thigh, that second thigh and
that left leg.

Tête de faune

Dans la feuillée, écrin vert taché d'or,
Dans la feuillée incertaine et fleurie
De fleurs spendides où le baiser dort,
Vif et crevant l'exquise broderie,

Un faune effaré montre ses deux yeux
Et mord les fleurs rouges de ses dents blanches.
Brunie et sanglante ainsi qu'un vin vieux,
Sa lèvre éclate en rires sous les branches.

Et quand il a fui—tel qu'un écureuil—
Son rire tremble encore à chaque feuille,
Et l'on voit épeuré par un bouvreuil
Le Baiser d'or du Bois, qui se recueille.

Faun's Head

In the foliage, green jewel box spotted with gold,
In the uncertain foliage flowering
With splendid flowers where the kiss sleeps,
Alive and rending the exquisite embroidery,

A frightened faun shows his two eyes
And bites the red flowers with his white teeth.
Brown and bloody like an old wine,
His lip bursts out in laughter under the branches.

And when he has fled—like a squirrel—
His laugh trembles still on each leaf,
And one sees frightened by a bullfinch
The golden Kiss of the Woods, communing with itself.

As in "Soleil et chair," the imagery in both poems
stresses the integration of animal and vegetable orders, the
splendid physicality of the *faunes,* a vibrancy of existence
that has overtones of inebriation, sexuality, and animal

health. "Antique" is a more complete version of these themes. It uses a musical motif to suggest the experience of harmonious existence within the body: "Ta poitrine ressemble à une cithare, des tintements circulent dans tes bras blonds." It also asserts the fuller, androgynous sexuality to which the homosexual is only a contributing element: "Ton cœur bat dans ce ventre où dort le double sexe. Promène-toi, la nuit, en mouvant doucement cette cuisse, cette seconde cuisse et cette jambe de gauche." In contrast to the aggressive assertion of the sexual in "H" and "Les Stupra," here an atmosphere of velvety self-assurance encompasses both the faun and the speaker. The exclamatory opening sentence, the present tense and descriptive mode throughout, the repeated intimate personal pronoun, the reference at the end to "la nuit," and finally the last sentence, in which direct address to the faun seems to cause it to come to life and movement before our eyes—all indicate how close this mythical being is to the consciousness and experience of the speaker and, by suggestion, to the intrigued awareness of the reader.

This reading suggests a function for the impressionism of "Tête de faune." The shimmering evocation of "la feuillée, écrin vert taché d'or," "la feuillée incertaine" in which "un faune effaré" is glimpsed, only to flee (as would a more familiar creature—"tel qu'un écureuil"), leaves behind a strange impression of a mythic presence in the consciousness, even *sight,* of the onlooker: "Et l'on voit épeuré par un bouvreuil / Le Baiser d'or du Bois, qui se recueille." "Tête de faune" is an effectively rendered glimpse of what "Soleil et chair" only asserted, and of what "Antique" later brings more fully to the threshold of awareness.

Techniques of discovery and communication, these, proposing to the reader possibilities not normally accessible in our world. And, in "Soleil et chair," "Tête de faune," "Les Stupra," "Antique," and "H" already quite a range of experience and modes of expression is involved. Pagan poems all, they insist on the bodily-sexual-animal as infused with intenser, quasi-divine life. But they accomplish this by attracting us through a combination of aggressiveness and self-possessed assurance. They differ in form as well, indicating something of the poetic-collective undertaking in which Rimbaud is engaged. Doctrinal in "Soleil et chair," the first of "Les Stupra," and "H," they are also proposed as realizable in our minds and experience—the impressionism and discovery in "Tête de faune," the riddle of "H," the presentness, intimacy, and awakening to life of "Antique."

From provocation to realization, then, Rimbaud's poetry presents the body as elementally animal and powerfully sexual; at the same time it strives to bring to consciousness the mythic figures of pagan experience. From attention to the body there comes a revitalized sense of the divine, indeed engenderings of superhuman figures in texts from "Voyelles" to "Génie," which we need now to explore, continuing to note forms of actualization, provocations and proclamations, celebrations and enactments.

Two verse poems, "L'Etoile a pleuré rose" and "Voyelles," so well known as not to require exhaustive commentary, when taken together illustrate how a reflection on the body (which is simultaneously a reflection on language) can engender a sense of divinity:

> L'Etoile a pleuré rose au cœur de tes oreilles,
> L'infini roulé blanc de ta nuque à tes reins;
> La mer a perlé rousse à tes mammes vermeilles
> Et l'Homme saigné noir à ton flanc souverain.

The Star has wept rose in the heart of your ears,
The infinite rolled white from your nape to your loins;
The sea has pearled ruddy on your vermilion breasts
And Man bled black on your sovereign flank.

Voyelles

A noir, E blanc, I rouge, U vert, O bleu: voyelles,
Je dirai quelque jour vos naissances latentes:
A, noir corset velu des mouches éclatantes
Qui bombinent autour des puanteurs cruelles,

Golfes d'ombre; E, candeurs des vapeurs et des tentes,
Lances des glaciers fiers, rois blancs, frissons d'ombelles;
I, pourpres, sang craché, rire des lèvres belles
Dans la colère ou les ivresses pénitentes;

U, cycles, vibrements divins des mer virides,
Paix des pâtis semés d'animaux, paix des rides
Que l'alchimie imprime aux grands fronts studieux;

O, suprême Clairon plein des strideurs étranges,
Silences traversés des Mondes et des Anges:
—O l'Oméga, rayon violet de Ses Yeux!

Vowels

A black, E white, I red, U green, O blue: vowels,
One day I will tell your latent births:
A, black hairy corset of shining flies
Buzzing, bursting around cruel stenches,

Gulfs of shadow; E, candors of vapors and tents,
Lances of proud glaciers, white kings, quivering of umbels;
I, purples, spit blood, laughter of beautiful lips
In anger or penitent drunkenness;

U, cycles, divine vibrations of viridian seas,
Peace of pastures sown with animals, peace of wrinkles
Which alchemy prints on great studious brows;

O, supreme Clarion full of strange stridors,
Silences traversed by Worlds and by Angels:
—O the Omega, violet ray of Her Eyes!

Critics like Emilie Noulet and Robert Faurisson have
very well grasped in these texts the interrelations between
language, the body, divinity, and nature or universal reality. Thus, although on one level "L'Etoile a pleuré rose" is
a *blason de la femme,* a stylized emblazoning and celebration
of woman, it also calls attention to its own verbal structure, "its squared composition . . . four times four words
which are read vertically as well as verse by verse, and of
which each quarter represents simultaneously a world and a
category of speech, in a doubly parallel succession: sub-
stance–action–colors–bodily zones of sexual pleasure."[3]
And "Voyelles" explicitly begins as a reflection on the
engendering power of language ("naissances latentes"). But
both texts through their language also give rise to a sense
of the body, and beyond it of the cosmos. Thus "L'Etoile a
pleuré rose" makes the powerful female body ("souverain")
appear to be produced not only through language and the
suffering erotic activity of men—and we should note the
suggestion of sexual substances, organs, and actions in
expressions such as "perlé rousse" and "saigné noir"—but
also by star and sea and the infinity of the universe. And in
"Voyelles" the alphabet generates a series of images that in
the quatrains are recognizable as particular objects, sensations, beings, and emotions, but open up in the tercets to
a global vision of the world and then, beyond that, to
some apocalyptic presence. Of course that presence is from

the beginning emphatically erotic, the sexualized body being suggested in this poem by such expressions as "noir
corset velu," "puanteurs cruelles," "lances," "frissons
d'ombelles," "sang craché, rire des lèvres belles." But
whereas "L'Etoile a pleuré rose" establishes almost static
connections between language, thought, body, and nature,
in "Voyelles" these same elements are active in a process
by which basic reality and bodily experience, and then the
totality of the universe and a great divine Being seem to be
generated: "O l'Oméga, rayon violet de Ses Yeux!"

Thus Rimbaud's attention to the body gives rise to a
sense of apocalyptic divinity (especially in "Clairon," "Silences traversés des Mondes et des Anges," "l'Oméga"),
re-enacting a mystical-alchemical version of the poetic
function (a sonnet embodies the universe) and recalling as
well the Illuminist-Blakean reconstitution of the single
universal Being. All the poems discussed thus far, in fact,
contribute to Rimbaud's creation of a more acutely animal,
multiply sexual, divine body; but it is "Voyelles" that
most clearly exemplifies the element of poetic engendering
as well as the tendency to transcendence or apocalypse. On
the contrary, in "Génie," which we must study with its
companion poem "Solde," the *process* of engendering and
the impulse to transcendence are absent. Instead, in a
magnificent culmination of the issues discussed here,
"Génie" returns us to programmatic form, obviates the
need for both provocation and for an unfolding of the
divine figure by giving us absolute presence from the beginning, and eschews transcendence in favor of a dynamic
immanence close to that which we see in Nietzsche.

But first "Solde," the ironic provocation that is the
necessary counterpart to the affirmations of "Génie."
"Solde" proposes many of the values of "Génie," but in a
provocative commercial mode whose ambiguity has led to

opposing interpretations of the poem. It opens by presenting positively the state of augmented being that we have
been discussing, in opposition to the Judeo-Christian ethic
and its social and intellectual extensions:

> A vendre ce que les Juifs n'ont pas vendu, ce que no-
> blesse ni crime n'ont goûté, ce qu'ignorent l'amour mau-
> dit et la probité infernale des masses; ce que le temps ni
> la science n'ont pas à reconnaître.

> For sale, what the Jews didn't sell, what nobility and
> crime have not tasted, what forbidden love and the infer-
> nal probity of the masses are ignorant of; what neither
> time nor science has to recognize.

In this late formulation, the negation of ethical-social
codes ("infernale" reverses ethical values), and of related
experiential-conceptual categories and methods (time, science) is augmented by a critique of forms of rebellion; this
critique recalls Nietzsche's "noble" ethic and "criminal"
acts of philosophical attack, as well as Rimbaud's own
homosexuality ("l'amour maudit"). But despite the sophistication as to means, the goal remains the same, the rediscovery of integral existence, expressed by familiar musical
and communal motifs as well as the imagery of sexual
profusion:

> Les Voix reconstituées; l'éveil fraternel de toutes les
> énergies chorales et orchestrales et leurs applications
> instantanées; l'occasion, unique, de dégager nos sens!
> A vendre les Corps sans prix, hors de toute race, de
> tout monde, de tout sexe, de toute descendance! Les ri-
> chesses jaillissant à chaque démarche! Solde de diamants
> sans contrôle!

The Voices reconstituted; the fraternal awakening of all choral and orchestral energies and their immediate application; the opportunity, unique, to free our senses!

For sale priceless Bodies, beyond all race, world, sex, lineage! Riches springing up at each step! Clearance on diamonds without control!

These multiple energies are achieved through an intellectual-esthetic effort, already encountered in "Jeunesse," and involve a dynamism of mankind and world such as we find in "A une raison" and "Génie." And later, in "Solde," there are expressions such as "les applications de calcul et les sauts d'harmonie inouïs" (the applications of calculus and unheard leaps of harmony); "les habitations et les migrations, sports, féeries et comforts parfaits, et le bruit, le mouvement et l'avenir qu'ils font" (the habitations and migrations, sports, enchantments and perfect comforts, and the noise, the movement and the future that they produce); "Elan insensé et infini aux splendeurs invisibles, aux délices insensibles" (Wild and infinite surge to invisible splendors, insensible delights). But these energies are primarily experienced in a multiple body of inestimable value ("les Corps sans prix"), which goes beyond the limits of the physical as we know them: "dégager nos sens!"; "hors de toute race, de tout monde, de tout sexe, de toute descendance!" These expressions celebrate what Rimbaud was pursuing throughout the earlier texts: renovation of the body, including suggestions of reconstitution, harmony, awakening; a curious communal enlargement; a victory over the limits of the physical, riches, and profusion.

However, the voice of total confidence that speaks in this poem is not lacking in ironic overtones. Housing, migrations, sports, light entertainment, perfect comfort—

these are the paltry versions of the search for integral existence provided in the modern world and satirized in poems like "Mouvement" and "Soir historique." Elsewhere in "Solde" the tone edges toward a mocking, semisadistic invocation of socioeconomic groups and corresponding ethical positions that contrasts with the "éveil fraternel" of musical energies already mentioned: "A vendre l'anarchie pour les masses; la satisfaction irrépressible pour les amateurs supérieurs; la mort atroce pour les fidèles et les amants!" (For sale, anarchy for the masses; irrepressible satisfaction for superior amateurs; atrocious death for the faithful and for lovers!); "Elan insensé . . . et ses secrets affolants pour chaque vice—et sa gaîté effrayante pour la foule" (Wild surging and its frightening secrets for each vice—and its terrifying gaiety for the crowd).

These lines illustrate the difficulty of estimating the tone of "Solde." They enthusiastically reverse ethical values, proposing death for the faithful and an enticing secret to satisfaction in reward for vice. But the ebullient suggestion of death for the good indicates that the element of provocation is not absent. Similarly the indiscriminately generous attitude toward various social and ethical groups seems ironic. The masses and the crowd, no less than the figures of power and self-indulgence ("les amateurs supérieurs"), are supposedly *all* to be satisfied. This passage evokes real class conflict, but scornfully (if the masses want anarchy, let them have anarchy). Indeed, since in the social and economic world all class interests cannot be satisfied, these lines in fact tend to devalue ethical and social categories. They are infused with an irony that is close to Nietzsche's and finally are punctuated by a brutal withdrawal: "A vendre les Corps, les voix, l'immense opulence inquestionable, ce qu'on ne vendra jamais. Les vendeurs ne sont pas à bout de solde! Les voyageurs n'ont pas à rendre leur commission de si tôt!" (For sale, the Bodies, the voices, the immense unquestionable opulence, what will never be sold. The sellers are not through with the sale! The travelers don't have to render accounts so fast!).

This concluding paragraph nicely summarizes the major features of the poem. By a technique of succinct, rhythmic recapitulation, which we will encounter again, it gathers up the themes of body, voice, and opulent power. All these remain beyond question—as experienced by the speaker. But immediately the commercial metaphor, through which the superior experience was supposedly to have been made available to all, is reintroduced and reversed. This reversal has been prepared by the earlier insinuation of the register of advertising discourse into the emphatic style of "Solde": "l'occasion, unique, de dégager nos sens!"; "les trouvailles et les termes non soupçonnés, possession immédiate" (the opportunity, unique, to free our senses!; the unsuspected finds and terms, immediate possession). In fact, the title and recurrent commercial formula, "à vendre," emphasize from the beginning the "come-on" structure of the poem, with its proposal to make available, through the techniques and vocabulary of the socioproductive order, an experience undermining that order and its modes of expression. "Solde" is in some sense an attack on its own public, a deflating of the notion of collectivity, at least as conceived in socioeconomic terms. What the speaker possesses with exuberant confidence is proffered and then refused to us, so long as we continue to exist in the mode of experience and discourse that seems natural to us and that the poem subverts.

We can see therefore that "Solde" is both presentation of and refusal to convey the superior state, a scornful withdrawal that nonetheless programmatically enumerates the central features of the revitalized mode of being. These qualities make "Solde" a good preparation for "Génie," for what is withdrawn in the former is fully affirmed in the latter.[4] Indeed "Génie" recapitulates all the elements that I have been tracing: anti-Christian ethics, celebration of body-self, world-divinity, and asocial collectivity. And it does so in a mode that surpasses the provocation of "H," "Les Stupra," and "Solde" as well as the necessity to engender divinity and the apocalyptic tendency of "Voyelles." "Génie" is a generous celebration of man and world as already present, immanent, dynamic, divine.

First then the negation of Christian divinity and ethics:

Et si l'Adoration s'en va, sonne, sa promesse sonne:
"Arrière ces superstitions, ces anciens corps, ces ménages
et ces âges. C'est cette époque-ci qui a sombré!"

   Il ne s'en ira pas, il ne redescendra pas d'un ciel, il
n'accomplira pas la rédemption des colères de femmes et
des gaîtés des hommes et de tout ce péché: car c'est fait,
lui étant, et étant aimé.

. . . .

   Sa vue, sa vue! tous les agenouillages anciens et les
peines *relevées* à sa suite.

. . . .

   O lui et nous! l'orgueil plus bienveillant que les
charités perdues.

And if the Adoration goes away, rings, his promise rings:
"Away with these superstitions, these bodies of old, these
households and these ages. It's this epoch that has
foundered!"

   He won't go away, he won't descend again from a
heaven, he will not accomplish the redemption of the
angers of women and of the gaieties of men and of all
this sin: for it's done, since he is, and is loved.

. . . .

His view, his view! all the ancient genuflections and penances *relieved* in his wake.

....

O he and us! pride more benevolent than lost charities.

Here the distant, punishing, redeeming Christian divinity and the related features of adoration, sin, guilt, humility, submission, and charity are presented as superstitions. Opposed to them is an instantaneous relationship with divinity—a relationship simultaneously of love and pride. This *orgueil bienveillant* is close to Blake's and Nietzsche's stance against Christian self-abasement and in favor of vigorous self-affirmation, which is seen as inevitably creating a celebration of reality as a whole. The promise and reality of that transformation, pursued through lifelong endeavor by those writers, are proclaimed by Rimbaud with a similar fervor. *If,* if the ancient superstitions are transcended, then the new promise will be realized: a whole era of human culture, with its false conceptions of body, relationships, and even temporality ("ces anciens corps, ces ménages et ces âges"), will have ended. This "si," somehow initiating a discourse asserting that this transformation *has* occurred ("C'est cette époque-ci qui a sombré"), and followed by more and more exclamatory affirmations of the reality of the change ("car c'est fait"; "Sa vue, sa vue!"; "O lui et nous!"), recalls the structure of realization in "Soleil et chair" and indicates the seriousness of Rimbaud's effort to negate effectively a restrictive morality, and to proclaim, found, bring about the new sense of ethics and reality.

Consequently the new reality, perceived as a divine presence, *is* proclaimed as *present,* from the opening words of the poem:

Il est l'affection et le présent puisqu'il a fait la maison
ouverte à l'hiver écumeux et à la rumeur de l'été, lui qui
a purifié les boissons et les aliments, lui qui est le
charme des lieux fuyants et le délice surhumain des stations. Il est l'affection et l'avenir, la force et l'amour que
nous, debout dans les rages et les ennuis, nous voyons
passer dans le ciel de tempête et les drapeaux d'extase.

He is affection and the present since he has made the
house open to the foaming winter and to the hum of
summer, he who has purified drinks and food, he who is
the charm of fleeting places and the superhuman delight
of stations. He is affection and the future, strength and
love which we, upright in rages and boredom, we see
passing in the stormy sky and the flags of ecstasy.

This paragraph is in the mode of entire affirmation, attaining a kind of generosity, without ignoring the realities of
suffering and unhappiness: "debout dans les rages et les
ennuis." This generosity is visible in the form, which is
presentational and definitional, telling us without irony
what the *génie* is and what he does. The most fully realized
of the giant beings that we have encountered in Rimbaud,
the *génie* is a superhuman, personalized, eroticized force,
who in his immanence and association with natural cycles
recalls Nietzsche's genius of the universe.[5] Here indeed
Rimbaud achieves his greatest celebration of the fundamental realities of human existence in the world—habitations, seasons, food, drink, movement, and activity.

By definition too, the *génie*'s energy is uniquely of the
present and future. To recognize the *génie* as essentially
presence and activity involves a transcendence of a past-
dominated mentality in favor of a capacity for encounter
and acceptance of present existence. In this respect, in

terms of content and form, "Génie" shows the ground covered by Rimbaud from the nostalgic myth of "Soleil et chair" and "Les anciens animaux." What those poems aspired to, what "Antique" and "Voyelles" and others brought nearer, is realized now as an encompassing and ceaseless energy, which involves change, progression, *and* suffering. Thus later: "O monde! et le chant clair des malheurs nouveaux!" (O world! and the clear song of new misfortunes!). Rimbaud's *génie* is the entire dynamic life of the world, viewed as supremely valuable, and humankind's unrestrained participation in it.

This participation is again rooted in the revalued ethic of the body, as the second paragraph of the poem makes clear (concluding ellipsis is Rimbaud's):

> Il est l'amour, mesure parfaite et réinventée, raison merveilleuse et imprévue, et l'éternité: machine aimée des qualités fatales. Nous avons tous eu l'épouvante de sa concession et de la nôtre: ô jouissance de notre santé, élan de nos facultés, affection égoïste et passion pour lui, lui qui nous aime pour sa vie infinie . . .

> He is love, measure perfect and reinvented, marvellous and unforeseen reason, and eternity: beloved machine of fatal qualities. We have all known the terror of his concession and of ours: O rapture of our health, surge of our faculties, egoistic affection and passion for him, he who loves us for his infinite life . . .

This passage emphasizes the body, self-joy, and once again an indispensable egoism, the self-affirmation that produces recognition of the value of existence and world. Not only is love thereby reinvented (asserting what "Délires I" of the *Saison* denies); so also is reason, which is redefined in sexual terms that also marvellously transcend the ordinary categories of our logic: "l'amour, mesure parfaite et réinventée, raison merveilleuse et imprévue."

Many significant features of a certain romantic literary tradition come together in this paragraph: innocent selfishness; reason reconciled with, identified with the erotic; a strong narcissism that celebrates the nonself. The values of childhood treated in chapter 1 are thus englobed in a larger project of renovation of self and world as erotic satisfaction. The power that accomplishes this renovation transcends the aggressive, bestial accents of "H" and "Les Stupra" without neglecting the frightening potential of the sexual. Expressions like "machine aimée des qualités fatales" and "l'épouvante de sa concession" reconcile power with satisfaction, just as the "affection égoïste" is seen to overflow into "passion pour lui," affirmation of self leading to appreciation of universal life: "lui qui nous aime pour sa vie infinie."

In keeping with this overflowing of self, the definitional opening paragraphs of the poem and the succeeding passages of ethical critique, which I examined first, give way to an exclamatory mode, in which the *génie*-world is celebrated:

> O ses souffles, ses têtes, ses courses; la terrible célérité de la perfection des formes et de l'action.
> O fécondité de l'esprit et immensité de l'univers!
> Son corps! Le dégagement rêvé, le brisement de la grâce croisée de violence nouvelle!
> ....
> Son jour! l'abolition de toutes souffrances sonores et mouvantes dans la musique plus intense.
> Son pas! les migrations plus énormes que les anciennes invasions.
> ....
> O monde! et le chant clair des malheurs nouveaux!

O his breaths, his heads, his racings; the terrible celer-
ity of the perfection of forms and of action.
O fecundity of the spirit and immensity of the universe!
His body! the dreamed-of deliverance, the shattering
of grace crossed by new violence!
....
His day! the abolition of all sonorous and moving sufferings in more intense music.
His step! the migrations more enormous than the ancient invasions.
....
O world! and the clear song of new misfortunes!

These lines continue the interplay of satisfaction and
power, but augmented by the exclamatory style and the
musical and *dégagement* motifs to an almost ecstatic intensity that prepares us for the texts we shall discuss in the
next sections. This intensity is conveyed by the union of
contraries like "terrible célérité" and "perfection des
formes," "grâce" and "violence." Something similar happens syntactically, for the action, power, speed, and energy of the world are expressed through a diminishing of
the verbal forms that normally describe action. Everything
has become present in a psychic-linguistic act of openness
to and celebration of universal energy. Acceptance of the
world so as to unite and enrich mind and universe ("O
fécondité de l'esprit et immensité de l'univers!"), calling
for the human response of vast collective movements that
are not explained but are not presented ironically either—
here self, collectivity, and universe are gathered up into a
totality in which all is experienced as supremely good.

The conclusion of the poem even more strongly asserts
the sense of totality and reciprocity, of world and man's
response to it:

Il nous a connus tous et nous a tous aimés. Sachons, cette
nuit d'hiver, de cap en cap, du pôle tumultueux au
château, de la foule à la plage, de regards en regards,
forces et sentiments las, le héler et le voir, et le renvoyer,
et sous les marées et au haut des déserts de neige, suivre
ses vues, ses souffles, son corps, son jour.

He has known us all and loved us all. Let us know how,
this winter night, from cape to cape, from the tumultu-
ous pole to the castle, from the crowd to the beach, from
gaze to gaze, strengths and tired feelings, to hail him
and to see him, and to send him away, and under the
tides and at the top of the deserts of snow, to follow his
views, his breaths, his body, his day.

Interaction, totality, circularity: these characteristics of the
entire poem here achieve a fulfilling expression that comes
close to Nietzsche's great wheel of being, the dance of all
things in the eternal return, the universe as the joyously
accepted vicious circle: *circulus vitiosus deus,* the world both
immediately present and eternally recurring, and accepted
by mankind as of divine value.

But the conclusion also raises issues of communication,
collectivity, and form. Absent is the aggression against the
reader of other texts, for in "Génie" there is no ironic
speaker, no explicit *je* or *vous* at all. Instead, everything is
nous. Early in the poem this *nous* is associated with a perception of the *génie* from a distance, from the profane existence of anger and boredom: "Il est l'affection et
l'avenir . . . que nous, debout dans les rages et les ennuis,
nous voyons passer dans le ciel de tempête et les drapeaux
d'extase." From this collectively attentive beginning the
poem moves on to assert the bond of *amour-orgueil* that
unites the *génie* and us: "lui qui nous aime pour sa vie

infinie"; "O lui et nous!" But the interaction is not one of
possession or identification; rather, in the conclusion the
nous of the poem are asked to recognize and respond to the
génie, in a kind of generous mental contribution to his
ever-active, coming-and-going presence: "Sachons, cette
nuit d'hiver, de cap en cap, du pôle tumultueux au
château, de la foule à la plage, de regards en regards, forces
et sentiments las, le héler et le voir, et le renvoyer, et sous
les marées et au haut des déserts de neige, suivre ses vues,
ses souffles, son corps, son jour." "Sachons": a rare and
immensely significant appeal to collective consciousness,
skillfully aware and active (the sense of the verb *savoir*
itself), unpossessive ("le renvoyer"), perceptive ("le voir"),
responsive ("le héler"). Note that the verb denoting responsive expression precedes that indicating awareness ("le
héler et le voir"), which suggests a communal act of speech
that actively contributes to the presence of the divine, that
helps to *constitute* the mythic reality.

Note too that, as in "Solde," the implied community
cuts across and subverts social and economic distinctions.
The chiastic "du pôle tumultueux au château, de la foule à
la plage" mixes social and natural categories, and ultimately
subordinates the societal entirely by locating the encounter
with the *génie* at the extremes of nature, recalling Nietzsche's debunking of the sociopolitical, his evocation of nature's Dionysian power, collectively experienced.

Such a communal response to divinity is shaped through
the form of "Génie," which passes from the definitional
and the critical to the exclamatory and the celebrational,
and which at the end gathers itself together, imitating and
also constituting for us its immensely simple subject, the
unity of the world, with the brief, rhythmic reprises that
we noted in "Solde": "O monde!"; "ses vues, ses souffles,
son corps, son jour." The poem's formal and functional

techniques (definitional, negational, celebratory, totalizing) correspond to a poetic-philosophical project of extraordinary interest—the analogies with Blake and Nietzsche help to demonstrate its scope and importance—and also coherence. "Génie" gathers together all that we have seen in the texts from "Soleil et chair" on.

But finally, what sort of poetic consciousness accomplishes such a linguistic-communal act? Hardly one that exists as self-divinized transformation, as ecstatic self-forgetfulness—note how distant are the "drapeaux d'extase" at the beginning of the poem. Rather it seems closer to the Zarathustrian or late Goethean soul as described by Nietzsche, the comprehensive soul that not only overflows into the world but also draws circles round itself, circles in which the life of the universe is seen to ebb and flow. Despite the danger of disintegration and failure apparent in other of Rimbaud's texts, and despite the troubling insistence on apolitical collectivity, "Génie" is the product of such a soul, a drawing of circles that reveals the oneness of all. It is an act of psychic and bodily health, a marvellously collective act of the poet who has transcended all that is negative and who encourages us to do the same, freeing us for an affirmation of ourselves, our bodies, and the divinity of the world.

Altered States of Consciousness: Varieties of Ecstatic Experience

"Génie" is thus a master poem, which in its universal compass includes a movement toward ecstasy without however dissolving into an expression of the ecstatic state itself. We need now to investigate those other, multiple versions of the attraction to and experience of altered states of consciousness in Rimbaud, to which in some sense the poems analyzed thus far may be considered preliminary. First I shall survey the range of Rimbaud's references to altered states, then show how comprehensible and even typical they are by reference to elements delineated by such students of the ecstatic as Blake, Nietzsche, and twentieth-century investigators.

Several of the texts already discussed contain expressions of transformed states, often attaining the intensity, burning pleasure, and transcendence or transformation of body and self associated with the term ecstasy. Recall, for example, the exuberant sense of demonic divinity in "Angoisse" and the paradoxical unbodying and multiplication of the body in "H" and "Solde." Thus, "H": "Là, la moralité des êtres actuels se décorpore en sa passion ou en son action—O terrible frisson des amours novices sur le sol sanglant et par l'hydrogène clarteux!" (There, the morality of present beings becomes disembodied in her passion or in her action—O terrible shudder of new loves on the bloody ground and through the transparent hydrogen!). And in "Solde":

> Les Voix reconstituées; l'éveil fraternel de toutes les énergies chorales et orchestrales et leurs applications instantanées; l'occasion, unique, de dégager nos sens!
>
> A vendre les Corps sans prix, hors de toute race, de tout monde, de tout sexe, de toute descendance! Les richesses jaillissant à chaque démarche! Solde de diamants sans contrôle!

> The Voices reconstituted; the fraternal awakening of all choral and orchestral energies and their immediate application; the opportunity, unique, to free our senses!
>
> For sale, priceless Bodies, beyond all race, world, sex, lineage! Riches springing up at each step! Clearance on diamonds without control!

In both these passages elements of liberation from the individual body produce an intensification of the physical. The heavily erotic emphasis of "H" is said to lead to a disembodying ("se décorpore"), that is, to a liberation from the limitations of morality and even of individual existence, temporality, and the dichotomy of activity and passivity ("moralité," "êtres actuels," "passion ou . . . action"). Through sexual activity, the ethically constricted, sensuously limited, individual body that we normally experience is to be transcended, producing a state in which the contraries of ordinary existence are erased. A violent experience ("terrible frisson"), this new state involves an elemental physicality but also, it seems, a kind of purified essentiality of being: "sur le sol sanglant et par l'hydrogène clarteux." In "Solde," too, the elements of transcendence ("dégager nos sens" and the formula "hors de") are insistent and again extend to the basic categories of individual physical existence in the world ("race," "monde," "sexe," "descendance"). But the violence of "H" is transformed into profusion ("Les richesses jaillissant. . . . Solde de diamants sans contrôle!"), and indeed into a multiplication of the body ("les Corps sans prix") that is equivalent to the rediscovery of enlarged, fully integrated human existence: "les Voix reconstituées," "l'éveil fraternel," "toutes les énergies chorales et orchestrales." A number of oppositions thus emerge from these passages: the body as transcended *and* intensified; an elemental physicality but also a purified, almost abstract state; an insistent voice that nonetheless proclaims a participation in, a reconstitution of, some larger experience—the expression of multiple, transpersonal ecstasy.

Though paradoxical, the ecstatic aspects of "H" and "Solde" are essentially coherent. More complex are other of Rimbaud's expressions of altered states, especially in the

lettres du voyant and the *Saison*. In those texts a much wider
range of reference to states of vision, trance, and frenzy is
involved, such that the persistence of several known elements does not eliminate the potential for confusion and
dichotomy.

The *voyant* letters, expressing an ecstatic poetics that we
shall examine later, can be considered also as involving
directly the desire to achieve a fundamental alteration of
consciousness. This aspiration is set within the clichés of
the pagan myth of history encountered earlier: the harmonious life of the Greeks and subsequent decadence; the
rediscoveries of romantic, Parnassian, and Baudelairean
poetry; and Rimbaud's attempt to progress further in the
transformation of consciousness:

> Je m'encrapule le plus possible. Pourquoi? Je veux être
> poète, et je travaille à me rendre *voyant.*
> [I am debauching myself as much as possible. Why? I
> want to be a poet, and I am working at making
> myself *visionary.*]
>   . . .
> il s'agit de faire l'âme monstrueuse
> [it's a matter of making the soul monstrous]
>   . . .
> il faut être *voyant,* se faire *voyant*
> [it is necessary to be *visionary,* to make oneself *visionary*]
>   . . .
> Le Poète se fait *voyant* par un long, immense et raisonné
> *dérèglement* de *tous les sens.*
> [The Poet makes himself *visionary* by a long, immense,
> and reasoned *derangement* of *all the senses.*]

Here the process of becoming a poet is identified with the
obliteration of ordinary consciousness and the accession to
a different state, which seems monstrous in comparison. In
particular, the attack at the level of sensation threatens the

illusory stability of rational awareness, and implies a more real, if infinitely more chaotic, vision.

The means to this transformation are briefly, but inclusively, sketched: "Toutes les formes d'amour, de souffrance, de folie; il cherche lui-même, il épuise en lui tous les poisons"—the varieties of sexual experience, self-inflicted suffering and mental derangement, and intoxicants, including explicitly alcohol and implicitly drugs. This program has both initiatory and communal overtones, for it will involve enormous suffering ("Les souffrances sont énormes") to the end that normal consciousness may be enlarged: "Enormité devenant norme, absorbée par tous, il serait vraiment *un multiplicateur de progrès!*" (Enormity becoming norm, absorbed by all, he would be truly *a multiplier of progress!*). Finally, it carries with it the danger that marks any extreme attempt to transcend the self, the risk not of ecstatic joy but of suffering and indeed of loss of personal awareness ("quand, affolé, il finirait par perdre l'intelligence de ses visions")—the negative ecstasy of madness.

So, in brief compass, the *voyant* letters suggest the myth, goals, techniques, individual and communal aspects, and dangers of a program to transform consciousness. Two years later *Une Saison en enfer* demonstrates in sardonic detail the multiple and contradictory aspects of this program as well as the deleterious effects that it produced.

The *Saison* in fact picks up, and deflates, virtually all the themes in the *voyant* letters. The heroic suffering foreseen there is now described as having been realized—as self-inflicted pain leading to the brink of literal insanity and death (Introduction, "Délires II"). The transformation of the self, with its erotic and surreal components, is debunked as ineffectual escapism, fear of reality, to which at the end the poet is forced to submit ("Mauvais Sang," "Délires I," "L'Eclair," "Adieu"). "Délires II" in particular criticizes

Rimbaud's ecstatic-poetic method, calling its various phases "folies," "enchantements," "hallucination," "sophismes magiques," "le désordre de mon esprit." Moreover, "L'Impossible" invokes the persistence of the pagan myth as well as the question of appropriate ecstatic techniques. There Rimbaud realizes that all along he had been trying to regain "la sagesse de l'Orient, la patrie primitive," but by inappropriate—that is, obscuring and intoxicating— means: "la brume," "l'ivrognerie! et le tabac! et l'ignorance! et les dévouements!" (fog, drunkenness! and tobacco! and ignorance! and devotions!). Thus the critique of the attempt to alter consciousness retains the features of myth, ecstatic techniques and danger, and even its negativism displays a continuing nostalgia as well as the hint of more appropriate methods of reaching the primal state of being.

This confusion as to states and means is borne out throughout the *Saison,* which alludes to a variety of experiences of trance, frenzy, dissociation, ecstasy, and quasi-mystical dissolution,[6] most associated with known cultures and historical periods, and most presented as harmful despite moments of exaltation. Thus in keeping with the attempt to leave civilized modes of existence, Rimbaud early on imagines a medieval witches' dance and then shortly later a more primitive state of unconscious trance:

> Le plus malin est de quitter ce continent, où la folie rôde pour pouvoir d'ôtages ces misérables. J'entre au vrai royaume des enfants de Cham.
>
> Connais-je encore la nature? me connais-je?—*Plus de mots.* J'ensevelis les morts dans mon ventre. Cris, tambour, danse, danse, danse, danse! Je ne vois même pas l'heure où, les blancs débarquant, je tomberai au néant.
>
> Faim, soif, cris, danse, danse, danse, danse!
>
> *("Mauvais Sang")*

The shrewdest thing is to leave this continent, where madness roams to provide hostages for these wretches. I am entering the true kingdom of the children of Ham.

Do I still know nature? do I know myself?—*No more words*. I bury the dead in my belly. Cries, drum, dance, dance, dance, dance! I don't even see the hour when, the whites disembarking, I will fall into nothingness.

Hunger, thirst, cries, dance, dance, dance, dance!

Complete with references to ancestor worship and ritual drum and dance, this passage is an extreme expression of the pagan myth, evoking the ability of the savage to withdraw from individual consciousness, through frenetic and repetitive rhythms to eliminate knowledge of self and external world, forget language, and transcend *all* awareness.

Unconscious savage trance—a radical form of altered consciousness indeed: the *obliteration* of awareness. But the whites do land, inevitably imposing the forms of the Western mentality that the poet has been attempting to suppress, and the rest of the *Saison* involves not simply Rimbaud's desire to flee such forms but also his attempt to transform them through his ethical-esthetic undertaking. References to states of trance and dissociation, often of a primitive sort, punctuate the work. Thus "Nuit de l'enfer," whose mention of hallucination and poison seems to describe the paroxysm of alienation from reality to which Rimbaud's *voyance* has led, is explicitly ecstatic: "Je ne suis plus au monde. . . . Extase, cauchemar, sommeil dans un nid de flammes." "Out of the world" is what Rimbaud wants to be in at least one of the *Illuminations* ("Jeunesse"), but here the exalted state, which fuses movement and rest, sleep and burning sensation, self-enclosure and dynamic energy, is a nightmare—hallucinatory, overwhelming, terribly painful. This is another extreme form

of altered consciousness, an ecstatic but infernal experience, a nearly complete dissociation that the poet has to
struggle to surmount: "Ah! remonter à la vie!" (Ah! to rise
again to life!).

In the self-analysis that follows, negatively colored
trance states are again evoked. As characterized by the
foolish virgin in "Délires I," the aspirations of the "époux
infernal" are in the direction of savage fury and quasi-
permanent somnambulism—but strangely mixed with in-
flated intellectual pretensions:

> "Je suis de race lointaine: mes pères étaient Scandinaves:
> ils se perçaient les côtes, buvaient leur sang.—Je me ferai
> des entailles partout le corps, je me tatouerai, je veux
> devenir hideux comme un Mongol: tu verras, je hurlerai
> dans les rues. Je veux devenir bien fou de rage."
> ....
> Il feignait d'être éclairé sur tout, commerce, art,
> médecine.
> ....
> Il n'a pas une connaissance, il ne travaillera jamais. Il
> veut vivre somnambule.

> "I come from a distant race: my fathers were Scandina-
> vian: they pierced their sides, drank their own blood.—I
> will make gashes all over my body, I'll tatoo myself, I
> want to become hideous like a Mongol: you'll see, I will
> howl in the streets. I want to become completely crazy
> with rage."
> ....
> He pretended to be enlightened on everything, commerce,
> art, medicine.
> ....
> He doesn't know anyone, he will never work. He wants
> to live as a sleepwalker.

The ramblings of the infernal husband continue the impulse to the savage, this time by reference not to African trance but rather to Arctic and Siberian-Asian experience. Note the persistence of the initiatory and magical techniques of transcending the body's sensitivity to pain, and the goal of hideous fury, a monstrous frenzy that would indeed be a shocking provocation in the streets of a modern European city. The other two sentences are developed in "Délires II," which debunks Rimbaud's visionary pretentions, in part because of the extended periods of literal dissociation that they produced:

Je finis par trouver sacré le désordre de mon esprit.
J'étais oisif, en proie à une lourde fièvre: j'enviais la félicité des bêtes
[At the end I found the disorder of my mind sacred. I was idle, in prey to a heavy fever: I was envious of the felicity of animals]

. . .

Mon caractère s'aigrissait. Je disais adieu au monde dans d'espèces de romances
[My character grew bitter. I said goodbye to the world in songlike poems]

. . .

Ma santé fut menacée. La terreur venait. Je tombais dans des sommeils de plusieurs jours, et, levé, je continuais les rêves les plus tristes. J'étais mûr pour le trépas, et par une route de dangers ma faiblesse me menait aux confins du monde et de la Cimmérie, patrie de l'ombre et des tourbillons.
[My health was threatened. Terror came. I would fall into sleeps lasting several days, and, awake, I continued the saddest dreams. I was ripe for death, and by a route filled with dangers my weakness led me to the confines of the world and of Cimmeria, the country of shadows and whirlwinds.]

"Vivre somnambule"[7] indeed: "Délires II" depicts an extended period of dissociation from the normal sense of reality, produced by systematic hallucinatory techniques, and experienced as profoundly destructive, as fatal if not discontinued.

It is in this context that Rimbaud (mis)quotes and comments on a number of texts from the *Derniers Vers,* which represent a still different form of exalted experience, this time of an ascetic and mystical kind. Thus the motifs of purification and deprivation of food in "Faim" or "Fêtes de la faim" and "Le loup criait" imply an asceticism far removed from the bountiful immanence of the divinity in our food and drink in "Génie." There is also the imagery of intense suffering in "Fêtes de la patience," clearer in the manuscript version:

> Ame sentinelle,
> Murmurons l'aveu
> De la nuit si nulle
> Et du jour en feu.
>
> Des humains suffrages,
> Des communs élans
> Là tu te dégages
> Et voles selon.
>
> Puisque de vous seules,
> Braises de satin,
> Le Devoir s'exhale
> Sans qu'on dise: enfin.
>
> Là pas d'espérance,
> Nul orietur.
> Science avec patience,
> Le supplice est sûr.
>
> *("L'Eternité")*

Sentinel soul,
Let us murmur the avowal
Of the night so null
And of the day on fire.

From human approvals,
From common impulses
Here you free yourself
And fly in accordance.

Since from you alone,
Embers of satin,
Duty is breathed
With no one saying: at last.

Here, no hope,
No orietur.
Science with patience,
Torture is sure.

Detachment from others, the motifs of flight, fusion of night and day, burning coals and cool satin, suffering accepted fatalistically: this is a complex of known motifs pointing to the fiery, painful, solitary experience of a mystical eternity. Indeed, there is a definite, though ambivalent, reflection on the relationship of such motifs to Christian experience in a stanza that is not quoted at all in "Délires II":

Ah! Mille veuvages
De la si pauvre âme
Qui n'a que l'image
De la Notre-Dame!
Est-ce que l'on prie
La Vierge Marie?

("*Chanson de la plus haute tour*")

Ah! Thousands of widowings
Of the so poor soul
That has only the image
Of Our Lady!
Does one pray
To the Virgin Mary?

Grudgingly perhaps, the refusal of the erotic, the traditional spiritual vocabulary, and the reference to the Virgin
create a relationship between Rimbaud's experience in
"Fêtes de la patience" and Christian ascetic mysticism.

These poems thus describe a mystical process and culmination, related to traditional forms of asceticism, and spiritual and transcendent in tendency. Consider expressions
such as "la plus haute tour" and "auguste retraite" (the
highest tower, august retreat) or "tu te dégages / Et voles
selon" and "le monde est vicieux" (you free yourself and fly
in accordance; the world is vicious) from the poems, and
Rimbaud's assertions in "Délires II": "Je disais adieu au
monde" (I said goodbye to the world) and "Enfin, ô bonheur, ô raison, j'écartai du ciel l'azur, qui est du noir, et je
vécus, étincelle d'or de la lumière *nature*. De joie, je pre-
nais une expression bouffonne et égarée au possible" (Finally, O happiness, O reason, I removed from the sky the
azure, which is blackness, and I lived, golden spark of the
light *nature*. From joy, I took on an expression clownish
and distracted in the extreme). The last of these, introducing the culminating stanzas of "L'Eternité," uses another
recognizable mystical code, that of alchemy. Note that
total transcendence is not yet in question; this is a highly
purified nature mysticism. Personal consciousness, while
radically transformed, is not obliterated either—existing as
"étincelle d'or de la lumière *nature*," the speaker nonetheless firmly retains his consciousness of self: "je vécus."

Finally, Rimbaud's phrase "une expression bouffonne et égarée au possible" beautifully conveys the qualities of poetic expression most appropriate to the immediacy and strangeness of this mystic experience—deceptively simple, almost foolishly joyful, distracted, lost, dissociated.[8]

The contrast between these ascetic texts of nearly total transcendence and the earlier versions of savage trance, fury, and drug-induced ecstasy is striking and reproduces the paradox of transcendent and immanent directions encountered earlier. These paradoxes are further emphasized at two other fascinating points in "Délires II." The first is a brief exclamatory sentence occurring in the midst of transcendent, ascetic, and immanent suggestions, and preceding the mystical culmination "de la lumière *nature*": "Oh! le moucheron enivré à la pissotière de l'auberge, amoureux de la bourrache, et que dissout un rayon!" (Oh! the drunken gnat at the urinal of the inn, in love with borage, and dissolved by a sunbeam!). So many features of Rimbaud's undertaking are condensed here: the background of human community ("l'auberge"); the existence of the elementally physical, fusing the organic, the vegetable and the insect, already seen in "Voyelles"; the experience of inebriation leading to dissolution in pure light. In miniature this sentence expresses much of the conflicting process of texts like "Voyelles" and "Fêtes de la patience"; it does so by uniting what elsewhere exists as dichotomous: immersion in the most physical identified with dissolution in pure light, immanence therefore equaling transcendence, and within which individual identity (not even here of the human, whose transformed state is best imagined by the insect) is finally dissolved.

The second point is the evocation, just before the poet. definitively distances himself from his mystical experience, of what he calls "le Bonheur":

Le Bonheur était ma fatalité, mon remords, mon ver: ma
vie serait toujours trop immense pour être dévouée à la
force et à la beauté.

Le Bonheur! Sa dent, douce à la mort, m'avertissait au
chant du coq,—*ad matutinum,* au *Christus venit,*—dans les
plus sombres villes.

Happiness was my fatality, my remorse, my worm: my
life would always be too immense to be devoted to
strength and to beauty.

Happiness! Its tooth, sweet to the death, warned me
at the song of the cock,—*ad matutinum,* at the *Christus
venit,*—in the darkest cities.

The reference to Christian experience persists, as does the
awareness of the human community, this time in its more
somber urban form. (The complex relation between the
visionary and the social, especially the urban, will be in-
vestigated in chapter 3). But even more significant is the
suggestion of an experience of overriding importance, involving joy so intense as to seem deathlike, and fatalistically accepted as dominating the speaker's existence.[9] Then
immediately the poet gives a version of one of his most
magically simple ecstatic-mystic poems:

> O saisons, ô châteaux!
> Quelle âme est sans défauts?
>
> J'ai fait la magique étude
> Du bonheur, qu'aucun n'élude.
>
> Salut à lui, chaque fois
> Que chante le coq gaulois.
>
> Ah! je n'aurai plus d'envie:
> Il s'est chargé de ma vie.

Ce charme a pris âme et corps
Et dispersé les efforts.

O saisons, ô châteaux!

L'heure de sa fuite, hélas!
Sera l'heure du trépas.

O saisons, ô châteaux!

O seasons, O chateaux!
What soul is without flaws?

I have made the magic study
Of happiness, which no one avoids.

Hail to it, each time
The Gallic cock sings.

Ah! I shall no longer have desire:
It has taken charge of my life.

This charm has taken soul and body
And dispersed endeavors.

O seasons, O chateaux!

The hour of its flight, alas!
Will be the hour of death.

O seasons, O chateaux!

This is the version given in "Délires II," whose divergences from the manuscript text are relatively minor, except for one important couplet that the *Saison* drops: "Que comprendre à ma parole? / Il fait qu'elle fuie et vole!" (How understand my words? It makes them flee and fly).

Here we have the problem of visionary language, its fundamental elusiveness, combined again with a strong sense of
disorientation. The poem itself in both versions illustrates
these themes, for its directness of exclamation, question,
statement and address, and its use of mysteriously universal elements ("saisons," "châteaux," "magique étude,"
"bonheur," "charme," "âme et corps") are extremely elusive. At the same time these qualities allow it to convey
one after another many facets of the mystical process of the
Derniers Vers: nature and human constructs, the falling
away of the dominance of ethical considerations, the systematic search for ecstatic joy, the attainment of an effortless, disinterested state of being, and also, finally, the
inevitability of losing it. "O saisons, ô châteaux!" is a
culminating, elemental expression of a state of dissociation, followed by the return to the normal: "Cela s'est
passé. Je sais aujourd'hui saluer la beauté" (That's past.
Today I know how to say hello to beauty).

The materials discussed here, from *Illuminations* like
"H" and "Solde" to the *lettres du voyant* and the *Saison,* are
various, even contradictory. The erotically oriented prose
poems, with their paradoxes of intensification, transcendence, and multiplication of the bodily, are different from
the pursuit of transformed consciousness in the *voyant* letters and the burning yet sleeplike ecstasy to which that
pursuit leads in "Nuit de l'enfer." And elsewhere the *Saison* alludes to still other states of trance and dissociation
ranging from the primitive to the mystical: the witches'
sabbat, the dance of the "enfants de Cham," the savage
Scandinavian or Mongol fury of the "époux infernal," the
desire to "vivre somnambule," the exalted contact with "la
lumière *nature*" of "Fêtes de la patience," and the extreme
disorientation expressed in "O saisons, ô châteaux!"

Despite their differences, if we take these expressions

together we see them as embodying an ecstatic syncretism, combining Greek, African, Scandinavian, Mongolian, Mohammedan, Christian, and alchemical elements—a range of altered states that the poet opposes to the limited rationality of the world he wishes to flee. Moreover, the oppositions that emerge from the juxtaposition of these diverging traditions turn out to be meaningful: the body versus the spiritual; immanence, physicality, and the savage versus ascetic traditions of purification and transcendence; the obliteration of consciousness in trance versus the lucid awareness of the self as a living part of "la lumière *nature*." At points even these contrasts seem to be overcome, as in the image of the "moucheron enivré à la pissotière de l'auberge, amoureux de la bourrache, et que dissout un rayon." Here the dichotomy immersion-transcendence gives way before an ungraspable unity to which all techniques of ecstasy may lead. But within that mysterious unification there emerges another conflict—between good ecstasies, which produce joy and affirmation, and bad ecstasies, which cause prolonged suffering, alienation from self, collectivity, and world, and which threaten madness and death.

From the variety of altered states some basic patterns therefore emerge, to which we can add several other informing elements. The myth of an original state of mankind is present throughout—in the pagan poems, the Greek harmony of the second *voyant* letter, the purified "sagesse de l'Orient, la patrie primitive" of "L'Impossible." There is also consistent reference to recognizable ecstatic techniques: sexual activity, stimulants, self-imposed suffering, dance and drum—in short many forms of sensory modification, at times by deprivation, as in some of the *Derniers Vers*. These differing tendencies produce several strands of ecstatic imagery: the barbarously elemen-

tal—earth, fire, blood; the motifs of *dégagement* and enlargement; the imagery of cosmic or polar reality and totality, as in "Voyelles" and "Génie," conveying a vision of
the entire world; the more spiritualized imagery of alchemy and Christian experience—the solitude, flight,
light, intense joy-pain of "Fêtes de la patience." Finally,
the dangers of the ecstatic project are emphasized, as well
as the likelihood of painful loss of the vision. Good or bad,
ecstasy may mean total dissolution or disorientation, as in
"O saisons! ô châteaux!" Good or bad, too, the ecstasy
ends, and in some sense the poet must step away from it:
"Cela s'est passé. Je sais aujourd'hui saluer la beauté."

Despite the intensity of these materials in Rimbaud,
they are therefore hardly incomprehensible or unique. Indeed, the work of Blake, Nietzsche, and twentieth-century
investigators of altered states can help us see Rimbaud as a
poet developing recognizable features of ecstatic experience
in a modern context. They make us aware of traditions
that constitute a quasi-universal phenomenon, but in
which certain cultures seem of privileged importance, traditions that exhibit fairly consistent myths, techniques,
and symbolism, as well as dichotomies similar to those we
have seen in Rimbaud.

First, then, the quasi-universal aspect of ecstatic experiences and techniques. When Blake has Ezekiel claim to
have practiced mind-transforming techniques as a means of
"raising other men into a perception of the infinite," adding "this the North American tribes practise," and when
Nietzsche asserts that in India, during the Christian
Middle Ages, in Greenland and Brazil, techniques of fast-
ing, sexual abstinence, and isolation led to states resembling epilepsy and madness, both writers alert us to widespread experiences, of a fundamentally ambivalent sort,
attained in many different cultures by recognizable tech-

niques.[10] Later students of religion and drugs, including
William James, Aldous Huxley, N. K. Chadwick, Mircea
Eliade, and Roland Fischer, similarly stress the universal
phenomenon and conflicting forms of altered states, produced by consciousness-modifying substances, by techniques of sensory deprivation, by music, drum and dance,
and by methods of meditation and spiritual discipline.
Some even argue for the mantic origin of all cultures,
including our own, whose rationalism would in such a
perspective represent a repression and sublimation of ecstatic states and systems of knowledge.

Rimbaud's syncretism can thus be seen as corresponding
to the history of ecstatic experience among the Greeks,
Siberian and Asian peoples, African cultures, Islamic and
Christian mystical traditions—and also as reproducing the
notion that the ecstatic, active at the origin of Western
culture, seems to have been lost. This last point explains
in part why Greek experience, especially the Dionysian, is
given such emphasis by writers like Hölderlin and
Nietzsche. Rimbaud's motif of Greek eroticism is to be
recalled here, and we should note as well that Dionysian
frenzy is collective, as Nietzsche stressed, and as we shall
see in discussing Rimbaud's "Villes I."

In contrast, another tradition, that of shamanism, is
essentially different. Strongest in Central and Siberian
Asia, this religion features a specialist of the ecstatic who
alone attains the exalted state, which he communicates to
his community in the form of a dramatic and musical
spectacle.

Thus there is considerable correspondence between Rimbaud's allusions and the actual history of ecstatic experiences, and several aspects of his work reflect similar issues
in ecstatic religions: universal states and techniques, ranging from the savage to more sophisticated forms of mysti-

cism; the contrast between collective frenzy such as the Dionysian and the individual ecstasy of the shaman; the relationship between altered states and the forms through which they are communicated to a public—the last an issue to which we return later in this chapter.

These paradoxes (primitive/mystical, collective/solitary, loss/rediscovery, experience/expression) reveal the ecstatic as marked preeminently by ambivalence if not contradiction. Thus in *Dawn* Nietzsche views the prevalence of such a tendency in history as a sign of madness and escapism— the product of a hatred of body and world—and this recalls the debilitating, nearly fatal, result of Rimbaud's ascetic mysticism in the *Saison*. Nonetheless, throughout his work Nietzsche balances lucid control, on the one hand, with a more positive kind of frenzy, on the other. Springing from health and strength, involving the unleashing of sexuality, associated with narcotics, cruelty, and the enormous power of nature, this more valuable tendency is said by Nietzsche to preserve our primitive history of animality, a potential for savage violence that never disappears, which according to him should never be forgotten, which is an essential element of his "noble" ethic and an indispensable feature of artistic psychology. Nietzsche's exposition serves as interesting commentary on the explosive sexuality and animality of texts such as "H", "Les Stupra," and the *Saison,* particularly regarding the desire in "Délires I" to attain and flaunt a primitive fury in the streets of a modern city.

The ambivalence of the ecstatic as deriving from a troubling re-experiencing of the savage and animal in our nature is visible not only in Nietzsche and Rimbaud but also in more recent students of exalted states. For example, Aldous Huxley's description of what he calls the visionary as an experience of the *not-self*—psychological, spiritual, collective, and also organic—corresponds to features of Rimbaud's

work. Consider the revelation in the *voyant* letters of a psychic reality transcending the conscious self, the spirituality
and identification with "la lumière *nature*" in "Délires II,"
and the collectivity of texts like "Solde" and "Génie," and
also the animality of "Les anciens animaux" and the dissolution into physicality in "H." For Huxley, this full *not-self,*
including the organic, transcends our limited consciousness
and opens up toward the mystical, an experience of oneness
and affirmation that Rimbaud expresses in "Génie." But
Huxley was also acutely aware of negative states of altered
consciousness—subhuman, "lower than personal," involving "consciousness of the body . . . heightened and continually degraded," in which self and body are experienced
as "progressively more tense, more tightly packed." These
formulas resemble descriptions in the *Saison,* notably in
"Nuit de l'enfer," and we should also note, in opposition to
Nietzsche's idealization of Dionysian frenzy, the criticism
by Huxley and others of the mass intoxication and savagery
of that cult and similar manifestations throughout history.
Indeed, the Bacchic frenzy involved dismemberment and
eating of living victims, including infants—in short, the
submersion of the rational, the human, the societal, the
ethical by the irresistible animality that Nietzsche praised
and to which Rimbaud was drawn.

The experience of animality in some forms of ecstasy is
therefore a revealing paradox, one indeed that provides a
link to an informing myth, paradisal in nature, which is
related to the pagan myth in Rimbaud. For as studied in
relation to the Dionysian, the shamanistic, and mind-
altering drugs, the ecstatic often involves a myth of history
with aspects of origins and loss, integration and contradiction, animality and humanness, decadence and return,
and—as in Rimbaud once more—an inevitable and self-
conscious syncretism.

Thus Roland Fischer analyzes various religious and drug experiences not in terms of animality and spirituality but in terms of a model of consciousness that emphasizes dichotomy and coherence, with the peak experiences of ecstasy and yoga *samādhi* achieving an oceanic oneness resulting from total psychic integration—an integration educated out of us in our culture but favored in other civilizations and at other moments in our own history (the last a "scientific" version of ecstatic myth). From a different perspective W. K. C. Guthrie emphasizes the mixture of traditions in Dionysian religion, which linked figures from a number of regions and sources, including Dionysus, Orpheus, Pythagorus, and even Apollo. The inclusion of Apollo seems to indicate the need not only to unify religious traditions in a syncretist way but especially to integrate animal-ecstatic elements with the rational.

Mircea Eliade in his study of shamanism more systematically interrelates a myth of origins, decadence and syncretism, contradictory forms of altered consciousness, and the experience of animality. He shows that shamanism harks back to mythic times, when man enjoyed total integration with reality; that the mythic origin, however, is never encountered, is always absent. The ecstatic is therefore a paradisal phenomenon, evoking an idealized time when man supposedly communed with the animals, such animal symbolism being united with other paradisal and "uranian" motifs—hunting, fire, flight, rainbows, mountains, cities, palaces, precious stones—which we also encounter in the poetry of Blake, Coleridge, Rimbaud, and Yeats. The shaman's assumption of animal qualities, his submission to animality, is therefore a preparation for the ecstatic, a transcendence of the merely human, a means of recreating the primordial unity of animal, human, and divine.

In discussing this unity, however, Eliade does not min-

imize dichotomous elements: the phenomenon of black and
white shamanism, representing divergent religious conceptions; the danger of literal possession and cataleptic trance;
an underlying conflict of ascensional spiritual purification
and infernal animal ecstatics. Finally, the paradisal myth
itself insinuates insufficiencies and contradictions: not only
that the collectivity does not experience ecstasy and that
the exaltation is impermanent but also the element of historical decadence. True ecstasy remains rare; actual shamans do not have the same spiritual powers as their prehis-
toric forebears; corrupt techniques, mainly intoxicants,
have replaced the attainment of ecstasy through religious
music, intellectual power, and spiritual discipline; degraded, fakiristic forms mimic true ecstasy with illusionistic theatrical performances.

Eliade's insistence on the paradisal myth at the base of
shamanism allows us to connect—in a perspective of decadence, nostalgia, and aspiration—a number of issues proposed by Nietzsche, Blake, Huxley, Fischer, and others:
the value and threat of animality, the impulse to psychic
integration and mastery, but also the persistence of dichotomy in the amalgamation of divergent traditions. How
relevant such themes are for Rimbaud is apparent from the
texts examined thus far, and particularly in the enigmatic
and sinister poem "Parade":

> Des drôles très solides. Plusieurs ont exploité vos
> mondes. Sans besoins, et peu pressés de mettre en œuvre
> leurs brillantes facultés et leur expérience de vos con-
> sciences. Quels hommes mûrs! Des yeux hébétés à la façon
> de la nuit d'été, rouges et noirs, tricolores, d'acier piqué
> d'étoiles d'or; des facies déformés, plombés, blêmis,
> incendiés; des enrouements folâtres! La démarche cruelle
> des oripeaux!—Il y a quelques jeunes,—comment regar-

deraient-ils Chérubin?—pourvus de voix effrayantes et de
quelques ressources dangereuses. On les envoie prendre
du dos en ville, affublés d'un *luxe* dégoûtant.

O le plus violent Paradis de la grimace enragée! Pas de
comparaison avec vos Fakirs et les autres bouffonneries
scéniques. Dans des costumes improvisés avec le goût du
mauvais rêve ils jouent des complaintes, des tragédies de
malandrins et de demi-dieux spirituels comme l'histoire
ou les religions ne l'ont jamais été. Chinois, Hottentots,
bohémiens, niais, hyènes, Molochs, vieilles démences,
démons sinistres, ils mêlent les tours populaires, maternels, avec les poses et les tendresses bestiales. Ils
interpréteraient des pièces nouvelles et des chansons
"bonnes filles." Maîtres jongleurs, ils transforment le lieu
et les personnes et usent de la comédie magnétique. Les
yeux flambent, le sang chante, les os s'élargissent, les
larmes et des filets rouges ruissellent. Leur raillerie ou
leur terreur dure une minute, ou des mois entiers.

J'ai seul la clef de cette parade sauvage.

Tough rascals. Some have exploited your worlds. Without needs, and in no hurry to make use of their brilliant
faculties and their experience of your consciences. Pretty
virile! Eyes listless like a summer night, red and black,
tricolored, steel studded with golden stars; features deformed, leaden, blanched, burned out; wild hoarsenesses!
The cruel gait of finery!—Some are young,—what would
they think of Cherubino?—with terrifying voices and dangerous tricks. They send them to town to strut, decked out
in revolting *luxury*.

O the most violent Paradise of raging grimace! No
comparison with your Fakirs and other theatrical buffoon-
eries. In costumes improvised in the style of bad dreams
they act out sad songs, tragedies of brigands and demi-
gods wittier than history or religions have ever been.
Chinese, Hottentots, gypsies, simpletons, hyenas, Mol-

ochs, old lunacies, sinister demons, they mix the popular
numbers meant for Mom with the bestial poses and caresses. They could do versions of new plays and "nice
girl" songs. Master jugglers, they transform place and
persons and use magnetic theater. Eyes flame, blood
sings, bones expand, tears and red filaments stream.
Their raillery or their terror lasts a minute, or whole
months.
  I alone have the key to this savage show.

At the climax of this poem, at the term of the bizarre
magico-theatrical activity of its threatening personages, is
a visceral ecstasy of the sort already glimpsed in "H" and
"Solde," in which person, time, and space are transformed,
and the body is enlarged and dissolved, taking on a burning, singing, streaming intensity of existence. This ecstasy
is set in a context that is both paradisal and degraded,
conscious of the contradictory history of mankind with its
oppositions of spirituality and bestial sexuality: "demi-
dieux spirituels"; "l'histoire ou les religions"; "Chinois,
Hottentots, bohémiens, niais, hyènes, Molochs, vieilles
démences, démons sinistres, ils mêlent les tours populaires, maternels, avec les poses et les tendresses bestiales."
Here the ecstasy, supposedly superior to all that has been
possible in the various religious traditions, at the same
time is characterized in a flagrantly demeaning fashion.
The analogy with Fakirism is particularly telling, in the
context of the ideas from Eliade, as is the theatrical analogy throughout. Despite the claim to the ability actually
to transform reality, the text *is* illusionistic ("comédie
magnétique"), a degraded form of the ecstatic-paradisal
myth: "O le plus violent Paradis de la grimace enragée!"
  Nonetheless "Parade" does tend to actualize its personages and their ecstasy through notational, exclamatory,
questioning, and outrageously assertive forms of expres-

sion: "Des drôles très solides"; "Quels hommes mûrs!";
"comment regarderaient-ils Chérubin?"; "Leur raillerie ou
leur terreur dure une minute, ou des mois entiers". "Parade" recalls in a darker vein the provocative realizations
seen earlier. Thus the last sentence ("J'ai seul la clef de
cette parade sauvage") is a more alienated version of the
end of "Solde": "Les voyageurs n'ont pas à rendre leur
commission de si tôt!" (The travelers don't have to render
accounts so fast!). And the entire tone of the poem is the
opposite of the generous community of *nous* in "Génie":
"Plusieurs ont exploité vos mondes . . . peu pressés de
mettre en œuvre leurs brillantes facultés et leur expérience
de vos consciences." Everything about "Parade," then—its
bestiality, self-conscious historical awareness, fakiristic
form and tone, and hostility toward its audience—makes it
look like a degraded form of ecstatic expression, an aggressive performance whose very success testifies to the alienation from which it proceeds.

The literary-religious-anthropological perspective of Eliade and others is thus revealing for a wide range of Rimbaud's writing—the *voyant* letters, the *Saison, Illuminations*
from "H" to "Parade." These texts are all dominated by
the impulse to ecstasy, but in the framework of paradisal
myth, with its structure of origin, loss, nostalgia, determination, rediscovery, and possibilities for failure and disintegration. This myth accounts for the syncretism, the divergent forms of trance and frenzy that Rimbaud evokes,
as well as for the conflicting methods that he suggests—
and also for his self-criticism in "L'Impossible," his
glimpse of a purer conception of spiritual discipline.[11]
Decadence and error, and the difficulty of winning
through to a satisfactory conception of the ecstatic undertaking therefore explain much in the *Saison* and "Parade."
Such features also explain why Rimbaud's work reproduces

so many typical oppositions of mankind's religious history—from the ascensional, ascetic mysticism of "Fêtes de la patience" to the savage, bodily, sometimes degraded expressions of other texts. They account as well for the contrast of generosity and aggression in "Génie" and "Parade," for the possibility both of positive accomplishments and destructive, alienated ecstasies. So much in Rimbaud's work corresponds to the impulses, successes, contradictions, and modes of expression of the ecstatic traditions themselves, because he represents a late, Western version of the attempt to achieve ecstatic experience in all its ambivalent forms. Having pursued this view and having characterized the difficulty of Rimbaud's enterprise, we need now to examine his effort to realize his project in poetry through the poetics and forms that, almost inevitably, he was led to develop.

Ecstatic Poetics: Self, Collectivity, Form

Indeed Rimbaud was most interested in altered states for the sake of writing poetry:

> Il s'agit d'arriver à l'inconnu par le dérèglement de *tous les sens*.
> [It's a matter of reaching the unknown through derangement of *all the senses*.]
>
>   . . .
>
> Le Poète se fait *voyant* par un long, immense et raisonné *dérèglement* de *tous les sens*. Toutes les formes d'amour, de souffrance, de folie
> [The Poet makes himself *visionary* by a long, immense, and reasoned *derangement* of *all the senses*. All forms of love, of suffering, of madness]
>
>   . . .

quand, affolé, il finirait par perdre l'intelligence de ses
visions, il les a vues!
[even if, maddened, he ends up losing the intelligence of
his visions, he has seen them!]

. . .

Le poète définirait la quantité d'inconnu s'éveillant en
sons temps dans l'âme universelle.
[The poet would define the quantity of unknown awakening in his time in the universal soul.]

. . .

Enormité devenant norme, absorbée par tous, il serait
vraiment *un multiplicateur de progrès!*
[Enormity becoming norm, absorbed by all, he would be
truly a *multiplier of progress!*]

These phrases from the *lettres du voyant* equate poetry with
the discovery, attainment and expression of altered states
of consciousness. Note that familiar elements recur here:
an intellectualist-spiritualist vocabulary, and yet the centrality of the senses as well as, paradoxically, a materialist
stance: "Cet avenir sera matérialiste" (This future will be
materialist). But all of this is mediated now by the need to
discover novel forms and language.

The issues of the self, the senses, language, form, and
by extension the ecstatic poet's communal function, are
therefore all of interest. Rimbaud's forceful view of the "I"
as other than what we normally assume can be placed in
the context of other poetic attempts to enlarge and transcend the self, from Blake's fourfold prophetic vision and
Coleridge's glimpse of some greater persona in dreams, to
doctrines of impersonality and mask in Keats, Mallarmé,
and Yeats. But it is again Nietzsche who is most relevant
to Rimbaud's assertions that "JE est un autre. Si le cuivre
s'éveille clairon, il n'y a rien de sa faute. Cela m'est évident: j'assiste à l'éclosion de ma pensée: je la regarde, je

l'écoute: je lance un coup d'archet: la symphonie fait son
remuement dans les profondeurs, ou vient d'un bond sur la
scène" (I is another. If brass wakes up trumpet, it's not at
all its fault. This is evident to me: I am present at the
birth of my thought: I watch it, I listen to it; I draw a
stroke of the bow: the symphony stirs in the depths, or
comes with a leap onto the stage). Contemporaneous with
Nietzsche, these sentences are close to his beliefs in *The
Birth of Tragedy*.[12] Both writers re-evaluate romantic literature, asserting against common prejudice that lyric is precisely *not* subjective, but rather an *unselving*. In both, this
unselving aims at increased contact with and expression of
the elemental reality of the world, which they believe has
been obscured by the historical growth of narrowly subjective modes of awareness. This effort implies a dialectic
between two poles of an enlarged experience. In Nietzsche,
there is the Dionysian, the unconscious element, and the
Apollonian, the principle of individuality. The latter, with
its ultimately dreamlike structures of thought and expression, includes almost all aspects of our ordinary mental
life—reason, morality, language, normal perception, plas-
tic and visual imagery. The brief phrases from Rimbaud's
letter correspond. An underlying activity of thought and
expression, not originated or understood by the conscious
self, is suggested by the reflexive "s'éveille," the expression
"rien de sa faute," and the spontaneous actions of unconscious forces—"fait son remuement," "vient d'un bond."
Second, there is an observing and structuring activity of
the "I": "Cela m'est évident: j'assiste à l'éclosion de ma
pensée: je la regarde, je l'écoute: je lance un coup
d'archet." Through this latter process unconscious material
comes to awareness. In particular, the progression *profondeurs, symphonie, scène* parallels Nietzsche's argument that
consciousness originates in the depth of Dionysian reality,

that it manifests itself first as music, thereafter attaining perceivable form in the Apollonian "dream spectacle."

So Rimbaud and Nietzsche sketch a model of experience involving conscious and preconscious elements, a progression to more structured forms of awareness that, however, are further removed from primitive reality. Hence the necessity of transforming these structures of the mind in favor of a more primordial kind of experience. In both writers this necessity raises questions bearing on ecstatic poetry, questions concerning sensation and reason—that is, relatively unmediated experience and the impositions of intelligence—and therefore also concerning disorder and form in the self and its expressions, indeed the unity and even existence of what we call the self.

Thus, when in the shorter *lettre du voyant* Rimbaud suggests that "C'est faux de dire: Je pense. On devrait dire: On me pense" (It's false to say: I think. One should say: I am thought), he expresses in rudimentary form a radical insight that is developed in the later writings of Nietzsche, namely that the supposedly stable ego is in reality made up of half-glimpses, falsifications, illusions. Indeed, Nietzsche's critique of the soul-ego-subject superstition is most compelling when he analyzes notions like "I think" and even "it thinks" (in me) as falsifying vestiges of a primitive fetishism of language. That is, he asserts the reality of consciousness as liberated from the illusion of the subject, which in effect is a more systematic and extreme version of what Rimbaud argues from direct experience in the creation of poetry.

In the longer of the *voyant* letters Rimbaud pursues the explosion of the self in terms of enlargement and transformation—through methodical deformation of experience at the root level of sensation. His belief in the possibility of thereby arriving at full self-knowledge and a real vision of the unknown (recall "sa propre connaissance, entière"; "il arrive à l'*inconnu*!"; "il les a vues!") betrays a youthful naiveté alien to the mature Nietzsche's demolishing of the subject and perspectivist argument that we can never escape the prison of the senses. But Nietzsche consistently attacks intellectual consciousness as most removed from the real, and in crucial passages he insists instead on the enormous value of the senses—if not distorted then refined, perfected, thought through—as the key to the most satisfying, even the truest version of reality. Indeed he argues that the supposed objects of the senses, *things,* are as illusory as the self, and that it is only grammar that makes us believe in self, God, *and* things. Thus, the senses do not lie in revealing dynamic flux, as opposed to the fixed, illusory things that are the creations of the intellect. Altogether there is, therefore, a significant convergence of Rimbaud's and Nietzsche's ideas on consciousness and sense experience. The notions of self and thing must be transformed, even exploded; the senses are to be reconstrued as conveying a more acute, dynamic, unstable world of experience; this world may be alive with an overmastering power and beauty of which normally we are unaware but which we can come to perceive.

In fact, a text like "Ce qu'on dit au poète à propos de fleurs" could be read as an interpretation of Nietzsche's philosophy of the senses. That poem's disconcerting imagery subverts and enriches our sense of things; one example: flowers that are snouts and chairs, that drool pommades yet are jewellike in possessing gem-tonsils and gem-ovaries. Such imagery also provides a starting point for the explosions of material reality and consciousness that we glimpsed in texts like "H" and "Parade"—"O terrible frisson des amours novices sur le sol sanglant et par l'hydrogène clarteux!" (O terrible shudder of new

loves on the bloody ground and through the transparent
hydrogen!); "Les yeux flambent, le sang chante, les os
s'élargissent, les larmes et des filets rouges ruissellent"
(Eyes flame, blood sings, bones expand, tears and red
filaments stream). Such lines prelude the ecstatic dissolution of "Being Beauteous" and "Barbare," and remind us
that Nietzsche's and Rimbaud's demolition of self and
things is motivated throughout by the attraction to states
of transport and frenzy.

But the subversion of rational consciousness in favor of a
sense-dominated, chaotic range of states at whose extreme
we encounter ecstasy and madness inevitably raises the
issues of control and form in the self and its expressions.
The interaction of frenzy with lucidity is both a hallmark
and a problem of visionary-ecstatic thinking, not only in
Rimbaud and Nietzsche but in other poets as well, and
perhaps generally in ecstatic religions. For example, shamans accede to ecstasy in part through exceptional physical
and intellectual discipline, attained through years of practice. The relationship between discipline and ecstasy concerned many poets of the romantic tradition. For example,
Yeats's attraction to trance and illumination is balanced by
a corresponding effort to control "all Asiatic vague immen-
sities," and his poetry is marked throughout by an ambivalent interaction of the body, spiritual trance, and sculp-
tural-architectural motifs that suggest the coolness of art.
These elements in fact characterize a certain poetic current.
Earlier, not to speak of Blake or Hölderlin or Keats, there
is Coleridge, whose "Kubla Khan" is similarly characterized by a mixture of orgasmic, ecstatic, musical, and visionary imagery and architectural elements. Coleridge
often moves between, on the one hand, the attraction to
states of trance, associated with Dionysian energy, involving absolute immediacy of perception and expression, and,

on the other, his fear of the madness that such states may bring, his awareness of the difficulty the imagination has in achieving totally unified control of the full range of our experience, his more realistic emphasis on the alliance of imagination with conscious will.

Both Nietzsche and Rimbaud celebrate frenzy more wholeheartedly than Coleridge, but neither downplays the structuring activities of the mind. For Nietzsche consciousness is *constituted* by the interactions between Dionysian and Apollonian elements, the Apollonian being necessary to save us from complete dissolution by providing perceivable form; the two forces must be in strict proportion. Despite increasing attention to the value of discipline and of the lucidly self-created soul, Nietzsche never stopped insisting on the value of frenzy, on the persistence of the savage-animal element of our nature, on frenzy as in fact an *indispensable* ingredient of artistic psychology, on the persistence therefore, even in late, civilized, specialized forms of art, of the original ecstatic forces.

Throughout his career Nietzsche emphasized the persistence of the ecstatic, as well as the power of genius to combine savage elements with superior lucidity, resulting in the apparently effortless dance of the great artist-thinker. The young Rimbaud, for his part, stressed an initial penetration to the state of frenzy—which is monstrous, bordering on insanity, and which threatens to dissolve consciousness: "quand, affolé, il finirait par perdre l'intelligence de ses visions" (even if, maddened, he ends up losing the intelligence of his visions); "Qu'il crève dans son bondissement par les choses inouïes et innommables" (Let him die leaping through unheard of and unnamable things). These statements point to a severe discontinuity between exalted states and normal consciousness. In response, there is a corresponding effort to join the two realms, an insistence on the systematic effort that is necessary to attain the ecstatic illumination, and then to express it. As the passages cited at the opening of this section show, Rimbaud believed that the poet must work, by means of reasoned derangement, to make himself visionary. Similarly, he asserts: "la première étude de l'homme qui veut être poète est sa propre connaissance, entière; il cherche son âme, il l'inspecte, il la tente, l'apprend. Dès qu'il la sait, il doit la cultiver" (the first study of the man who wants to be a poet is understanding himself, complete; he searches his soul, he inspects it, he tests it, learns it. As soon as he knows it, he must cultivate it).

What emphasis, in a poet pursuing exalted states to the point of dissolution of individual consciousness, on work, method, rational control! And most revealing of all is Rimbaud's emphasis on the unknown, which is close to Nietzsche's argument on the relationship between the Dionysian chaos and the absorbing and structuring function of the Apollonian that brings it to conscious form. Let us leave aside for the moment Rimbaud's confident claim to integrate the visionary and the sociocultural (a claim undermined variously by the *Saison,* "Solde" and "Génie"); still we cannot here minimize the poet's desire, having reached the unknown, to absorb it into normal consciousness, not for himself alone but especially for others.

The attempt to transcend normal consciousness, the attainment of peaks of exaltation, the problems of lucidity, discontinuity, and loss—these features in Rimbaud and other writers can be recapitulated and interrelated through arguments proposed by Roland Fischer. The bipolar model of consciousness that he constructs (one element to receive experience and the other to be conscious of it, to interpret it) applies an age-old epistemological pattern to the ecstatic experience. The polarities that Fischer stresses are

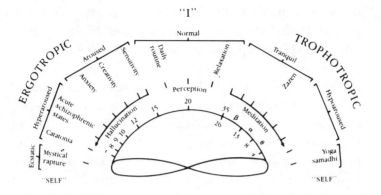

Fig. 1. Bipolar Model of Consciousness

NOTE: Fischer's explanation of this figure is as follows: "Varieties of conscious states mapped on a perception-hallucination continuum of increasing ergotropic arousal (*left*) and a perception-meditation continuum of increasing trophotropic arousal (*right*). These levels of subcortical hyper- and hypoarousal are cortically interpreted by man as normal, creative, psychotic, and ecstatic states (*left*) and *zazen* and *samadhi* (*right*). The similarity between horizontally corresponding states of hypo- and hyperarousal is borne out by the fact that the coefficient of variation is in the same low range of magnitude during deep meditation . . . as it is in catatonia, i.e., 7 to 8. . . . With increasing hypoarousal, i.e., from relaxation to *samadhi,* there is a preponderance of beta, alpha, and then theta EEG waves with their characteristic hertz frequencies of 26 to 13, 12 to 8, and 7 to 4 cps. The loop connecting ecstasy and *samadhi* represents the trophotropic rebound which is observed in response to intense ergotropic hyperarousal."

---

those between subcortical levels that register experience and cortical interpretation of it, between left and right hemispheres of the brain, and between the mutually exclusive ergotropic and trophotropic systems, illustrated in the diagram in figure 1 and involving respectively increasing psychic arousal whose term is ecstasy, and decreasing arousal, to the point of attaining the ultimate peace of the yoga experience.[13]

The value of this model lies in Fischer's attempt, based on study of many religious and drug experiences, to represent the full continuum of states of consciousness; without minimizing discontinuities, he nonetheless stresses the impulsion to psychic integration. The parallels with Rimbaud are striking: the normal, dichotomous experience of separate "I" and external world (at the center of the diagram); the creative moments of withdrawal from that normal state; the emergence, as in the *voyant* letters, of another, larger self (Fischer calls it the mental dimension of exalted states); the negative states on the way to ecstasy, corresponding perhaps to some of the painful experiences recounted in the *Saison;* the bipolarity of ecstatic excitement and the peace of *samādhi,* illuminating the contrast between the peace sought in poems like "Fêtes de la patience," "Marine," and "Mystique," on the one hand, and the raging energy of "Villes I" and "Barbare" on the other; and finally, the disappearance of the normal world and with it the impulse to motor activity, and the oceanic experience of unity and fulfillment, paralleling the opposition between ordinary reality and the ecstatic state in Rimbaud and particularly revealing for a text like "Barbare," as we shall see.

Indeed, Fischer's delineation of a continuous progression toward ecstasy and *samādhi* proves generally useful in discussing Rimbaud's ecstatic poems in the *Illuminations,* which are marked by a similar sense of process and culmination. The presence of both discontinuity and integration in Fischer's model also provides insight into Rimbaud's linking of achievement and loss in the *voyant* letters as well as similar features in his poetry and that of others. Thus the opposition between subcortical and cortical allows Fischer to distinguish between experience itself and the accompanying circumstances or symbolism that we associate with it and by which we recognize and interpret it. A version of associationism or objective correlative, this distinction suggests a persuasive mechanism for the persistence of recognizable motifs characteristic of ecstatic literature. It also accounts for various phenomena relevant to ecstatic poetry: amnesia (peak moments that can be recalled only when the accompanying conditions are present); déjà vu (the subcortical only, feeling without corresponding interpretation); flashback (subcortical and cortical elements integrated); and the special ability of ecstatics, in the absence of peak experience, to recall it completely—a sign, according to Fischer, of the ultimate in psychic integration attained in the ecstatic experience and *samādhi* and persisting into more normal states of consciousness. These elements are indeed close to preeminent features of Rimbaud's writing: immediacy and integration of the ecstasy; loss, fragmentation, the forlorn return to the normal "I" of waking life, a pervasive disorientation; and persistence of the vision in poetic forms that continue to render it present.

Fischer's ideas and model therefore provide a useful way to organize significant features of ecstatic poetics: multiple, divergent mental states, and the effort to integrate them; the fading of normal reality, that is, the dissolution of the world of sense perception (Rimbaud's and Nietzsche's subversion of *things*) in favor of experiences of transport or peace in which subject and object are fused; and, permeating ecstatic experience *and expression,* the coexistence of frenzy and lucidity, dispersion and conscious structure. That is, any discussion of the ideas of ecstatic *poetry* leads to the problem of ecstatic *form,* to the conceiv-

ing of words capable of conveying, evoking, enacting ecstatic experience.

Thus, although in the second *voyant* letter Rimbaud
considers that he is attempting an experience of the ineffable—"les choses inouïes et innommables"—the young
poet nonetheless sets out to find an appropriate language
in which to express the vision, and to do so for others:

> Il est chargé de l'humanité, des *animaux* même; il
> devra faire sentir, palper, écouter ses inventions; si ce
> qu'il rapporte de *là-bas* a forme, il donne forme; si c'est
> informe, il donne de l'informe. Trouver une langue;—Du
> reste, toute parole étant idée, le temps d'un langage uni-
> versel viendra! Il faut être académicien,—plus mort qu'un
> fossile,—pour parfaire un dictionnaire, de quelque
> langue que ce soit. Des faibles se mettraient à *penser* sur
> la première lettre de l'alphabet, qui pourraient vite ruer
> dans la folie!
>
> Cette langue sera de l'âme pour l'âme, résumant tout,
> parfums, sons, couleurs, de la pensée accrochant la pensée
> et tirant. Le poète définirait la quantité d'inconnu
> s'éveillant en son temps dans l'âme universelle: il donne-
> rait plus—que la formule de sa pensée, que la notation
> de *sa marche au Progrès!* Enormité devenant norme,
> absorbée par tous, il serait vraiment *un multiplicateur de
> progrès!*

> He is responsible for humanity, for the *animals* even;
> he will have to make his inventions smelled, touched,
> heard; if what he brings back from *over there* has form, he
> gives form; if it's formless, he gives formlessness. Find a
> language;—Besides, every word being idea, the time of
> a universal language will come! You have to be an acade-
> mician,—deader than a fossil,—to complete a diction-
> ary, in whatever language. Were weak people to start

thinking about the first letter of the alphabet, they could
quickly stampede to madness!

This language will be of the soul for the soul, sum-
ming up everything, perfumes, sounds, colors, thought
catching onto thought and pulling. The poet would define the quantity of unknown awakening in his time in
the universal soul: he would give more—than the formulation of his thought, than the notation of his *march toward Progress!* Enormity becoming norm, absorbed by all,
he would be truly *a multiplier of progress!*

Here the predominance of the poetic intention is clear
(as is the magical view of language encountered in "Voyelles"). Yet a curious mixture of conceptions of language
insinuates the paradoxical nature of such visionary expression. The poem is to translate faithfully what is perceived
in the exalted state, even supposedly to the point of transcending form, or at least recognizable form: "si ce qu'il
rapporte de *là-bas* a forme, il donne forme; si c'est informe,
il donne de l'informe." This intention goes as far as possible in the direction of not imposing Apollonian structure,
with the word "inventions" in this context retaining something of its traditional meaning of *discovery*. But Rimbaud
later adds, "les inventions d'inconnu réclament des formes
nouvelles" (inventions of the unknown call for new forms),
which points to a second, distinctly nonecstatic poetic activity, the methodical search for a language adequate to
express the vision. Hence, "Trouver une langue," and the
intentional, definitional, even ethical implications of "Il
est chargé de," "il devra faire sentir," "Le poète définirait." Dionysian and Apollonian functions are thus combined in Rimbaud's formulations.

Coleridge proposes for "Kubla Khan" a trance state in
which reality, the content of consciousness, and expression

are perfectly coincident ("all the images rose up . . . as *things,* with a parallel production of the correspondent expressions, without any sensation or consciousness of effort"), and Hölderlin in "Brod und Wein" evokes an illumination of the divine among the Greeks in which words responsively emerge with the organic necessity of natural growths ("nun müssen dafür Worte, wie Blumen, entstehn"). But Rimbaud, somewhat differently, suggests a poetic activity of two essential moments: first vision, then the devising of a language in which to express it.

Rimbaud's scheme, debatable in its supposition of the possibility of experience completely prior to language, is still apparently less idealized than the formulations by Coleridge and Hölderlin, in which words arise spontaneously, with no gap whatever between themselves and either consciousness or reality. Note, however, that Hölderlin's and Coleridge's texts evoke that ideal of language as impossible for us. Both imagine a past ecstatic experience—Dionysian-Christian for Hölderlin, a drug-initiated illumination expressed by a conflation of Greek and Asian elements for Coleridge. And both involve a more or less successful effort to move closer to the exalted state through the operation of the poem itself, but also final alienation from the ecstatic condition, return to normal consciousness (nostalgia, despondence, memory, hope, determination), return also to normal language (inadequate, arbitrary, intentional). In the *voyant* letters Rimbaud is still at the beginning, projecting the movement toward the ecstatic experience, but the potential gap between vision and expression is great, and it insinuates possibilities for serious problems and failures.

Finally, though, in Rimbaud's formulations a third moment emerges, that of the reader, to whom the vision must become palpably present, experienced, absorbed into his enriched consciousness. In "Brod und Wein" Hölderlin evokes the Dionysian possession of the Greeks, denied to us; "Kubla Khan" closes with a hypothetical imagination of a frenzied poet figure, from whom onlookers shrink in terror. Both texts therefore raise the possibility of our reaction to or involvement in the state of ecstasy, but do so in a distanced, skeptical way. Rimbaud's youthful belief in the identity of word and idea, in the approaching era of a universal language, hardly to be attained by the scholar's etymological approach, a language capable of *creating madness,* is projected toward the future and is comparably distanced. This ironically colored evocation of the ecstatic power of poetry, together with the more moderate formulations about the poet's disciplined composition and the reader's gradual absorption of the abnormal into consciousness, suggest both the ultimate goal and the recurrent limitation of Rimbaud's poetry. The *Saison* mercilessly exposes the latter, debunking Rimbaud's effort to invent new realities, ironically deflating his claim to have created a universal language: "je me flattai d'inventer un verbe poétique accessible, un jour ou l'autre, à tous les sens. Je réservais la traduction" (I flattered myself that I invented a poetic language accessible, one day or another, to all the senses. I withheld the translation). The *Saison* insists on the persistence in his work of the known resources of poetic language ("la vieillerie poétique"), which hardly seem to attain the desired immediacy.

Thus the true poetic effort is to actualize exalted states that have been inaccessible to normal consciousness, have been precisely mythic, through literary forms sufficiently original to conjure up these states in the mind of the reader, but which upon analysis appear to partake of the normal functions of language in our conscious, Apollonian world. As we shall see in the next section, a group of *Illuminations* fascinatingly reveal these ambiguities of ex-

alted and normal consciousness and language, proposing
ecstatic intensity through highly crafted and intentional
imagery, structure, and convention. These *Illuminations*
constitute a repertory of ecstatic forms, which we cannot
see fully until we consider in a larger context the ecstatic
poet's vocation and societal function, and the kinds of
imagery and structures that this function might be said
archetypally to generate.

For in a literal way Rimbaud reproduced features of
mantic poetic activity despite his living in a modern, de-
mythified culture. These features include: recognition of
the mantic vocation; initiation involving extreme states,
prolonged suffering, with the concomitant dangers of ill-
ness or madness; an extended period of study with experienced shamans, training in ecstatic techniques and in an
impressive body of philosophical, religious, esthetic, and
cosmological knowledge; the individual attainment of ecstasy and the conveying of it to the rest of the community;
a variety of forms in which to do so, involving music,
narrations of spiritual or underworld journeys, spectacles or
dramatic enactments of the exalted experience.

Rimbaud's *lettres* correspond closely to these mantic
themes. They are first a declaration of the recognition of
the poetic vocation and a realization of the necessity of
painful initiation: "Les souffrances sont énormes, mais il
faut être fort, être né poète, et je me suis reconnu poète"
(The suffering is enormous, but it is necessary to be
strong, to be born a poet, and I have recognized myself as
a poet). The ecstatic techniques and the danger of madness
have already been mentioned. As for training by experienced mantics, Rimbaud is in the isolated position of any
ecstatic in modern Western culture. His initiation and
training are represented by his reading of the poetic tradition, his judgment as to which writers are truly visionary.

The phenomenon of literacy, the transformation of the communal-oral into the solitary act of reading thus characterizes the poet's situation, and the concluding portion of the second letter, with its comments on romantics, Parnassians, Baudelaire, and others, functions as Rimbaud's recognition of poetic initiation, training, and mastery. The prestige and range of the traditional shaman's knowledge and function are only implied in Rimbaud's letters, mainly in hyperbolic statements such as "Il est chargé de l'humanité, des *animaux* même." Aside from recalling the shaman's intimate connection with the animal world, this statement introduces a strong sense of communal responsibility, expressed elsewhere in the letters as Rimbaud's desire to have a productive function in a just and responsive society. But it is the *Saison* that (ironically) demonstrates the extent of Rimbaud's pretensions—as in this previously cited description of the infernal husband in "Délires I": "Il feignait d'être éclairé sur tout, commerce, art, médecine" (He pretended to be enlightened on everything, commerce, art, medicine). Even more clearly, the *Saison*'s most ecstatic chapter, "Nuit de l'enfer," expresses a global poetico-religious function of sardonically mythic proportions: "Je vais dévoiler tous les mystères: mystères religieux ou naturels, mort, naissance, avenir, passé, cosmogonie, néant. Je suis maître en fantasmagories." Earlier, in "Nuit," Rimbaud spoke of being richer than poets and visionaries but of maintaining total silence; later in the chapter his pretensions lead him to a mad imagination of himself as a Christ figure. But in the sentences cited here he is closest to the underlying mantic function, revealer of all natural and supernatural mysteries, from birth to death, from time to a cosmological vision of the universe—but all finally in a cynical and negating perspective: nothingness, phantasmagories.

Thus the *Saison* indicates the full extent of the communal function that we may conceive as the outcome of the
poetics of exalted states announced in the *lettres du voyant*,
irony being the inevitable mode concerning such a function in a desacralized culture such as ours. As for the forms
of expression generated by Rimbaud's poetic goals, the
lettres provide little help, aside from the materials on language and form already discussed. The *Saison* ("Délires II")
is more suggestive, designating an initial *notational* effort
("je notais l'inexprimable. Je fixais des vertiges"), followed
by hallucination of vision and language, the phenomenon
of leaving the world and mystic fulfillment, then a kind of
theatrical dissociation: "Je devins un opéra fabuleux: je vis
que tous les êtres ont une fatalité de bonheur: l'action n'est
pas la vie, mais une façon de gâcher quelque force, un
énervement" (I became a fabulous opera: I saw that all
beings have a fatality of happiness: action is not life, but a
way of bungling some force, an enervation).

These indications are of less than total significance,
however, since they so much concern the mystic asceticism
of "Fêtes de la patience." They need to be completed by
certain other kinds of art Rimbaud says he imagined, for
example, "voyages de découvertes dont on n'a pas de relations, républiques sans histoires, . . . révolutions de
mœurs, déplacements de races et de continents" (voyages
of discovery for which we don't have the account, republics
without history, revolutions in morals, displacements of
races and continents). Relevant also are the overall form of
the *Saison,* a narration of an ecstatic-spiritual experience
explicitly called a descent to hell, and the forms of provocation and realization that we saw in the first section of
this chapter. Together these elements resemble the pattern
of mantic art described by Eliade and Chadwick and comparable, as we shall see, to certain features of the ecstatic

Illuminations: celestial ascensions and underworld journeys, presentations of ecstatic states, musical and dramatic spectacles for the community. Chadwick and Eliade, like Nietzsche, locate the roots of the major art forms of music and literature in the mantic, shamanistic, or Dionysian state. The predominance of the ecstatic-lyric, of presentational-spectacular realizations, of narrative-dramatic-musical celebrations in Rimbaud comes close to these formulations, suggesting that many formal aspects of his poetry, so unique and so apparently difficult to categorize, are engendered by his ecstatic goals.

Two aspects of ecstatic form deserve further attention before we turn to the *Illuminations.* The first is the imagery, which may be viewed as archetypal in psychological terms, such as those used by Fischer, and also as a function of religious and poetic tradition; both senses bear directly on an audience's experience of ecstatic literature.[14] I earlier alluded to some of this imagery, but we need to summarize it now in order to appreciate its thoroughgoing relevance for Rimbaud. As we would expect, despite certain unifying tendencies (the motif of leaving the self, or the body, or even the human), dichotomies once again are visible. In fact, in their full scope such motifs correspond to the range of conflicting traditions that we found, earlier in this chapter, to be relevant for Rimbaud's work.

In spiritual, ascensional forms, but in many drug experiences as well, the following five characteristics are of note. (1) Modification of learned perceptual constancies, with near space initially foreshortened and with space-time progressively transformed, until in the extremes of ecstasy and *samādhi* the spatial-temporal disappears entirely. This feature is stressed as well by Baudelaire on drugs and by Blake throughout his work, and in a different form is visible in the progression of Rimbaud's

"Matinée d'ivresse," "Being Beauteous," "Barbare." (2)
The experience of heightened luminosities, complex and
living geometrical patterns of an extremely absorbing sort
such as Coleridge noted, that are responsible perhaps for
the intense yet artificial quality of the imagery in Rimbaud's "Fleurs," some of his city poems, and "Veillées,"
especially part II—the last expressive of some initial and
intermediate phases, perhaps drug-induced, of the process
of altering consciousness. (3) Penetration to an archetypal
area of the psyche in which one encounters the uranian
imagery of heightened natural scenery, the city—cosmic
mountain—palace complex, the buried precious stones
and rainbows that link ancient religious and poetic traditions from Dante to Blake, and Hölderlin and Coleridge
to Rimbaud and Yeats. (4) The experience of larger-than-
life figures, angels, and divinities, a feature strong in
Blake and remarkable in the "êtres supérieurs" engendered frequently in Rimbaud's poetry. (5) Finally, total deindividualization, transcendence of the subject-object dichotomy, the experience of undifferentiated being,
expressed by the imagery of dissolution and by motifs of
global, polar, universal totality (variously in "Fêtes de la
patience," "Génie," "Barbare").

A second group of motifs is connected with what might
be called *body ecstasies*. It includes Rimbaud's strongly sexual emphasis in connection with Greek divinities such as
Venus and Pan. The Dionysian is also relevant, with its
motifs of intoxication, sexual abandon, a frenzy in which
the god's female votaries first suckle animals and children,
then rend and devour them. The savage and animal are
associated as well with hunting motifs. In addition, the
Dionysian penetration to the heart of reality is suggested
by imagery of water and all other life-giving fluids, as well
as by the attraction to nature in its most violent and

powerful manifestations. Finally, Dionysus is the god of sudden appearances and disappearances; thus the orgiastic ecstasy he provokes also emphasizes the impermanence common to exalted experiences. As we shall see, many of these elements are especially relevant for Rimbaud's "Villes I" and "Barbare."

In some sense Eliade's description of the symbolism of shamanistic ecstasy unites the preceding two groups, with the qualifications that shamanism downplays the specifically sexual and that it always involves individual ecstasy. The spiritual tendency of the shamans is apparent in uranian imagery, in the experience of mystic light, and especially in the insistence on the shaman's magical power of flight. The shaman also reaches the realm of the dead, encounters divine beings, and speaks to the spirits. But black shamanism follows another direction on the mystic voyage, and all shamanism, even the ascensional, emphasizes identification with the animal as a preparation for the ecstatic. As in the Dionysian, hunting motifs are thus central, in combination with the exaltation of fire and the figures who control it, the smiths. Perhaps even more important is the stress on the transformation of the body— widespread symbolism of destruction of the body, numbering of the bones, introduction of painful but magical substances into the flesh, the undergoing of ritual death involving great suffering, and finally the experience of bodily rebirth, bones covered by new flesh, and the like. Once again, this motif of painful ecstatic bodily transformation (for which we will see close analogies in "Matinée d'ivresse," "Being Beauteous," and "Barbare") indicates the paradoxical interconnections of the bodily and the spiritual, of transcendent and immanent impulses in the ecstatic experience.

This recapitulation of imagery, all of which is relevant

to Rimbaud, indicates how far-reaching are the problems of self, sensation, language, dispersion, and control discussed earlier. For the ecstatic aims at opening up *all* the domains of experience associated with such divergent imagery, and therefore raises the questions of dichotomy and unity in consciousness as well as in expression.

One final convention of ecstatic form is the theatrical in its various modalities, which involves similar complexity in that it can be viewed as actual enactment of ecstatic immediacy or as fictional imitation, as utter coherence or complete separation of ecstatic experience and language. In this connection it is interesting that "Délires II" describes a kind of musico-theatrical dissociation ("Je devins un opéra fabuleux") at the term of at least one phase of Rimbaud's evolution. The dramatic and the musical as ambivalently related to the immediacy of the exalted state are central to arguments about the derivation of ecstatic literature in Nietzsche, Eliade, and Chadwick.[15] Eliade describes a range of performances, from actual trance (accompanied or induced by music) to increasingly theatrical, and finally degraded, fakiristic spectacles, the last of these a phenomenon that we linked to "Parade" and that is suggestive as well for "Solde."

Nietzsche, too, is preoccupied by the relations of actual trance and various modes of musico-theatrical performance. In *The Birth of Tragedy,* he describes the hypothetical historical stages whereby the Dionysian revelers, who supposedly once experienced themselves as literally transformed into satyrs, later became simply members of the dramatic chorus, so that the satyr comes to represent a variety of nonecstatic, or quasi-ecstatic, and also markedly *esthetic* functions: musician, poet, dancer, visionary. A later formulation derives all artistic activity from the original frenzies (both Apollo and Dionysus are now conceived as producing frenzy), placing what Nietzsche calls Dionysian histronicism, the actual physical embodying of the trance experience, at the beginning, prior to its more specialized later appearance as music.

Extremely interesting views of Rimbaud, who of course wrote no actual plays, emerge from such speculations: the literal, bodily experience of trance, giving way to musical-verbal presentations, self-conscious creations of the civilized-ecstatic, musician-poet-visionary (and fakiristic?) writer. Ecstasies of the body, the varieties of poetic-musical-dramatic language, lyric-narrative-dramatic forms of presentation, movements toward the intensity of ecstasy and away from it to the sterility of loss, are therefore all of great importance for the study of the ecstatic *Illuminations*.

Realizations and Transcendences: The Illuminations *and Romantic Ecstatic Poetry*

Several important *Illuminations* exemplify, more closely and completely than the work of other romantic visionary poets, the argument I am pursuing. The erotic and the element of realization, together with the experience of superior beings, remain central to these *Illuminations,* just as in the pagan poems treated in the first section of this chapter. At the same time, a more global project of consciousness-transformation ending in ecstasy, with techniques and symbolism such as we saw in the second and third sections, is also strikingly apparent. The transfiguration of self and senses, of consciousness and external world, from the modification of spatial-temporal perceptual categories to oceanic dissolution, is pursued in a progression toward more extreme forms of exaltation.

Nonetheless, typical paradoxes remain, and the prob-

lems of discontinuity and loss, the complexities of the self
and the bereft experience of the isolated "I" fallen from the
exalted state, are also insistently present. Finally, the issue
of ecstatic form, glimpsed in the *voyant* letters and the
Saison, is marvellously illustrated in these texts, which
variously employ elemental and archetypal symbolism,
syncretist accumulations, and tactics of enactment, to
render present the search for, accession to, and disintegration or persistence of ecstatic states. The problematic features of language and structure, experience and expression,
consciousness, artifact and public thus prevail in these
strange poems, which seem in part to commemorate, to
designate as absent, in part somehow to enact through
language the altered states of consciousness to which Rimbaud so evidently aspired.

Though perhaps unique in accumulating so many ecstatic elements, Rimbaud is hardly alone among poets in
pursuing exalted states, as I have already suggested.
Writers such as Blake, Hölderlin, Nerval, and Yeats,
among others, reveal similar myths of history as well as the
pursuit of altered states, though in ways that differ from
Rimbaud and that can therefore help us to perceive the
originality of the *Illuminations.* For example, a series of
ecstatic elements—animal, erotic, sadistic, Dionysian—
and numerous uranian motifs (notably city and architectural imagery) are integrated in Blake's long prophetic
works in a progression toward an apocalypse in the traditional religious sense. That is, various ecstatic moments
take their place in an overarching system that perhaps
makes Rimbaud's individual poems seem partial or inadequate in comparison, but in which the intensity of each of
these moments is thereby diminished, the exalted experience being enmeshed in mythology, the infernal finally
becoming ascensional, the ecstatic being absorbed into a

larger, prophetic perspective. Blake indeed only sporadically attains the remarkable immediacy of Rimbaud's brief pieces, which are quite correctly called "illuminations."[16]

In Nerval and Hölderlin some similar issues are involved, together with an overriding sense of failure in the visionary project. Both the sybilline density of *Les Chimères* and the unsuccessful effort of the protagonist of *Aurélia* to articulate a vast mythological system of the universe contrast with Rimbaud's capacity for ecstatic enactment. And one could argue that this is the case because Rimbaud's psychology, sexual temperament, historical circumstances, and ecstatic conception of poetry together favor such enactment, as opposed to the sense of inadequacy, nostalgia, and finally madness that color these elements in Nerval.

Hölderlin's madness similarly compels us to confront the tragic seriousness of his life and poetry, just as his elegiac and celebrational forms testify to an ambivalent combination of nostalgia and projected realization. In Hölderlin ecstatic and prophetic experiences are brought closer to our awareness by the structure of the poems themselves and by the poet's sense of the necessity of a communal awakening. Nonetheless, the divine remains characteristically absent. In "Brod und Wein" it is said that Dionysus gives not only hope and a sacramental (that is, nonimmediate) reminder of the divine in our food and drink—the contrast with the direct presence of Rimbaud's "génie" is typical—but also forgetfulness *and* lucidity, the ability to stay awake through the night of history in anticipation of a return of the gods. This superhuman task, whose quasi-impossibility is revealed by a text like "Patmos," indicates the distance that Rimbaud, so to speak, has come, as well as the enormous difficulties that attend any effort to surmount the process of history and to reenact ecstasy for a public through poetry.

The romantic tradition thus provides examples of poets preoccupied by visionary-ecstatic themes in ways that are different from Rimbaud but capable of elucidating his work. The example of Yeats indicates the persistence of this tradition. His myth of history, his doctrine of the mask and of the enlarged self, his thematics of trance and self-absorbed or frenzied dance, show his affinities with earlier ecstatic poetry. Typically, however, Yeats is far more given than is Rimbaud to emphasize the spiritual, the intellectual, the element of conscious control. Yeats is therefore most useful as a contrasting example, as well as reminding us of those elements of control and artifice that the *lettres du voyant* do not ignore.

Thus in Yeats the body and sexuality are abundantly emphasized, but hardly with the surreal immediacy of Rimbaud's imagery. Trance may have some inherent relation to the body, since "All dreams of the soul / End in a beautiful man's or woman's body," but characteristically in the ecstatic state body and soul alike are "cast out and cast away / Beyond the visible world." The bodily origin of exalted experience thus leads in Yeats to ascensional formulas, notably in texts like "The Double Vision of Michael Robartes" and "All Souls' Night." Indeed, the "Supernatural Songs" explicitly evoke Celtic and Indian mysticism to unmask the unreality of all except the spiritual beyond, in the process suggesting corresponding forms of religious ecstasy. Similarly, "Sailing to Byzantium" strives to transcend nature through changeless art. And its more complex companion piece "Byzantium," though powerfully evoking the mire and blood of material existence, still surmounts them through imagery of spiritual or artistic mastery. The progression in "Byzantium" is again recognizably ascensional, moving beyond the bodily, then beyond an initial level of vision and spirituality (motifs of religion, drunkenness, nocturnal modes of perception), and attaining a realm that transcends the categories of man, shade, or image—a realm of superior vision and structure ("a starlit or a moonlit dome"), a veritable fusion of life-in-death, an intensity of flame, dance, and trance so far transcending ordinary existence as to be quite literally immaterial. Finally, the golden smithies who "break" the flood of ordinary reality, and the Emperor for whom they labor, admirably figure the control for which Yeats strove, and recall the masterful voice that confidently declaims in his poems, in this respect so different from the dissolved self and the enacted frenzy in Rimbaud's work.

The imagery of frenzy, architecture, and imperial power in "Byzantium" inevitably harks back to a text that haunts the English poetic tradition and that also provides a most useful integrating analogy with Rimbaud's work: Coleridge's "Kubla Khan." The differences between Coleridge and Rimbaud are clear enough, and might generally be expressed as a function of Coleridge's conservatism in theology, psychology, ethics, and overall poetic theory and form. The last issue is particularly relevant, for the traditional meters and self-conscious preface of "Kubla Khan" differ markedly from Rimbaud's prose poems. One could, however, argue that the *Saison* and other ironic texts provide a distancing commentary for Rimbaud's ecstatic writing that is comparable to Coleridge's preface. Moreover, the poem "Kubla Khan" itself contains many features directly related to ecstatic poetics and to Rimbaud's poems, features that can be summarized as follows.

First, Coleridge's poem is a fascinating treatment of the relation between poetic creation and altered states. The preface reports a supposedly drug-induced, trancelike "vi-

sion" and "composition." Stanza three evokes first a lost
visionary state, then a poetic frenzy that is fearful in intensity. And the second stanza describes a "deep romantic
chasm," the locus of a Dionysian-like energy that is powerfully sexual, attractive to human beings, and perceivable in
nature as an orgasmic force:

> A savage place! as holy and enchanted
> As e'er beneath a waning moon was haunted
> By woman wailing for her demon-lover!
> And from this chasm, with ceaseless turmoil seething,
> As if this earth in fast thick pants were breathing,
> A mighty fountain momently was forced.

This erotic power, calling forth human expectation, pain,
and frenzy, and perceived in the natural world, is extended
throughout the poem by the imagery of sublime nature
("sacred river," "caverns measureless to man," "forests ancient as the hills," "deep romantic chasm," "caves of ice").
Evocative of erotic-religious-poetic forms of frenzy, these
motifs together anticipate not only Nietzsche but also very
directly the universal ecstasies depicted in "Villes I" and
"Barbare."

Drugs, dream, vision, trance, and human frenzy within
an eroticized perception of nature thus link Coleridge's
poem to ecstatic traditions in general and to Rimbaud in
particular. A second feature of resemblance is the way in
which "Kubla Khan" shows in miniature the syncretist and
paradisal tendencies discussed earlier. Its ecstatic motifs
involve a conflation of Greek (Platonic, Orphic, perhaps
Dionysian), Asian (indeed Tartar, that is, shamanistic),
Biblical, Miltonic, and many other elements, all finally
emerging in a paradisal perspective: "For he on honey-dew
hath fed, / And drunk the milk of Paradise."

But we have seen that such self-conscious tradition—consider especially in the preface the allusion, even to the point of direct quotation, to Purchas—is the sign of a loss, and this is the third fashion in which "Kubla Khan" has an archetypal significance for ecstatic poetry. In ways closely related to the arguments of Fischer, Coleridge in the preface speaks of "Kubla Khan" as a fragment, all that remained of an ecstatic unity that was disrupted by everyday interactions and concerns. The poem itself is similar, insinuating first the threat of loss ("Kubla heard from far / Ancestral voices prophesying war!"), then rupture (the "I" who unexplainedly emerges in the last stanza, recounting how once he had poetic vision and how he would like to recreate it). Loss and possession, unity and rupture, normal "I" as opposed to ecstatic "Self," amnesia following loss of the exalted state, yet persistence of the vision in the poem—all these features further indicate the centrality of "Kubla Khan" and its relevance for much in Rimbaud.

Fourth, the multiple dimensions of consciousness are related to structuring and uranian imagery characteristic of religious and poetic traditions. The Emperor, the demon-lover, the poet figure at the end, and also the thresher evoked in stanza two, are embodiments of the multifaceted poetic self, illustrative of mastery, erotic power, failure, and aspiration, as well as the successful harvesting of the poem. The architectural imagery shows a similar range and ambivalence. Initially, Kubla simple *decrees* the creation of the dome, walls, and towers whose function it is to girdle round, enfold, and transform nature into a bright, sensuous, incense-bearing garden. The sovereignty of the mind and art is thus suggested, whereas after Kubla's intuition of destruction the same motifs reappear with a different resonance:

> The shadow of the dome of pleasure
> Floated midway on the waves;
> Where was heard the mingled measure
> From the fountain and the caves.
> It was a miracle of rare device,
> A sunny pleasure-dome with caves of ice!

Reflection, harmony, the reconciliation of opposites—
these lines well exemplify the miraculous unifying capacity
of art stressed in Coleridge's theoretical pronouncements.
But "shadow," "device," and, in the last stanza, "I would
build that dome in air," emphasize also the artificial, unsubstantial, commemorative aspects of a poetry that, in
contrast to the ideal of spontaneous immediacy in the preface, finds its realm after, and in the absence of, the exalted state.

Fifth, however, despite its qualifications and framings,
"Kubla Khan" does include elements of enactment for a
public, elements that differ from Rimbaud's primarily in
being less forceful but, as such, illuminate the paradoxes of
ecstatic poetry. The preface, with its appearance of circum-
stantial detailing of dates, places, and persons, and its
presentation of the poem not as a work of art but as a
"psychological curiosity," is the first of these, arousing our
interest in some mysterious, supposedly not merely poetic
and therefore fully *real,* transformation of consciousness.
And the poem, described as a remnant of the lost state,
tends to render such a state as present. Thus the past
tense—one might say the mythic-historical past tense—is
modified, made more intense, brought closer to a kind of
present by exclamations ("But oh!", "A savage place!"),
subtle variations of demonstratives (the initial "that deep
romantic chasm" modulates to "And from this chasm"),
effective evocation of natural and man-made objects, spa-

tial indicators ("where," "down to"), awesome and sensuous adjectives ("measureless," "fertile"), and open-ended simile ("As e'er beneath a waning moon was haunted / By woman wailing for her demon-lover!"). The last of these has both superlative and engendering functions, asserting a sacred absolute and materializing the erotic-ecstatic personages before our eyes.

This tendency to make present, for which we shall find more intense analogies in Rimbaud, is illustrated in relation to an image of the audience of ecstatic poetry at the end of the poem. Having asserted that he no longer has the vision, the poet figure then indicates what he would do were he to regain it:

> To such a deep delight 'twould win me,
> That with music loud and long,
> I would build that dome in air,
> That sunny dome! those caves of ice!
> And all who heard should see them there,
> And all should cry, Beware! Beware!
> His flashing eyes, his floating hair!
> Weave a circle round him thrice,
> And close your eyes with holy dread,
> For he on honey-dew hath fed,
> And drunk the milk of Paradise.

By a subtle shift of speakers, Coleridge here manages to generate a semblance of ecstatic presence from a situation of loss and absence. He does this by inserting, within the continuing conditional expression of the "I," a direct quotation, the text from "Beware" on representing the speech of an invented audience in the face of the speaker's imagined ecstasy. The lack of quotation marks favors this tactic, which has the effect of replacing conditional verbs by

exclamatory, verbless forms, and by imperatives—by the
forms that imply present experience and urgent response to
it.

But this very enactment stresses the ambiguous status of
ecstatic poetry, of language in relation to exalted experience. It occurs only in and through the poem ("with music," "in air"), within a discourse that is at most a hypothetical approximation of the ecstatic state, and also
through the reaction of an imagined audience to that state
and to the threatening forms through which it may be
expressed. Evocation and enactment of a necessarily absent
realm, "Kubla Khan" epitomizes the paradoxes of romantic ecstatic poetry.

Coleridge's poem, more than any other, can therefore
stand as a paradigm in relation to Rimbaud's work as well as
to the recurrent features of ecstatic experience and expression discussed in preceding sections. Exalted states, related
to drugs, dream, vision, sexual frenzy; the self-conscious
amalgamation of traditions revealing the nostalgia and aspiration of a paradisal myth; the experience of loss, rupture,
fragmentation of "I" and "Self," reflected in structure and
imagery; and yet rhetorical tactics of realization in the consciousness of the audience—all these features of "Kubla
Khan" reproduce essential elements and help us to recognize
comparable features of *Illuminations* like "Matinée d'i-
vresse," "Being Beauteous," "Dévotion," "Barbare," and
"Villes I." If in these texts Rimbaud's realizations of ecstasy
are more powerful and apparently more immediate than
Coleridge's, Rimbaud's failures are correspondingly more
overwhelming. "Kubla Khan" points the way to the prose
poems of the *Illuminations,* in which the enigma of ecstatic
poetry as realization and absence is progressively revealed.

The contrast with Coleridge and the predominance of
enactment are already visible in a text that presents itself

as the unmediated expression of a triumphant achievement, the inauguration of a superior mode of being:

Matinée d'ivresse

O *mon* Bien! O *mon* Beau! Fanfare atroce où je ne
trébuche point! Chevalet féerique! Hourra pour l'œuvre
inouïe et pour le corps merveilleux, pour la première fois!
Cela commença sous les rires des enfants, cela finira par
eux. Ce poison va rester dans toutes nos veines même
quand, la fanfare tournant, nous serons rendus à
l'ancienne inharmonie. O maintenant nous si digne de ces
tortures! rassemblons fervemment cette promesse surhumaine faite à notre corps et à notre âme créés: cette promesse, cette démence! L'élégance, la science, la violence!
On nous a promis d'enterrer dans l'ombre l'arbre du bien
et du mal, de déporter les honnêtetés tyranniques, afin
que nous amenions notre très pur amour. Cela commença
par quelques dégoûts et cela finit,—ne pouvant nous saisir sur-le-champ de cette éternité,—cela finit par une
débandade de parfums.

Rire des enfants, discrétion des esclaves, austérité des
vierges, horreur des figures et des objets d'ici, sacrés soyez-
vous par le souvenir de cette veille. Cela commençait par
toute la rustrerie, voici que cela finit par des anges de
flamme et de glace.

Petite veille d'ivresse, sainte! quand ce ne serait que pour
le masque dont tu nous as gratifié. Nous t'affirmons,
méthode! Nous n'oublions pas que tu as glorifié hier chacun
de nos âges. Nous avons foi au poison. Nous savons donner
notre vie tout entière tous les jours.

Voici le temps des *Assassins*.

Morning of Drunkenness

O *my* Good! O *my* Beautiful! Terrible fanfare where I
don't stumble! Magical rack! Hurrah for the unheard-of

work and for the marvellous body, for the first time! It
began under the laughter of children, it will finish with
them. This poison is going to remain in our veins even
when, the fanfare changing, we will be returned to the
earlier disharmony. O now us so worthy of these tortures!
let us gather fervently together this superhuman promise
made to our created body and soul: this promise, this
insanity! Elegance, science, violence! They promised us to
bury in shadow the tree of good and evil, to deport tyrannical proprieties, so that we may bring forward our
very pure love. It began with feelings of disgust and it
finishes—since we are unable to seize this eternity on
the spot—it finishes in a stampede of perfumes.

Laughter of children, discretion of slaves, austerity of
virgins, horror of faces and objects here, may you be consecrated by the memory of this night. It began in lout-
ishness, here it is ending with angels of fire and ice.

Little night of drunkenness, holy! if only for the mask
that you bestowed on us. We affirm you, method! We
don't forget that you glorified yesterday each of our ages.
We have faith in the poison. We know how to give our
life entirely every day.

Now is the time of the *Assassins*.

Here we encounter many familiar elements of ecstatic
experience, technique, and expression: the methodology of
inebriation through drugs, in its negative and positive moments ("ivresse," "poison," "veines," "dégoûts," "débandade de parfums," "méthode," "*Assassins*"); the nearly unbearable intensity of the exalted state, conveyed by musical
and torture motifs ("Fanfare atroce," "Chevalet féerique,"
"tortures," "démence"); the centrality of the body and of
the erotic, associated with a transformation of being similar
to that in the pagan poems leading to "Génie" ("corps
merveilleux," "promesse surhumaine," "corps et . . . âme

créés," "L'élégance, la science, la violence," "l'arbre du bien et du mal," "honnêtetés tyranniques," "notre très pur amour"); a satisfaction so great that the world is transformed ("Rire des enfants, discrétion des esclaves, austérité des vierges, horreur des figures et des objets d'ici, sacrés soyez-vous"); and perhaps most importantly, the magnification and transfiguration of the self: the progression from "*mon* Bien" to the mask and enlarged existence of the conclusion, "Nous t'affirmons, méthode! Nous n'oublions pas que tu as glorifié hier chacun de nos âges."

But such ecstatic motifs are all the more powerful because of the high degree of presentness that differentiates Rimbaud's writing from a text like "Kubla Khan" or, for that matter, from the work of the other poets mentioned earlier. From the opening word the discourse of "Matinée d'ivresse" is marked by overwhelming presentness—it is exclamatory, iterative, personally experienced, so immediate as to dispense frequently with verbs, expressive of celebration and confidence: "O *mon* Bien! O *mon* Beau! Fanfare . . . où je ne trébuche point! Chevalet féerique! Hourra pour l'œuvre"; "O maintenant nous si digne"; "Nous t'affirmons, méthode! Nous n'oublions pas . . . Nous avons foi . . . Nous savons donner notre vie tout entière tous les jours."

Such formulations amount to a convention of present discourse while under the influence of exalted experience, though after its peak. For example, consider especially the opposition between "veille d'ivresse" and "matinée d'ivresse," and a sentence like "Ce poison va rester dans toutes nos veines même quand, la fanfare tournant, nous serons rendus à l'ancienne inharmonie." The emphatic presentness of the discourse cannot therefore hide the fact of a slight but important gap. The poem does not involve full coincidence of ecstatic experience and utterance, largely

because of its preliminary and partial nature ("pour la
première fois," "ne pouvant nous saisir sur-le-champ de
cette éternité"). Instead we have a convention of postecstatic speech concerning near-ecstatic experience. But the
gap, in contrast with "Kubla Khan," seems neither very
large nor of great moment; by presenting itself as an inau-
gurating success, "Matinée d'ivresse" confidently resolves
the discrepancies of experience and expression within an
encompassing continuity.

Continuity, primarily temporal, is a notable feature of
the poem, both thematically and formally. The experience
of transport is represented as a smoothly integrated temporal process, involving past, recent past, progressively more
present realizations, and an immediate future that opens
up rich possibilities; witness "On nous a promis"; the
slight modifications in "Cela commença . . . cela finira,"
"Cela commença . . . cela finit," "Cela commençait . . .
voici que cela finit"; and the assurance concerning the
future that disarms the impending loss of the exalted state:
"Ce poison va rester"; "O maintenant . . . rassemblons
fervemment cette promesse surhumaine"; "Nous savons
donner notre vie tout entière tous les jours." Such confidence is justified by the fact that the experience partici-
pates in a different temporal modality, that of the ecstatic,
ultimately paradisal order, to which the speaker implicitly
will accede through his practice of traditional techniques.
This expectation explains the suggestions of apprenticeship, promise, purpose ("On nous a promis . . . afin que
nous amenions notre très pur amour"), method, and the
mythic time-scheme in which individual existence is enlarged and a new order inaugurated ("ancienne inharmonie," "tu as glorifié hier chacun de nos âges," and the
concluding "Voici le temps des *Assassins*").

The final sentence thus gathers up the poem's central

elements: time in all its modalities ("le temps"), and inauguration ("Voici") of mythic, drug- and sex-induced, ecstatic being ("*Assassins*"). Such summarizing simplicity underlines the artistry of the poem's near-ecstatic discourse. Everything noted so far reveals how carefully Rimbaud incorporates recognizable ecstatic motifs, how deliberately he delineates both the intensity and the unfolding process of exalted experience. Additionally, the device of repetition with variation both represents that process and also unifies the poem formally; so that, in the terms of the *lettres du voyant,* one can say that if "Matinée d'ivresse" almost attains an ecstatic "beyond," it does so by giving a considerable degree of form. In particular, paragraph two, with its accumulating rhythm ("Rire des enfants, discrétion des esclaves, austérité des vierges"), not only expresses the significance of the materials presented in the first paragraph but also pulls the poem together for us, even while announcing its end ("souvenir de cette veille"). This device is deepened in the actual conclusion of the poem, which from pastness and apparent loss ("hier") derives confidence for the entire future ("tous les jours"), a future evoked as imminently present by the pregnant, and recapitulating, last sentence.

Within that sentence the word "*Assassins*" obviously plays a major role, again revealing Rimbaud's artistry. It insinuates a self-conscious, paradisal myth as underlying the poem's supposedly spontaneous discourse. For *Assassins* is derived from *Haschischins,* the name of an ancient Persian sect in whom willingness to kill for the faith was supposedly induced by the illusion of paradisal experiences produced by drugs and sexual experience. Thus "*Assassins*" alludes to motifs of Orientalism, destruction, drug-altered consciousness, intense sexual pleasure, and the fanaticism of a new conception of reality; it is a recognizable allusion to a paradisal-ecstatic tradition—involving etymology, literary history, ecstatic lore. Rimbaud likely learned of it in Michelet, and it has been argued that the myth of this sect also contributes to the imagery at the end of "Kubla Khan."[17] "*Assassins*" thus involves conscious allusion, the desire to re-enact the experience of an ancient ecstatic community through drugs and sexual experience—but most of all through historical knowledge and verbal expression, similar to Coleridge's combination of drugs and reading Purchas. There is also the importance of the *reader's* awareness of this tradition once he has understood the meaning of "*Assassins*"—the last sentence therefore functioning somewhat like the riddle of "H." So in a carefully plotted way, "Matinée d'ivresse" reveals not only symbolism typical of ecstatic states but also the elements of myth, tradition, initiation, and representation for a public. All these highly crafted features combine with the poem's convention of spontaneous utterance in a formal structure that enacts the near-ecstatic state and opens up to the reader the troubling possibility of a revolution in the nature of human existence.

"Matinée d'ivresse" thus subsumes aspects of technique, symbolism, legend, and even programmatic pronouncements into a quasi-ecstatic speech that seems to be instantly responsive to exalted experience. In comparison, "Being Beauteous" is even more immediate and also more elemental. It seems to present directly, with no gap in time, the unfolding of an ecstatic experience as well as its loss, with only hints as to the logic of the experience and the reasons for its abrupt termination:

Devant une neige un Etre de Beauté de haute taille.
Des sifflements de mort et des cercles de musique sourde
font monter, s'élargir et trembler comme un spectre ce

corps adoré; des blessures écarlates et noires éclatent dans les chairs superbes. Les couleurs propres de la vie se foncent, dansent, et se dégagent autour de la Vision, sur le chantier. Et les frissons s'élèvent et grondent, et la saveur forcenée de ces effets se chargeant avec les sifflements mortels et les rauques musiques que le monde, loin derrière nous, lance sur notre mère de beauté,—elle recule, elle se dresse. Oh! nos os sont revêtus d'un nouveau corps amoureux.

***

O la face cendrée, l'écusson de crin, les bras de cristal! Le canon sur lequel je dois m'abattre à travers la mêlée des arbres et de l'air léger!

Before a snow a Being of Beauty of tall stature. Whistlings of death and circles of muffled music cause to rise, expand, and tremble like a specter this adored body; scarlet and black wounds erupt in the superb flesh. The colors natural to life deepen, dance, and disengage around the Vision, in the making. And the shiverings rise and rumble, and the frenzied flavor of these effects taking on the mortal whistlings and the raucous music that the world, far behind us, hurls at our mother of beauty—she recoils, she rears up. Oh! our bones are reclothed with a new erotic body.

***

O the ashen face, the horsehair escutcheon, the arms of crystal! The cannon on which I must fall through the melee of trees and light air!

In contrast to "Matinée d'ivresse," this text makes no reference to drugs. Rather sexuality is the impelling energy of the speaker's exaltation: "Un Etre de Beauté de haute taille," "comme un spectre," "ce corps adoré," "des blessures écarlates et noires . . . dans les chairs superbes," "la Vision," "notre mère de beauté." This progression indicates how "Being Beauteous" engenders a divine female figure, highly eroticized, similar to what we saw in "Voyelles" and "L'Etoile a pleuré rose." But the engendering in "Being Beauteous" is clearly ecstatic, using elements of dissolution, enlargement, transcendence, and transfiguration: "s'élargir," "se foncent," "se dégagent," "nos os sont revêtus d'un nouveau corps amoureux." The last of these, close to shamanistic formulas (though differing in highlighting the sexual), effectively conveys the experience of utter physical transformation. And it is combined with other typical motifs—ascension, music, leaving the normal perceptual dimensions of life, finally transcending the world itself: "monter," "les couleurs propres de la vie se foncent, . . . se dégagent," "les frissons s'élèvent," "rauques musiques," "le monde, loin derrière nous." "Being Beauteous" is thus a synthesizing version of familiar, and often conflicting, experiences and motifs: dissolution of ordinary reality, transcendence and transformation, ascension above the world, yet also bodily ecstasy.

But impermanence, a problem treated optimistically in "Matinée d'ivresse," here is more disturbing. The break in the text makes rupture visible; the ascensional theme becomes a literal fall; the rich erotic imagery gives way to sterility, as sexuality becomes compulsive and self-directed ("cendrée," "le canon sur lequel je dois m'abattre"). Most significantly, the enlargement of self effected in "Matinée d'ivresse" is reversed; the ecstatic *nous* abruptly shrinks back to the normal *je,* just as at the end of "Kubla Khan" an "I" unaccountably appears, illustrating once more the problem of discontinuity between normal I and exalted Self.

This rapid, unexplained, apparently inevitable loss perhaps becomes comprehensible in terms of hints that the text, despite its almost exclusive character of enactment, furnishes. The predominance of the sexual, potentially too limited and merely personal, provides a clue, particularly because of its association with what in the text are precisely death impulses. The "mère de beauté" (with "mère" energizing themes of childhood, suggesting a link between Rimbaud's ecstatic poetry and the materials treated in chapter 1) is in part engendered by "des sifflements de mort," "les sifflements mortels." Analogously, it is "les couleurs propres de la *vie*" that "se dégagent," implying that the exalted realm, being beyond life, is a kind of death. In a directly physical way, too, the expression "des blessures écarlates et noires éclatent dans les chairs superbes" both creates and explodes the body of the "Etre de Beauté." Finally, in the disarray of loss and fall, the word "canon" fittingly evokes both sexual organ and instrument of warfare, reversing the promise of a poem like "Guerre," reinstating the conditions of ordinary experience, asserting the defeat of sexuality-ecstasy by the tendencies of death and negation.

Even if this interpretation is correct, the ambivalent erotic and death elements are not presented as part of an argument but as active forces, indeed as sounds and explosive events ("Des sifflements de mort . . . font monter"; "des blessures . . . éclatent"). For "Being Beauteous" is even more emphatically characterized by dynamic presence than is "Matinée d'ivresse." It involves the unfolding, entirely in the present—*all* the verbs are present—of the accession to, experience, and loss of an ecstatic state. Thus the title and first sentence are exclusively, if strangely, notational. There is no main verb; instead descriptive and locating elements alert us to a setting and a being of unaccustomed qualities ("devant," "une neige," "un Etre de Beauté de haute taille"). The second sentence, by its

compound subject, causative construction, and triple in-
finitive, embodies the process by which this "corps adoré"
comes to consciousness—comes to consciousness with a
violent intensification of sensual presence, as color and
flesh, exploding in our awareness.

But the stage of physicality is quickly modified by
another succession of verbs asserting a transcendence of
normally perceived color. Note also that the expression "la
Vision, sur le chantier" implies active creation of the divinity, not simply passive perception of her—an indication
within the text of the artist's constructive function, recognized in the *voyant* letters and evidenced by the features
of "Being Beauteous." Rhythmic accumulations, like those
noted in other texts, then take over, in a long sentence
that recapitulates what has preceded, distances it, and
states the moment at which the "mère de beauté" takes on
full life: "elle recule, elle se dresse." Immediately there is
the exclamatory reaction of self-transformation, followed
by the break in the text and the statement-exclamation
(again with no main verb) of the now-limited speaker's fall
from the peak of ecstasy.

So everything in "Being Beauteous" is enactment, revelation of the evolving and ending ecstasy. The convention
of the poem implies no gap whatever between exalted experience and the language that conveys it. The words and
the erotic physicality are so intimately connected, body
and language seem so close, so nearly identical, that one
can almost sympathize with Antoine Adam's literalistic
sexual reduction of the poem.[18] The error of that kind of
reading is to be excessively referential, to be taken in by
the poem's convention, to view the text as simply a record
of a prior state (which in part it may be), to ignore the
connection between Rimbaud's evident intentionality of
form and the issue, in ecstatic religion and poetry, of

performance for an audience. The power of "Being Beauteous" comes from tactics of realization, through which the
onset, culmination, and loss of an ecstatic state are dramatized with an immediacy and an inevitability that are at
once irresistible and fleeting, accessible to our imaginations yet elusive to our minds, despite our effort of analysis
finally marked by mystery.

The combination of mystery, enactment, and impermanence provides an entry to texts such as "Dévotion" and
"Barbare," the first of which is certainly mysterious but
nonetheless clearly prepares the second, itself an expression
of cosmic and permanent frenzy. First, "Dévotion":

A ma sœur Louise Vanaen de Voringhem:—Sa cornette
bleue tournée à la mer du Nord.—Pour les naufragés.

A ma sœur Léonie Aubois d'Ashby. Baou—l'herbe
d'été bourdonnante et puante.—Pour la fièvre des mères
et des enfants.

A Lulu,—démon—qui a conservé un goût pour les
oratoires du temps des Amies et de son éducation
incomplète. Pour les hommes! A madame ***.

A l'adolescent que je fus. A ce saint vieillard, ermitage
ou mission.

A l'esprit des pauvres. Et à un très haut clergé.

Aussi bien à tout culte en telle place de culte
mémoriale et parmi tels événements qu'il faille se rendre,
suivant les aspirations du moment ou bien notre propre
vice sérieux.

Ce soir, à Circeto des hautes glaces, grasse comme le
poisson, et enluminée comme les dix mois de la nuit
rouge,—(son cœur ambre et spunk),—pour ma seule
prière muette comme ces régions de nuit et précédant des
bravoures plus violentes que ce chaos polaire.

A tout prix et avec tous les airs, même dans des voyages métaphysiques.—Mais plus *alors*.

To Sister Louise Vanaen de Voringhem:—Her blue
coif turned toward the North Sea.—For the shipwrecked.
    To Sister Léonie Aubois d'Ashby. Baou—the summer
grass buzzing and stinking.—For the fever of mothers
and children.
    To Lulu,—demon—who has conserved a taste for the
oratories of the time of the female Friends and for her
incomplete education. For men! To madame***.
    To the adolescent that I was. To that holy old man,
hermitage or mission.
    To the spirit of the poor. And to a very high clergy.
    Also to every cult in such place of memorial cult and
among such events as it may be necessary to go, following the aspirations of the moment or else our own serious
vice.
    This evening, to Circeto of the high mirrors, plumb as
a fish, and illuminated like the ten months of the red
night,—(her heart amber and spunk),—for my sole
prayer mute like these regions of night and preceding
bravuras more violent than this polar chaos.
    At all costs and with all airs, even in metaphysical
journeys.—But no more *then*.

The element of obscurity is apparent enough here—in
the unexplained female names and conversely the "madame
***" who recalls similar nameless females in "Après le
déluge" and other texts, as well as in foreign words or
coinages like "Baou" and "Circeto." But there is a deeper
mystery, that of a secret cult and prayerlike form, which
critics like Albert Py and Nick Osmond convincingly link
to Rimbaud's homosexuality and drug taking. "Vice
sérieux," paragraph three with its allusions to male and
female homosexuality and to homosexual writing by Verlaine, and the sexual associations of Circe and the English
word "spunk" certainly insinuate the erotic as a major

preoccupation, although I would emphasize not homosexuality alone but the polymorphous sexuality that "H," with comparable mysteriousness, asserts. And Py is doubtless correct in linking the litany-structure of the poem to the vertigo of hashish and in reading the "à tout prix" of the conclusion as expressing the desire definitively to fulfill the promise of "Matinée d'ivresse."[19]

In fact, "Dévotion" by near-allusion or similarity of theme and imagery looks backward to the corpus of Rimbaud's child and ecstasy poems and also projects forward to realization of their aspirations. Thus in a general way the text has commemorative notes, for example, "Lulu . . . qui a conservé un goût pour les oratoires du temps des Amies" and "place . . . mémoriale." More particularly, paragraphs two and four recall the *Saison,* "Enfance," "Jeunesse," and "Vies" in evoking childhood, adolescence, and the aged saintly figure who is one of the emblems of the poet's continuing quest: "la fièvre des mères et des enfants"; "A l'adolescent que je fus. A ce saint vieillard, ermitage ou mission." Similarly, "l'herbe d'été bourdonnante et puante" recalls the progression in "Délires II," "Fêtes de la patience," and "Voyelles" from the world of nature, the seasons, insects, and the organic to a transcendent realm—those "voyages métaphysiques" that the end of "Dévotion" brings to consciousness. Again, Py's reference to "Matinée d'ivresse" is apt, although he does not mention the "bravoures plus violentes" that recall that poem's "fanfare atroce" nor the further realization of the motif in "Villes I" ("au milieu des gouffres les Rolands sonnent leur bravoure"). Thus, cryptically and sardonically ("A l'esprit des pauvres. Et à un très haut clergé"), "Dévotion" recapitulates the essential features of Rimbaud's project in connection with the childlike and visionary components of his imagination.

But recapitulation is for realization; the structure of the poem is that of magical incantation, "prière muette," readiness for some definitive event. Certainly this is the implication of the religious vocabulary, the ritual form, the attitude of expectant readiness—"à tout culte . . . et parmi tels événements qu'il faille se rendre, suivant les aspirations du moment ou bien notre propre vice sérieux." A religious seriousness, openness to the inevitability of the moment prepared by systematic method—these motifs convey the intensity of the speaker's preparation of his project. And, in the last two paragraphs, that project approaches the verge of realization.

Recognizable elements convey this imminent fulfillment. Circeto suggests sexuality, animality, and myth, and the polar setting extends the "devant une neige" of "Being Beauteous" in the direction of the arctic frenzy of "Barbare." The conception of time also becomes polar, as the "dix mois de la nuit rouge" carry us beyond the expectant present instant ("Ce soir"), opening up ("précédant") the perspective of a definitively *other* time. This recalls the mythic temporality of "Matinée d'ivresse" and again projects toward the transcendence of time-space in "Barbare." Like the polar scene, the words "Mais plus *alors*" imply a break with the conditions of normal experience. Abrogation of time-space, sexuality, violence, musicality, ecstatic heroism ("spunk," "bravoures . . . violentes," "A tout prix") all therefore contribute to an expression of ecstatic method and transport—the "voyages métaphysiques" glimpsed throughout Rimbaud's poems, of which "Barbare" is the final realization.

Thus "Dévotion," which at first glance interrupts the sequence of enactments, in fact prepares the ultimate transcendence. For in "Barbare" ecstatic sexuality, the polar setting, and the transformation of experience begun in

"Matinée d'ivresse" converge to express a frenzy that seems both universal and eternal (final ellipsis is Rimbaud's):

> Bien après les jours et les saisons, et les êtres et les pays,
> Le pavillon en viande saignante sur la soie des mers et des fleurs arctiques; (elles n'existent pas.)
> Remis des vieilles fanfares d'héroïsme—qui nous attaquent encore le cœur et la tête—loin des anciens assassins—
> Oh! Le pavillon en viande saignante sur la soie des mers et des fleurs arctiques; (elles n'existent pas.)
> Douceurs!
> Les brasiers, pleuvant aux rafales de givre,—Douceurs!—les feux à la pluie du vent de diaments jetée par le cœur terrestre éternellement carbonisé pour nous.—O monde!—
> (Loin des vieilles retraites et des vieilles flammes, qu'on entend, qu'on sent,)
> Les brasiers et les écumes. La musique, virement des gouffres et choc des glaçons aux astres.
> O Douceurs, ô monde, ô musique! Et là, les formes, les sueurs, les chevelures et les yeux, flottant. Et les larmes blanches, bouillantes,—ô douceurs!—et la voix féminine arrivée au fond des volcans et des grottes arctiques.
> Le pavillon . . .

> Long after days and seasons, and beings and countries,
> The banner of bleeding meat on the silk of seas and of arctic flowers; (they do not exist.)
> Recovered from old fanfares of heroism—which still attack our heart and head—far from the old assassins—
> Oh! The banner of bleeding meat on the silk of seas and of arctic flowers; (they do not exist.)
> Sweetness!

The blazing fires, raining in gusts of frost,—Sweetness!—the fires in the rain of the wind of diamonds
flung out by the terrestrial heart eternally carbonized for
us.—O world!—
(Far from the old retreats and the old flames, that one
hears, that one smells,)
The blazing fires and foam. Music, veering of abysses
and shock of ice against the stars.
O Sweetness, O world, O music! And there, the
forms, the sweat, the hair and the eyes, floating. And
the white tears, boiling,—O sweetness!—and the feminine voice reaching to the bottom of volcanoes and arctic
grottoes.
The banner . . .

In so many ways this text is a culmination of the elements of Rimbaud's ecstatic poetics. Consider its extreme
subversion of normal experience: "Bien après les jours et
les saisons, et les êtres et les pays"; "Remis des vieilles
fanfares d'héroïsme—qui nous attaquent encore le cœur et
la tête—loin des anciens assassins"; "Loin des vieilles retraites et des vieilles flammes, qu'on entend, qu'on sent."
These expressions situate "Barbare" at the term of a process
("encore," "vieilles"), a process initiated in "Matinée
d'ivresse" ("anciens assassins") and now fulfilled as abrogation of the perceptual constancies of normal "I"-world consciousness; witness "bien après," and the transcendence of
sensation, time, space, and personal being in "qu'on entend, qu'on sent," and "jours . . . saisons . . . êtres . . .
pays."
Even more radically, a recurrent complex of images extends the transformation of consciousness to the point of
abolishing the ultimate distinction, that between existing
and not existing, real and unreal: "Le pavillon en viande
saignante sur la soie des mers et des fleurs arctiques; (elles

n'existent pas.)." Architecture, nationality, bodily organs and the visceral reality of flesh, delicate natural growths and fabrics, and the elemental, polar forces of nature, sea and arctic regions—all coexist here, liberated from the divisions and constraints of the rational mind. This liberated coexistence corresponds to Nietzschean and Rimbaldian explosions of the senses, treated earlier in this chapter, and gives explicit expression to the subversion of the reality principle, a characteristic of ecstatic traditions and visionary literature from Blake to Breton: "elles n'existent pas." For normal consciousness such elements do not coexist; but, in formulas that represent both an enlargement and a subversion of the normal, "Barbare" shows them as simply *there* ("Et là"), as repeatedly forcing themselves on our awareness. There could be no more fascinating evocation of ecstatic consciousness, overpowering the categories of ordinary experience, against them asserting itself as having direct presence and reality.

Once the categories of the real are demolished, "Barbare" progresses rapidly toward the culmination of frenzy by combining and intensifying familiar motifs and structures. The volcanoes, arctic imagery, sexual and musical motifs, barbarous savagery, and ethereal sweetness of other ecstatic poems all reappear in the last half of the poem. And the orgasmic frenzy of the last full paragraph, together with the title and the recurrent image of the bloody meat, recall in part "Kubla Khan," in part Nietzsche's doctrine of the persistence of the savage, as well as Blake's doctrine of energy as eternal delight and comparable themes in Rimbaud from "Mauvais Sang" and "Délires I" to "Parade."

"Barbare" is thus a cosmic enactment of an elementally ecstatic state, from which the civilized veneer has been stripped away. At the same time, the poem's imagery proposes a high degree of coherence. Chadwick, who generally minimizes the evidence for trance in shamanistic religion, grants its increasing reality in the arctic regions, and "Barbare" would seem to represent a poetic parallel, a culmination in which extremes are united and there is penetration to an ultimate integration, with its accompanying archetypal imagery.[20] Hence the expression of an experience so intense as to combine boiling white tears and sweetness; the union of ice, fire, rain, wind, diamonds, and volcanoes; the perception of the enormous forces at the *heart* of the earth as giving forth diamonds *for us;* the orgasmic and penetrating imagery at the end, embodying total ecstasy: utter dispersal *and* absolute unification. *Identification* with Nietzsche's eternal joy of becoming, a literally experienced erotic sense of reality—"bodily erotic union with the world"—such formulations help to express the astonishing experience that "Barbare" enacts. The poem achieves the extreme experience of Fischer's ergotropic pole: maximum excitation, dissolution of the self-world dichotomy, direct participation in the world as dynamic totality.

This experience of universal frenzy is represented in the poem by structures of enactment that constitute an extension of features observed in other texts, for "Barbare" is the most absolute of Rimbaud's ecstatic realizations. First, there are the elements that distance the experience from the normal and install as present the contradictory visionary reality, the ecstatic scene. Then familiar exclamatory elements intensify the emotional tonality: "Oh!"; "Douceurs!"—the latter forming a full paragraph in this rapidly evolving text. Next, at the precise center of the poem, the underlying unity of existence is glimpsed through the union of contraries and the motifs of heart and world: "le cœur terrestre éternellement carbonisé pour nous.—O monde!" Here a solitary, completely dissociated *nous* perceives itself as the recipient of the dynamic energy of the entire world. The "all is gratitude" of the exalted state, glimpsed in "Matinée d'ivresse" and affirmed in "Génie," is more fully realized, the ecstatic self coming to awareness at the same time that all earthly reality is comprehended as rounded totality: "O monde!"

Then, quickly, after a further distancing formula ("Loin des vieilles retraites"), the perspective, as in "Voyelles," transcends the earth and becomes cosmic, again through accumulating structures and musical imagery: "Les brasiers et les écumes. La musique, virement des gouffres et choc des glaçons aux astres." This is followed by a final recapitulating and totalizing formula ("O Douceurs, ô monde, ô musique!") that expresses all that has preceded—the experience of the entire world, perceived as Dionysian music, producing ecstatic sweetness. Immediately the text carries us even beyond this, as reference to both person and world cease, and all is dissolved in the energy that *is* reality: "Et là, les formes, les sueurs, les chevelures et les yeux, flottant. Et les larmes blanches, bouillantes,—ô douceurs!—et la voix féminine arrivée au fond des volcans et des grottes arctiques." Rimbaud capitalizes to the maximum here on the recurrent arctic and orgasmic imagery, refining as well the earlier female deities into a universal sexualized voice that reaches the extremes of existence. This dispersion of physical forms, bodily yet disembodied, represents the ultimate ecstatic state, engulfing all of reality, and simply, absolutely, present: "Et là."

By the end of the poem, then, universal ecstasy is absolutely enacted. Even more interestingly, it is perhaps inappropriate to speak of the end of "Barbare." Far from implying the loss of ecstasy, the parting and partial reintroduction of the formula for the ecstatic scene ("Le

pavillon . . .") implies an ongoing, perhaps eternal, recurrence of the exalted state—the "éternité" recognized in
"Matinée d'ivresse" and which "Dévotion" aspires to possess. The most surprising convention of the poem, therefore, is that it does not end, but ceaselessly recurs, a
suggestion again close to Nietzsche's notion of eternal
return—consciousness so wholly fused with reality as to
participate in its timelessly ongoing existence. Another
way to understand this is to recall Fischer's discussion of
ecstatic states as marked by complete psychic integration,
transcending amnesia, somehow experiencing a single,
eternal reality. What this means will certainly continue
to elude us. But in "Barbare," Rimbaud's most definitive
enactment-presentation, the poet uses language, imagery,
and structure so compellingly and so archetypally that we
are afforded what is perhaps the ultimate insight into a
kind of ecstatic state that can be provided by words
alone.

But inevitably the words on the page do end, suggesting if not a trailing off of the ecstasy itself then at least an
end to verbal expression about it, insinuating once again
the ineluctable discrepancy between ecstatic experience and
language. Another major ecstatic text, "Villes I," dramatizes such discrepancies, indeed enacts again the utter loss
of the superior state more tragically even than a poem like
"Being Beauteous." Moreover, if "Barbare" is archetypal in
an elementally simplifying way, evoking a vast, solitary
dissociation, "Villes I" in contrast is archetypally syncretist, seemingly articulating the entirety of known ecstatic
traditions, recreating them as present, then brutally asserting their loss:

> Ce sont des villes! C'est un peuple pour qui se sont
> montés ces Alleghanys et ces Libans de rêve! Des chalets

de cristal et de bois qui se meuvent sur des rails et des poulies invisibles. Les vieux cratères ceints de colosses et de palmiers de cuivre rugissent mélodieusement dans les feux. Des fêtes amoureuses sonnent sur les canaux pendus derrière les chalets. La chasse des carillons crie dans les gorges. Des corporations de chanteurs géants accourent dans des vêtements et des oriflammes éclatants comme la lumière des cimes. Sur les plates-formes au milieu des gouffres les Rolands sonnent leur bravoure. Sur les passerelles de l'abîme et les toits des auberges l'ardeur du ciel pavoise les mâts. L'écroulement des apothéoses rejoint les champs des hauteurs où les centauresses séraphiques évoluent parmi les avalanches. Au-dessus du niveau des plus hautes crêtes, une mer troublée par la naissance éternelle de Vénus, chargée de flottes orphéoniques et de la rumeur des perles et des conques précieuses,—la mer s'assombrit parfois avec des éclats mortels. Sur les versants des moissons de fleurs grandes comme nos armes et nos coupes, mugissent. Des cortèges de Mabs en robes rousses, opalines, montent des ravines. Là-haut, les pieds dans la cascade et les ronces, les cerfs tettent Diane. Les Bacchantes des banlieues sanglotent et la lune brûle et hurle. Vénus entre dans les cavernes des forgerons et des ermites. Des groupes de beffrois chantent les idées des peuples. Des châteaux bâtis en os sort la musique inconnue. Toutes les légendes évoluent et les élans se ruent dans les bourgs. Le paradis des orages s'effondre. Les sauvages dansent sans cesse la fête de la nuit. Et une heure je suis descendu dans le mouvement d'un boulevard de Bagdad où des compagnies ont chanté la joie du travail nouveau, sous une brise épaisse, circulant sans pouvoir éluder les fabuleux fantômes des monts où l'on a dû se retrouver.

Quels bons bras, quelle belle heure me rendront cette région d'où viennent mes sommeils et mes moindres mouvements?

These are cities! This is a people for whom these
dream Alleghanys and Lebanons have sprung up! Chalets
of crystal and wood that move on invisible rails and
pulleys. The old craters circled by colossi and copper
palms roar melodiously in the fires. Love festivals sound
on the canals hung behind the chalets. The pack of
chimes cries in the gorges. Guilds of giant singers rush
up in clothes and oriflammes dazzling like the light of
the summits. On the platforms in the middle of the
chasms the Rolands sound their bravura. On the footbridges over the abyss and the roofs of the inns the ardor
of the sky decks out the masts. The collapse of apotheoses joins the fields on the heights where the seraphic
centauresses move about amid the avalanches. Above the
level of the highest peaks, a sea troubled by the eternal
birth of Venus, brimming with orphic choral fleets and
with the murmur of precious pearls and conches,—the
sea dims sometimes with mortal flashes. On the slopes
harvests of flowers big as our arms and our goblets, bellow. Processions of Mabs in ruddy dresses, opaline, as-
cend from the ravines. Up there, feet in the waterfall and
brambles, the deer are suckled by Diana. The Bacchantes
of the suburbs sob and the moon burns and howls. Venus
goes into the caves of blacksmiths and hermits. Groups
of belfries sing the ideas of the peoples. From castles
built of bone emerges the unknown music. All the leg-
ends circulate and the elks stampede into the towns. The
paradise of storms collapses. The savages dance ceaselessly
the festival of night. And one hour I went down into the
movement of a boulevard of Bagdad where groups of
companions sang the joy of the new work, under a heavy
breeze, circulating without being able to avoid the fabulous phantoms of the mountains where one must have
met again.

What good arms, what fine hour will render back to
me that region from which come my slumbers and my
slightest movements?

In this extraordinarily dense text, it is difficult to isolate elements for discussion. For we seem to encounter everything ecstatic as overwhelming movement and interaction. But if the discourse seems invulnerable to analytic procedures, a sober commentary can nonetheless emphasize recurrent—but still surprising—features. First, indeed, the poem's energy—its breathtaking enumeration of bizarre elements infused with superhuman vigor—cities, mountains, buildings, volcanoes, avalanches, "fêtes amoureuses," "chanteurs géants," Rolands, centauresses, Venus, Mabs, Diana, Bacchantes, savages, to name only some. The way in which these personages, settings, and events emerge endows "Villes I" with an even greater degree of activity than the other poems treated. Exclamatory, present verbs of movement and action rapidly succeed one another. There is also a transcendence of perceptual constancies common to the initial stages of altered states, notably the foreshortening of nearby space that leads to an elevation of the horizon—canals hung above chalets, the sea higher than the loftiest peaks.[21]

Similarly, outrageously exaggerated synesthesia transforms perception: "des moissons de fleurs grandes comme nos armes et nos coupes, mugissent." And normal oppositions such as that between up and down are radically energized: apotheoses (spiritual and upward-moving) are described as crashing down like buildings and yet leading upward to where centauresses evolve among other downward forces, avalanches. Surreal and infused with great power, such subversions of ordinary consciousness are the modes of perception proper to a realm in which the principle of contradiction is inoperant, in which singular and plural, old world and new, reality and dream, nature, humanity and its constructions all partake of an existence that is supremely present and that drives upward toward the culminating heights of the poem: "Ce sont des villes! C'est un peuple pour qui se sont montés ces Alleghanys et ces Libans de rêve!"; "Au-dessus du niveau des plus hautes crêtes"; "Là-haut."

So, first of all, "Villes I" is a representation of ecstatic consciousness and energy, transforming the real and imbued with supernatural vigor and direction. Second, in this flow of energy, recurrent motifs attain a heightened power but also an unusual completeness: the linking of city and nature; the amalgamation of music with the forces of fire, volcanoes, avalanches; the fusion of animal-human-divine; the combining of erotic experience, the hunt, the constructive, and the ascetic in personages such as Venus, Diana, hermits, and smiths; and an overwhelming sense of multiplicity and community. We observed such features variously in Nietzsche, poets from Coleridge to Yeats, and students of the ecstatic such as Eliade. In "Villes I," a totalizing expression of ecstasy, Rimbaud uses them all.

These motifs are separable for purposes of analysis, although in the poem they are characterized by interaction and also by increasing intensification as the text nears its end. Thus, the city-nature dialectic runs throughout, from the opening conflation of cities and mountains to the linking of chalets, platforms, footbridges, roofs, suburbs, chateaux, and towns with volcanoes, peaks, sky, avalanches, sea, ravines, waterfalls, and caverns. This interfusion of the human and natural is in its essence *religious,* transcending the divorce between man and world not only by returning to simpler modes (though this too is involved, as we shall see) but also by almost exaggerating the human potential for creation. At times highly artificial, the multiple efflorescences of human constructivity elsewhere produce a harmony between the natural world and that of mankind: "Les vieux cratères ceints de colosses et de palmiers de cuivre rugissent mélodieusement dans les feux"; "l'ardeur du ciel pavoise les mâts." In the second of these, human creativity stretches toward an ennobling beautification that nature reciprocally confers upon it. In the first, man's taste for the artificial and the colossal satisfyingly encompasses an elemental natural power rendered benign by age; consider "vieux," "ceints," "mélodieusement," and the connection of the gigantic with intimately felt synesthesia—"cuivre," "rugissent mélodieusement," "feux."

But volcanoes are known to erupt, and the poem plunges onward to evocations of human constructions that encounter the immensity of nature: "Sur les plates-formes au milieu des gouffres"; "Sur les passerelles de l'abîme." Danger, immensity, the abyss—here the city-nature fusion leads beyond the known, to the encounter with divinity, to a surreal transformation of both nature and architecture ("la lune brûle et hurle"; "Des châteaux bâtis en os sort la musique inconnue"), and ultimately to an ecstatic dispersion: "Le paradis des orages s'effondre." We recognize a particularly dynamic version of Eliade's paradisal symbolism, suspending the merely human, stretching through nature to the sacred, culminating in ecstatic dissolution.

It is not surprising therefore that the architectural motifs in "Villes I" are connected with the imagery of the extremes of nature. Nor is it surprising that we encounter other recurrent symbolism—music, fire, the hunt, the erotic, the animal, and the superhuman. Thus "Villes I" is permeated by strange music—not only the animalized sounds made by flowers and volcanoes, not only the "chanteurs géants" and Rolands sounding their "bravoure" that make the poem a magnification of the project begun in "Matinée d'ivresse," but finally also the hallucinatory sound and music experienced at the point of culmination: "Les Bacchantes . . . sanglotent et la lune . . . hurle";

"Des groupes de beffrois chantent les idées des peuples. Des châteaux bâtis en os sort la musique inconnue"; "Les sauvages dansent sans cesse la fête de la nuit." The musical techniques and symbolism of ancient ecstatic traditions once more come bizarrely to awareness, with an explicit reference to the Dionysian and with a characteristic final experience of dance-induced transport.

The musical motif is also connected with other strands of symbolism. For example, an early evocation of the hunt ("La chasse des carillons crie dans les gorges") is echoed by this later prelude to transport: "Là-haut, les pieds dans la cascade et les ronces, les cerfs tettent Diane." The first of these uses music and the hunt to evoke an activity in which the divine, the human, and the natural are indistinguishable. For the hunting music is played on church bells, and a single *cri* unites the realms to which "gorge" may refer: the baying of dogs, the human body, mountainous features of nature. These elements are picked up in the later sentence: dizzying height ("Là-haut"), immersion in nature ("les pieds dans la cascade"), the human-animal body ("tettent"), the contact of animality and divinity ("les cerfs," "Diane"). The connection between Dionysus and Diana, between the hunt and Bacchantic ecstasy, in Greek tradition is inescapable here, and we should not forget either Eliade's insistence on the link between shamanism and hunting as a means of transcending the human and participating in the life of nature. "Villes I" thus corresponds to much in the traditions of Greece and Asia in liberating a bodily energy that is at once animal and of divine value.

This energy is related to the erotic, which like the hunt unites the realms of nature, divine being, and human activity, from the early "fêtes amoureuses" to the introduction of Venus in relation to water and fire: "une mer troublée par la naissance éternelle de Vénus, chargée de flottes orphéoniques"; "Vénus entre dans les cavernes des forgerons et des ermites." These phrases link the elemental and extreme in nature to the sense of divinity as a ceaseless erotic energy. They also involve human activities, with an emphasis on the dialectic of solitude and community. "Flottes orphéoniques" evokes the themes of voyage, war, music, poetico-musical tradition, and choral or group activity, whereas in the second sentence the divine sexual energy is seen to extend to figures of isolated asceticism and creativity. In these personages the libidinal implications of fire and volcanoes are enlarged to include the mastery of the smiths and the spiritual disciplines of traditional holy men.

The significance of this conjunction is great. As in shamanistic religion, the arguments of Nietzsche, and the symbolism of romantic and post-romantic poetry, Rimbaud shows us the fiery energy of ecstasy interacting with the mind's capacity for isolation, meditation, discipline, structuring, creativity. Erotic power, unbounded transport must by implication be experienced, but must also be mastered and expressed, and the smiths and hermits are Rimbaud's symbols within the poem of the capacity to accomplish this feat. This suggests an authentic, if difficult, communal function for the ecstatic artist, one ambiguously related to the *voyant* letters and the *Saison* and also to the "flottes orphéoniques" that appear earlier in "Villes I."

Thus the strands of imagery are linked by a problematic of solitude and community. "Villes I" is thoroughly a poem of collective frenzy,[22] explicitly Dionysian and implicitly Nietzschean, as opposed to the vast dissociation of "Barbare." From the opening "Ce sont des villes!" the poem is emphatically plural ("les Rolands," "les centauresses") and collective ("un peuple," "des corporations," "des cortèges,"

"des groupes," "les idées des peuples"). Here again is a
progression toward culmination, for the last in the series of
groups are the savages, dancing in nocturnal frenzy. All
categories are thus subverted, all lead to the frightening
collectivity whose persistence in us Nietzsche continued to
emphasize. And, of course, much of the conclusion's poi-
gnancy comes strangely from the loss of this troubling collectivity, from the return to the isolated "I."

But before considering the loss to which the poem's
frenzied rhythm ultimately leads, on the other side of ecstasy, we need to reassert another way in which "Villes I"
is collective. It is so as well in being a collection of so
many different elements—by its syncretism. Those Rolands from French tradition that intrude upon more familiar ecstatic personages alert us to this eclecticism, as does a
sentence that occurs just before the culmination: "Toutes
les légendes évoluent et les élans se ruent dans les bourgs."
The invasion of the human by the animal is clear here, but
so is a liberation of the legendary, an explosion of the
mythical. "Toutes les légendes"—the phrase might describe the universal mythologizing of Blake, Hugo, and
Nerval; Coleridge's mixture of elements from the Bible,
Plato, Purchas, Milton, and much more; the syncretist
element of Dionysian religion; the self-conscious myth of
origins Eliade finds in shamanism.

Similarly, "Villes I," despite its surreal intensity, is allu-
sive and self-conscious, a paradoxical combination of spontaneity and insistence on tradition. Eastern origins and references to the new world ("ces Alleghanys et ces Libans") are
mixed in it; national traditions, European folk legend, and
Greek myth and religion (Roland, centauresses, Venus,
Mabs, Diana, Bacchantes) coexist throughout it. As in the
fusion of nature and city, of erotic and artistic, the immediacy of the text cannot be dissociated from its literary-mythi-

cal-religious self-awareness. "Villes I" is a universal recapitulation of ecstatic traditions, a re-enactment of what is
ancient and lost in the present of the text.

So this second major feature, the poem's presentation
of a wide range of ecstatic thematics and symbolism, can
be seen as a version of a third element, that of enactment. In looking at the forms of presentness and activity
at the beginning of the poem, we recall especially the
opening verbs of evolutive presence and spontaneous self-
generation and movement, and the enumeration, favored
by subtle shifts of demonstratives, partitives, and definite
articles, of elements that rapidly constitute a strange geography: "Ce sont des villes! C'est un peuple pour qui se
sont montés ces Alleghanys et ces Libans de rêve! Des
chalets de cristal . . . qui se meuvent sur des rails . . .
Les vieux cratères . . . Des fêtes amoureuses . . . La
chasse des carillons crie dans les gorges." Thereafter, all
drives upward from the city to the intensification, fulfillment, and loss of the ecstasy. It is worth quoting the
concluding sentences again in order to study these culminating movements more thoroughly:

> Là-haut, les pieds dans la cascade et les ronces, les cerfs
> tettent Diane. Les Bacchantes des banlieues sanglotent et
> la lune brûle et hurle. Vénus entre dans les cavernes des
> forgerons et des ermites. Des groupes de beffrois chantent
> les idées des peuples. Des châteaux bâtis en os sort la
> musique inconnue. Toutes les légendes évoluent et les
> élans se ruent dans les bourgs. Le paradis des orages
> s'effondre. Les sauvages dansent sans cesse la fête de la
> nuit. Et une heure je suis descendu dans le mouvement
> d'un boulevard de Bagdad où des compagnies ont chanté
> la joie du travail nouveau, sous une brise épaisse, circu-
> lant sans pouvoir éluder les fabuleux fantômes des monts
> où l'on a dû se retrouver.

> Quels bons bras, quelle belle heure me rendront cette
> région d'où viennent mes sommeils et mes moindres
> mouvements?

"Là-haut": the highest point of what is later called the ecstatic region is here attained. Here all the elements are given a more explicit and hallucinatory intensity. Initially the Dionysian is stressed, not only in the hunting, erotic, and Bacchantic allusions but also through the suckling of animals, leaving of the civilized, and invasion of the city by the animal—which are also features of Dionysian frenzy. But the nature of the Dionysian is to defy such categorization, to unleash instead an undifferentiated and savage state: "Les Bacchantes . . . sanglotent et la lune brûle et hurle"; "Le paradis des orages s'effondre. Les sauvages dansent sans cesse la fête de la nuit." Human beings and nature are alike caught up in a sobbing, burning, screaming frenzy; then there is a paradisal loosing of waters, a dissolving of all; finally a primal state, anterior to any recognizable cultural milieu, the elemental nocturnal trance experience, is revealed. Beyond the learned allusions, something timeless and primitive emerges. Like "Barbare," "Villes I" carries us to the core of ecstasy.

But of course "Villes I" also dramatizes the hopeless loss of the ecstatic state, and in this re-enacts motifs central to ecstatic poetics. The very access to ecstasy in this poem, the dissolving of waters, is ambivalent. "Le paradis des orages s'effondre" equates paradise with storms, and a similar ambiguity is enforced by the verb, which conveys both a liberation of pent-up energy and a collapse, the onslaught and the end of ecstasy, culmination *and* return to ordinary consciousness. This instantaneous access to and loss of the ecstatic make "Villes I" a more troubling treatment of the problem of discontinuity than "Matinée d'ivresse" and "Being Beauteous." In both those poems a speaker, more or less transformed, distinctly describes, recounts, exclaims, even comments. But the convention of "Villes I," in this resembling the beginning of "Kubla Khan," is to be without visible speaker until the moment of descent from the ecstasy. Until that point the text offers us a compelling sense of the ecstatic figures; the reader's consciousness is absorbed by their activities. Then, virtually without warning, a *narrating* "I" appears—more surprisingly even than in "Kubla Khan." For the Rolands, "flottes orphéoniques," and "éclats mortels" of the sea halfway through the text insinuate tragedy, destruction, and mortality more subtly than Kubla's "Ancestral voices prophesying war." And the *je* who appears at the end is more astonishing for not having been foreshadowed by preface, commentary, or break in the text (as in "Being Beauteous" or the stanzaic form of "Kubla Khan"). That is, in "Villes I" there is no gradual process of movement from ecstatic to normal state, no temporal *progression* whatever.[23] There is simply exalted plenitude and, rudely set beside it, the vacuity of normal consciousness. "Villes I" is a tragic embodiment of Rimbaud's ecstatic project, totally fulfilled, inexplicably—and *simultaneously*—lost.

And notice the representation of this state of loss, the characteristics of the reduced *je*. They correspond closely to Fischer's discussion of the "I" of normal consciousness in relation to the real world of activity and its possibilities for fulfillment. All the features of ordinary perception and existence suddenly return: time, person, objects, space, movement, geography—"Et une heure je suis descendu dans le mouvement d'un boulevard de Bagdad." The isolated self, the intrusion of clock time, and the return to downward movement are reinforced by a mode of discourse that contrasts sharply with the previous ecstatic presence and plenitude. This postecstatic discourse features a succession of three past tenses, emphasis on isolated particularity ("une heure," "un boulevard"), forms of submission ("dans," "sous"), incapacity ("sans pouvoir éluder"), supposition ("l'on a dû"), plaintive interrogation, and passivity ("Quels bons bras . . . me rendront?"). As for the real world perceived by such an enfeebled consciousness, it is characterized positively, pointedly parallel to the lost world, yet lacking in interest for the despondent speaker. Sensuous nature, exotic city, energy, collectivity, productive activity, heightened expression and response ("le mouvement d'un boulevard de Bagdad où des compagnies ont chanté la joie du travail nouveau, sous une brise épaisse")—all are present, all seem full of promise, yet none holds the attention of the speaker. They are representative at most of the satisfaction to be found within the confines of the real—the world that from the beginning Rimbaud wants to surmount. The pursuit of the ecstatic in some sense here leads to a debilitating dissociation, an incapacity for activity in the normal world.[24]

The relation of the speaker to the lost ecstatic region is even more troubling. There is a sense of abrupt discontinuity in the sentence beginning "Et une heure." The conjunction "et" has a disconnected quality, allowing no explanatory link between the real and the other realm, whose inhabitants are reduced to a vague and impersonal "on" and whose mountains now appear as "fabuleux fantômes" to a mind submitted to ordinary constraints. Nonetheless there is a remarkable persistence—intimate, even bodily— of ecstatic memory: "sans pouvoir éluder," "fabuleux fantômes," "monts où l'on a dû se retrouver," "cette région d'où viennent mes sommeils et mes moindres mouvements." The full ecstatic integration of self and world for which "Barbare" may furnish one image is lacking here; indeed the conclusion is one of appalling loss. Yet memory persists; and the entire first portion of the poem serves as an enactment of the ecstatic that is in a sense victorious over any subsequent disappearance. In this, "Villes I" is just as significant as "Barbare." The convention of the latter implies a complete triumph over the real, an eternization of global ecstasy. The exalted, tragic lesson of "Villes I" rather resides in its presentation of absolutely present ecstasy as also utterly lost. No more compelling exemplification of the paradoxes of ecstatic poetry can be imagined.

The Ecstatic Paradox: Lucid Frenzy, Failure and Success, Poem and Collectivity

To the point therefore of illustrating the contradictions of the ecstatic in language, the group "Matinée d'ivresse," "Being Beauteous," "Dévotion," "Barbare," and "Villes I" embodies virtually all the themes of nineteenth-century ecstatic-visionary poetry. The revitalization of the animal-divine, progressing through provocation to engenderings of superhuman figures in texts like "Voyelles" and "Génie" that do not entirely resolve the dialectic of transcendence and immanence; the multiplicity of similar oppositions in the range of altered states and ecstatic traditions that we saw in the *Saison;* the systematic transformation of self, sensation, and world together with the attempt to balance the chaotic with appropriate forms; the recurrent imagery and progression of states from normal perception to disso-lution, which are part of the poetics sketched in the third section—these elements are energized in the extraordinar-ily intense poems just discussed. Note, however, that the ascetic phases of Rimbaud's odyssey tend to disappear from these ultimate ecstatic *Illuminations,* making "Fêtes de la patience" and "Délires II" seem but one moment in an underlying and essentially pagan movement that unifies Rimbaud's early poems, the *lettres du voyant,* and major *Illuminations.* Nonetheless, the culminating poems "Barbare" and "Villes I," while illustrating Fischer's argument on the synthesizing nature of ecstasy—the progression through intermediate states to an experience of absolute coherence—at the same time perpetuate certain polarities. There is the contrast between the solitary polar dissociation of "Barbare" and the collective dynamism of "Villes I." And each poem within itself also encompasses flagrant dichotomies—the antagonism of reality and transformed consciousness, the contradiction of the existence and non-existence of the ecstatic region, the paradox of the poem that ends but is also eternally ongoing, the coexistence within the same text of presence and absence, of possession and hopeless loss.

Such oppositions become most meaningful in the context of the ancient traditions that Rimbaud attempted to re-enact. And the comparisons with nineteenth- and twentieth-century writers allow us to perceive how indeed he tried to carry out his enterprise, help us to see his particular combination of ardor and despair, lucid effort and abandonment, succinct yet totalizing forms, varieties of attenuation, enactment, and loss. Both the careers and the forms—extended, disruptive, variously successful and tragic—of Blake, Hölderlin, Nerval, Nietzsche, Breton, and Yeats throw into relief such features in Rimbaud and reveal what is most individual in his achievement. The ecstatic *Illuminations,* like much else in his production, thus emerge as original and traditional, as both archetypal and unique.

Some difficult issues persist and need to be recapitulated

before we move on to other phases of Rimbaud's work.
There is the experience itself of failure and loss, an inherent feature of the historical myth and process of shamanism
according to Eliade, a function of discontinuous mental
states for Fischer, a difficulty met in the lifelong struggle
of Blake and Nietzsche and the artistry of Yeats, one that
in contrast cut off the lives and productivity of figures like
Hölderlin and Nerval. Failure and loss are especially pro-
nounced in Rimbaud, despite his contrasting and extraordinary capacity for ecstatic affirmation, especially in
"Villes I" and in "Being Beauteous." Elements in the latter imply a link between sexuality, a death tendency, and
the power of reality itself, a combination discernible in the
Saison and other *Illuminations.*

Thus in "Adieu" Rimbaud couches his attack on his
visionary project in terms of a harsh notion of the real, and
there is a parallel critique in "Délires I" of the sexual
component of his ecstatic writing. "Vagabonds" resembles
"Délires I" in scornfully evoking a Verlaine-like homosexual partner and in describing as long concluded the desire
to regain the "état primitif de fils du Soleil" (primitive
state of son of the Sun). "Royauté" uses the desire of a
couple to attain a superior state, the metaphor of sexuality
("Ils se pâmaient l'un contre l'autre"—They swooned
against each other) being linked to motifs of illumination
and royalty: "Je veux qu'elle soit reine"; "Il parlait . . . de
révélation, d'épreuve terminée" (I wish her to be queen; he
spoke of revelation, of a trial completed). But the realization of desire in this text is limited in duration and neu-
tralized by being situated so far in the past as to be recounted in laconic fashion: "En effet, ils furent rois toute
une matinée où les tentures carminées se relevèrent sur les
maisons, et toute l'après-midi, où ils s'avancèrent du côté
des jardins de palmes" (Indeed, they were monarchs for a

whole morning, as crimson hangings were raised up on the houses, and for the entire afternoon, during which they advanced toward the garden of palms).

The pastness of this poem indeed contrasts with the modes of actualization in other poems—and so does its use of a parablelike form that elsewhere expresses the failure of Rimbaud's effort. For example, "Bottom" combines sarcasm about self, a resolutely past mode of narration, and the metaphor of sexual conflict—the last extended to symbolize the poet's unsuccessful struggle against reality: "La réalité étant trop épineuse pour mon grand caractère,—je me trouvai néanmoins chez Madame" (Reality being too thorny for my great character,—I nevertheless found myself at Madame's). The almost Blakean nameless female, identified with reality itself, takes on her full role of unconquerable antagonist—like the Witch in "Après le déluge" who will never reveal her secrets, and the mysterious "Elle" of "Métropolitain" with whom a strangely dissociated *vous* struggled, in a polar setting reminiscent of "Dévotion" and "Barbare." But the cosmic frenzy of those texts is again seen as definitively past: "Le matin où avec Elle, vous vous débattîtes parmi les éclats de neige, ces lèvres vertes, les glaces, les drapeaux noirs et les rayons bleus, et les parfums pourpres du soleil des pôles,—ta force" (The morning when with Her, you struggled among the bursts of snow, those green lips, the ice, the black flags and blue rays, and the purple perfumes of the polar sun,—your strength).

But among these debunking texts, "Conte" and "Angoisse" are the most devastating. Together they argue, in absolute terms, that neither the self nor reality can be transformed. "Angoisse" does so by presenting the nameless female in her most powerfully negating form (ellipsis is Rimbaud's):

Se peut-il qu'Elle me fasse pardonner les ambitions continuellement écrasées,—qu'une fin aisée répare les âges d'indigence,—qu'un jour de succès nous endorme sur la honte de notre inhabilité fatale?

(O palmes! diamant!—Amour, force!—plus haut que toutes joies et gloires!—de toutes façons, partout,— démon, dieu,—Jeunesse de cet être-ci: moi!)

Que des accidents de féerie scientifique et des mouvements de fraternité sociale soient chéris comme restitution progressive de la franchise première? . . .

Mais la Vampire qui nous rend gentils commande que nous nous amusions avec ce qu'elle nous laisse, ou qu'autrement nous soyons plus drôles.

Rouler aux blessures, par l'air lassant et la mer; aux supplices, par le silence des eaux et de l'air meurtriers; aux tortures qui rient, dans leur silence atrocement houleux.

Is it possible that She can make me forgive the continually crushed ambitions,—that a comfortable end can make up for the ages of indigence,—that one day of success can put us to sleep on the shame of our fatal incapacity?

(O palms! diamond!—Love, strength!—higher than all joys and glories!—in every way, everywhere,—demon, god,—Youth of this being: me!)

That accidents of scientific fantasy and movements of social fraternity can be cherished as progressive restitution of the first franchise? . . .

But the Vampire who makes us behave commands that we amuse ourselves with what she leaves us, or else that we be more amusing.

Roll in wounds, through the wearisome air and the sea; in torments, through the silence of the murderous waters and air; in tortures that laugh, in their horribly swelling silence.

Early on in this chapter I used the second paragraph to illustrate the transfiguration of self that Rimbaud strove for, but within the poem it appears as a parenthetical, impossible outcome of a mere supposition, of a rhetorical question that is obviously to be answered in the negative. The emotion of the poem, as the title indicates, is the opposite of ecstatic joy. Our human situation is one of submission—the interplay of singular and plural pronouns being distinctly nonecstatic—a horribly painful immobility in which elements that elsewhere had a positive function are now wholly evil (the torture and nature imagery, rhythmic structure, absence of finite verbs, and hallucinatory quality of the last paragraph).

The "franchise première" is therefore not to be regained; instead, the poet must deal with an incapacity in our nature, "notre inhabilité fatale," which no amount of method and discipline can surmount. Furthermore, the satisfactions affordable within the conditions of reality, whether personal ("une fin aisée," "un jour de succès"), or proposed as valid for humanity (the myths of scientific and social progress), can in no way compensate for the more fundamental failure. "Angoisse" is therefore even more absolute in rejecting the conditions of reality, which at the conclusion of the *Saison* Rimbaud wanted to accept, than is the end of "Villes I" and, in fact, approaches "Jeunesse" in viewing science and social developments as transitory and accidental ("accidents," "mouvements"). Once again the ecstatic impulse, which when successful challenges sociopolitical concepts, as in "Jeunesse," "Solde," and "Génie," in its despairing phase seems to incapacitate Rimbaud, to eliminate all possibility of satisfactory personal or collective activity within a world reduced to derisive and torturing insignificance—"aux tortures qui rient, dans leur silence atrocement houleux."

"Conte," which uses the parable form, the motif of royalty, and a familiar sadistic and homosexual rebellion against the female, is another deflating of Rimbaud's undertaking:

Un Prince était vexé de ne s'être employé jamais qu'à la perfection des générosités vulgaires. Il prévoyait d'étonnantes révolutions de l'amour, et soupçonnait ses femmes de pouvoir mieux que cette complaisance agrémentée de ciel et de luxe. Il voulait voir la vérité, l'heure du désir et de la satisfaction essentiels. Que ce fût ou non une aberration de piété, il voulut. Il possédait au moins un assez large pouvoir humain.

Toutes les femmes qui l'avaient connu furent assassinées. Quel saccage du jardin de la beauté! Sous le sabre, elles le bénirent. Il n'en commanda point de nouvelles.— Les femmes réapparurent.

Il tua tous ceux qui le suivaient, après la chasse ou les libations.—Tous le suivaient.

Il s'amusa à égorger les bêtes de luxe. Il fit flamber les palais. Il se ruait sur les gens et les taillait en pièces.—La foule, les toits d'or, les belles bêtes existaient encore.

Peut-on s'extasier dans la destruction, se rajeunir par la cruauté! Le peuple ne murmura pas. Personne n'offrit le concours de ses vues.

Un soir il galopait fièrement. Un Génie apparut, d'une beauté ineffable, inavouable même. De sa physionomie et de son maintien ressortait la promesse d'un amour multiple et complexe! d'un bonheur indicible, insupportable même! Le Prince et le Génie s'anéantirent probablement dans la santé essentielle. Comment n'auraient-ils pas pu en mourir? Ensemble donc ils moururent.

Mais ce Prince décéda, dans son palais, à un âge ordinaire. Le Prince était le Génie. Le Génie était le Prince. La musique savante manque à notre désir.

A Prince was vexed at never having employed himself at anything save the perfection of vulgar generosities. He foresaw astonishing revolutions in love, and suspected his wives of being capable of more than that complaisance adorned by heaven and luxury. He wanted to see the truth, the hour of essential desire and satisfaction. Whether or not this was an aberration of piety, he wanted it. At least he possessed rather considerable human power.

All the women who had known him were murdered. What slaughter in the garden of beauty! Under the saber, they blessed him. He ordered no new ones.—The women reappeared.

He killed all who followed him, after the hunt or libations.—They all kept following him.

He amused himself by cutting the throats of beasts of luxury. He had palaces set on fire. He hurled himself at people and cut them to pieces.—The crowd, the golden roofs, the beautiful animals still existed.

Can one reach ecstasy in destruction, rejuvenate through cruelty? The people did not murmur. No one offered the assistance of his opinions.

One evening he was galloping proudly. A Genie appeared, of an ineffable beauty, unavowable even. From his physiognomy and bearing emerged the promise of a multiple and complex love! of a happiness unspeakable, unbearable even! The Prince and the Genie probably annihilated themselves in essential health. How could they not have died from it? Together therefore they died.

But this Prince died, in his palace, at an ordinary age. The Prince was the Genie. The Genie was the Prince. There is no masterful music for our desire.

Here the sexual slaughter, which is generalized to include subjects and possessions, is a metaphor for the impulse to erase the constraints of the real. But ordinary power, even the "assez large pouvoir humain" of a tyrant, can accomplish no such thing: "Les femmes réapparurent!" "La foule, les toits d'or, les belles bêtes existaient encore."

As often in Rimbaud, then, the quasi-impossible attack on reality is couched in terms of the disappointing nature of heterosexual experience, the search for "d'étonnantes révolutions de l'amour," and the definition of truth as erotic fulfillment, "l'heure du désir et de la satisfaction essentiels." The homosexual "Génie" seems to embody this "amour multiple et complexe," "bonheur indicible," "santé essentielle"—all familiar Rimbaldian ecstatic formulas (not to speak of "Peut-on s'extasier dans la destruction" and "Le Prince et le Génie s'anéantirent probablement"). But with this "probablement" (and the following mock question and affirmation) the tone becomes openly sardonic, as a prelude to the sober conclusion, in which time and morality are shown to be ineluctable, the "Génie" is dismissed as a projection of subjective desire, and such desire is shown to be ineffectual: "La musique savante manque à notre désir." Ecstatic method, the magical music of "Guerre" and "Matinée d'ivresse," are seen as unattainable, in formulas that seem to belie the existence of poems such as "Barbare" and "Génie."

So the *Saison* and these sardonic *Illuminations* deflate the ecstatic enterprise, undermining almost all its characteristic features: the state of ecstasy itself; the transformation of self and reality; ecstatic myth and erotic method; the musical, torture, city, nature, and polar motifs; the possibilities of solitary and collective joy; the giant male and female figures that emerge in "Génie" and "Barbare"; and the forms of enactment themselves. If Rimbaud's ecstatic writing is an extension of his child poetry, then at the term of the one as of the other we encounter a devastating self-critique, which again recalls Freud's dichotomous principles of mental functioning, dividing psychic activity in terms of the polarities of the real and the pleasurable. Rimbaud's poetry aims at transcending this dichotomy, at surmounting what is thought to be an implacable reality and achieving totality of being. And yet the *Saison* and texts like "Angoisse" and "Conte" embody a bitter reality principle that denies the possibility of such transfiguration of self and world.

We have nonetheless gained some insights that enable us to challenge the absoluteness of this denial. First, there is Rimbaud's overemphasis on the sexual as both metaphor and actual method. Eliade and others accord the erotic only a limited role in the panoply of ecstatic techniques, and poems such as "Being Beauteous," "Vagabonds," "Royauté," "Bottom," "Angoisse," and "Conte" may be accurate in promulgating failure precisely to the extent that they accord an excessive privilege to the sexual, whereas Rimbaud's successful ecstatic texts are more inclusive. This feature is linked to another element, stressed by Eliade, present as well in Blake, Nietzsche, Fischer—the problem of historical decadence, the separation of Western culture from a mythical origin, the existence therefore of degraded techniques, the fading of belief in the divine in the face of rational and scientific modes of intelligence. A problem for all these writers, this situation is evidently crucial for Rimbaud, as the *Saison* demonstrates, and as a fakiristic text such as "Parade" also makes clear. But even against such obstacles that poem breaks out of the constraints of the normal and explodes toward ecstasy, and beyond "Parade" are the affirmations of "Barbare," "Villes I," and especially "Génie."

To comprehend the unimpaired impact of those poems, we do best to relate the thinking of Blake and Nietzsche and the findings of Fischer to Rimbaud, emphasizing the elements of discontinuity and persistence as well as the convergence of systematic effort and frenzy. All these writers emphasize the continued existence of ecstatic energies, the methodical struggle to liberate them, the possibility of attaining culminating states and expressions of such states, the inevitably intermittent quality of such attainment, yet also the possibility of persistence, of overcoming amnesia, of psychic and linguistic coherence. Rimbaud expresses a lucid, tragic awareness of these issues in the longer *lettre du voyant,* foreseeing the dissolution of his enterprise but insisting that this would in no way invalidate his visions, which would remain accessible in the form of poems and which would contribute to similar future experiences: "Il arrive à l'inconnu, et quand, affolé, il finirait par perdre l'intelligence de ses visions, il les a vues! Qu'il crève dans son bondissement par les choses inouïes et innommables: viendront d'autres horribles travailleurs; ils commenceront par les horizons où l'autre s'est affaissé!" (He reaches the unknown, and even if, maddened, he ends up losing the intelligence of his visions, he has seen them! Let him die leaping through unheard of and unnamable things: there will come other horrible workers; they will begin at the horizons where the other one collapsed!).

The adolescent bravado here perhaps betrays insufficient awareness of the necessity for lifelong discipline such as Blake's or Nietzsche's, but Rimbaud's insistence on suffering and derangement has its own integrity, and the price he paid for it is evident in the *Saison.* We earlier noted as well his sense of the difficulties of devising appropriate forms for the expression of the *innommable*—his thinking on ecstatic language, form, function, and public, and the actualizations of that thinking in the *Illuminations.* Those actualizations need to be thought of now as including the poems just discussed, that is, as incorporating a high degree of honesty, the ability for self-criticism, an awareness of the coexistence of failure and achievement—as intense and inherently discontinuous forms, capable of setting side by side absence and presence, possession and loss, absolute frenzy, and a comparably absolute denial of that same ecstasy.

Only such a poetry is faithful to the nature of the ecstatic for modern consciousness, as delineated in part by Blake but more by Coleridge, Nietzsche, Eliade, and Fischer, and most of all by Rimbaud himself. The struggle for the ecstatic, the resistance of the real, *simultaneous* success and failure, fragmented and fantastic forms that trouble our sense of the implacability of the world—the *Illuminations* most of all exemplify such a poetry. In their tragic way they embody Nietzsche's model of Apollonian consciousness somehow absorbing the experience of the Dionysian, Fischer's paradoxical and precious *discontinuous ecstatic totality:* "Enormité devenant norme, absorbée par tous, il serait vraiment *un multiplicateur de progrès!*" (Enormity becoming norm, absorbed by all, he would be truly *a multiplier of progress!*).

But this optimistic early formulation reintroduces a recurrent problem, that of the function of ecstatic poetry for the collectivity. The allusions to the events of the Paris Commune of 1871 in the longer *voyant* letter propose an uneasy yet idealistic view of the social function of the visionary poet, out of phase with a repressive society, hoping to be a contributing force in a future modality of political life. The poems from "Angoisse" to "Génie" are more troubling, in a way more realistically Nietzschean, in proposing an opposition between ecstatic states and social organization. The joyous collectivity of "Villes I" gives way to indifference or hostility toward group activity in the real world at the end of that poem and in "Angoisse." And the most permanent of the ecstatic realizations are comparable: "Barbare" involves a vast dissociation of person and reality, whereas in "Génie" the appeal for a collective responsiveness to immanent divinity reaches out to the extremes of nature, by-passing altogether the sociopolitical. These two poems are the most definitive and victorious of Rimbaud's achievements, and in the face of the attacks in the *Saison* and other texts, we need to recall them, recognize how astoundingly they embody the transcendent and immanent aspects of his ecstatic imagination. But if in the one we glimpse a cosmic and eternalized ecstatic reality, and if in the other we stretch toward an encounter with the generous, dynamic, divine reality of the world and of our lives, in neither can we avoid a challenge to our notions of society, to our sense of collectivity itself. In chapter 3 we therefore need to pursue Rimbaud's poetry in terms of the dialectic between nature and city as having conflicting claims to be the locus of human existence, and to deal with Rimbaud's estimate of and place in the society against which he so violently felt himself in opposition.

THREE

Visions and Habitations: Nature, City, and Society

Nature: we are surrounded and wrapped about by her—unable to break loose from her.

Johann Wolfgang von Goethe

This colossal centralization, this heaping together of two and a half millions of human beings at one point, has multiplied the power of this two and a half millions a hundred-fold. . . . But the sacrifices . . . become apparent later. . . . The very turmoil of the streets has something repulsive. . . . The hundreds of thousands of all classes and ranks crowding past each other. . . . The brutal indifference, the unfeeling isolation of each in his private interest, becomes the more repellent and offensive, the more these individuals are crowded together.

Friedrich Engels

Inextricable Unities: Nature, City, Consciousness

From the child to the ecstatic in Rimbaud, the connections are clear; and these categories are related to those of nature and the city as well. The child inhabits a more thrilling natural scene, while at the term of ecstasy, as in "Barbare" and "Villes I," the universe overflows with bursting energy. But as the title of the latter indicates, nature and city, the natural and the human there converge in some nearly incomprehensible divine mode that redeems the specifically urban suffering endured by the child-poet at the end of "Enfance." Blake's Innocence-Experience, Wordsworth's encounter with London, the conflict of natural innocence and urban suffering that persists in Baudelaire's "Le Cygne" and "Mœsta et errabunda"—Rimbaud's poetic curve is a variation of a recurrent structure. Indeed, the terms child, ecstasy, nature, and city incorporate elemental components of human life: the origin and continuity of personal existence; the desire for ultimate satisfaction; consciousness of and existence in the natural and man-made world—with the latter inevitably involving the themes of creativity and society.

"Nature and the city" is thus a phrase with a large range of multiple and complex significance. The number of Rimbaud's texts in which nature figures is high, not to speak of the importance of the theme throughout romantic poetry and after, in René Char to mention only one striking contemporary example. And the city plays a central role in nineteenth-century literature, not only in fiction but in poetry as well. Why this emphasis on the dialectic of nature and the urban in our major literature? Writers like Lewis Mumford and Henri Lefebvre and Raymond Williams, and behind them Marx and Engels, provide a good basis for studying, and perhaps answering, this question.

They argue that history preeminently involves the forms of man's interactions with nature; that the development of civilization has increasingly been a history of the urban; that the city has always implied man's perceptions of reality as both material world and cosmos; that it therefore represents our spiritual nature—culture, art, religion, utopia, while its history and structure also record the hard facts of economic and social existence—property, poverty, war, exploitation; that the modern industrial city, the seat of worldwide industrial economy, constitutes a quantitatively and qualitatively new and destructive form of human relationship with the natural.

Literature, according to this argument, has imaged the phenomenon of urbanization, from Greek poetry and theater and the satires of Juvenal to the interplay of country and city throughout English literature and the fascination with Paris that is not limited to the modern myth of Paris in French letters. But that myth is crucial, for in connection with what Lefebvre calls the fetishism of nature in the late eighteenth and early nineteenth centuries, it points to literary reverberations of the emergence of the industrial city, threatening for the first time in history the quasi-universal destruction of the natural world. Clearly many of the writers discussed in chapters 1 and 2—Rousseau, Blake, Hölderlin, Wordsworth, Hugo, Baudelaire—are related to this historical phenomenon. Rimbaud, witness to the urban revolution of the Commune of 1871, is equally involved. Rimbaud, of peasant/small *propriétaire* background, came to Paris in the early 1870s, different from some of the displaced peasant characters in Zola's novels, for example, in being possessed of extraordinary talent. *And also insight:* consider the worker in "Ouvriers" who laments the conditions of the industrial city and shows how it ravages nature, and the section of "Mauvais

Sang" in which Rimbaud reveals a pattern whose significance transcends the individual and achieves more generally historical significance:

> Dans les villes la boue m'apparaissait soudainement rouge
> et noire, comme une glace quand la lampe circule dans la
> chambre voisine, comme un trésor dans la forêt!
> [In the cities the mud would suddenly appear to me red
> and black, like a mirror when a lamp is being moved in
> the room next door, like a treasure in the forest!]
>
> . . .
>
> Mais je puis être sauvé. Vous êtes de faux nègres, vous
> maniaques, féroces, avares. Marchand, . . .
> magistrat, . . . général, . . . empereur, vieille
> démangeaison, tu es nègre
> [But I can be saved. You're fake negroes, you maniacs,
> ferocious, miserly. Merchant, . . . magistrate, . . . gen-
> eral, . . . emperor, old mange, you're a negro]
>
> . . .
>
> Le plus malin est de quitter ce continent. . . . J'entre au
> vrai royaume des enfants de Cham.
> [The shrewdest thing is to leave this continent. . . . I
> am entering the true kingdom of the children of Ham.]

It is astonishing how much is implicit in these lines:
childhood and nature; the movement to the city; the ambivalence of the urban, its squalor (compare Rousseau and
Balzac's *Le Père Goriot* for Paris's mud as symbol of economic deprivation, substandard conditions of life, and
moral corruption), yet the city's potential for illumination
(significantly a substitutive analogue of a rich discovery in
the natural world); solitude, perhaps comparable to the
isolation in the great cities that shocked Wordsworth, Engels, Baudelaire; the dissection of and attack on the power
figures of ideologically mystified Western culture ("faux

nègres": merchant, magistrate, general, emperor—capital, law, war, despotic government); the flight from that culture to the pagan existence of Africa.

In its innocence, that flight is, of course, streaked with ambivalence. Rimbaud earlier dreamed, in "Mauvais Sang," of going to and returning from the non-European world, in a brutally exploitative prefiguring of his actual later life:

> Je reviendrai, avec des membres de fer, la peau sombre, l'œil furieux: sur mon masque, on me jugera d'une race forte. J'aurai de l'or: je serai oisif et brutal. Les femmes soignent ces féroces infirmes retour des pays chauds. Je serai mêlé aux affaires politiques. Sauvé.

> I will come back, with limbs of iron, dark skin, furious eyes: from my mask, I'll be judged to be of a powerful race. I will have gold: I will be idle and brutal. Women nurse these ferocious invalids back from hot countries. I will be involved in political affairs. Saved.

The innocent revulsion against French society is here inseparable from the colonizing instinct. So a later section of "Mauvais Sang" dramatizes the landing of the whites, the submission of the colonized people: "Les blancs débarquent. Le canon! Il faut se soumettre au baptême, s'habiller, travailler" (The whites disembark. The cannon! It is necessary to submit to baptism, clothes, work). Note the characteristic elements that we shall encounter again: the link between the religious and the military in Western oppression, as well as between repression of the body and enslavement to work. Proto-Conradian, these passages relate the nature-city movement to a reflection about Western capitalist society in its global, colonial outreach—and in this Rimbaud's insight is as revealing as the novelistic tradition.[1]

"Nature and city" therefore must be seen as opening out onto the sense of European society in a worldwide context, a historical formulation, as is apparent in the passages from "Mauvais Sang" which I have been discussing. But nature and city are not only historical "content." They are inherently related as well to issues of perception, consciousness, and imagination. Nature and city are not only the world we live in; they are also the world that we perceive, that we make through perceiving as well as through activity. Indeed, as M. H. Abrams re-emphasizes, the romantic felicity of existence in nature begins with a satisfying *consciousness* of natural things. In response to the dominant epistemology of "modern" philosophy (the great Renaissance scientists, Descartes' validation of mind over matter, the English empiricist reversal of that position—stressing the mind's passivity and the unknowability of the external world in mysteries of primary and secondary qualities), post-Kantian philosophy and theory of the imagination stresses the mind as creative *and also* integrative with nature. Thus Coleridge, using both Berkeley and Kant, attempts to solve the subject-object dichotomy by an idealist tactic that nonetheless asserts the *concrete reality* of what we perceive.[2]

The paradoxes of this formulation, which is strictly faithful to Coleridge, persist through romantic poetics and are relevant to critical debates over Rimbaud's writing. Thus Abrams's survey of the romantic *marriage* between mind and world draws together, among others, a Baconian stress on concreteness, objects, freshness of perception (the early Wordsworth, Wallace Stevens) and a neoplatonic tendency (German romantic philosophy, Novalis, Coleridge, Wordsworth's later position on the superiority of mind).

We could extend the contrast in time by linking more recent versions of concrete and idealist emphases—namely the phenomenological approach of Sartre, Bachelard, J.-P. Richard, and the language-centered, antimimetic argument of linguistic and post-structuralist formalism, which characterizes so much recent writing on Rimbaud. Adding the perspective of these recent critics to the earlier views of François Ruchon and René Etiemble, we arrive at a kind of poetry that seems ferociously hyperreal and yet often insists on its own inherent quality of being *language*. This "paradox," which isn't one, exacerbates the romantic insistence on both concreteness and creation in nature poetry; in its most flagrant (anti-romantic? super-romantic?) form, it gives us a text like "Fleurs":

D'un gradin d'or,—parmi les cordons de soie, les gazes grises, les velours verts et les disques de cristal qui noircissent comme du bronze au soleil,—je vois la digitale s'ouvrir sur un tapis de filigranes d'argent, d'yeux et de chevelures.

Des pièces d'or jaune semées sur l'agate, des piliers d'acajou supportant un dôme d'émeraudes, des bouquets de satin blanc et de fines verges de rubis entourent la rose d'eau.

Tels qu'un dieu aux énormes yeux bleus et aux formes de neige, la mer et le ciel attirent aux terrasses de marbre la foule des jeunes et fortes roses.

From a step of gold,—among the silk cords, gray gauzes, green velvets and disks of crystal that blacken like bronze in the sun,—I see the digitalis opening on a carpet of filigree of silver, of eyes and of heads of hair.

Pieces of yellow gold sown on the agate, pillars of mahogany supporting a dome of emerald, bouquets of white satin and fine rods of ruby surround the water rose.

Like a god with enormous blue eyes and forms of
snow, the sea and the sky draw to the terraces of marble
the crowd of young and strong roses.

This remarkable poem, read in a representational way,
has led to simple-minded attempts at rationalization: a
natural scene described as if it were in a theater, a theater
viewed as a natural scene, and so forth. Clearly, however,
we have to read what it literally says; only then can we
appreciate its force, as both language and as consciousness,
as mind and relationship to nature. For example, the title
creates an expectation of the natural, indeed the vegetal,
but in the first paragraph we get instead a succession of
artificial, man-made, nonvegetal, and eventually disembodied human substances, structures, and forms: steps,
metals, cordons, fabrics, curtains, disks, rugs, filigree,
eyes, heads of hair—just about everything, we might
think, except flowers. And paragraph two is similar,
though more architectural ("piliers," "dôme") and more
uranian ("émeraudes," "rubis")—at one level this is clearly
a poem asserting, against naive nature, the creativity of
mind, art, the nonnatural intentionality and constructive-
ness of the human. This assertion is exemplified by the
opening emphasis on perspective and vision ("D'un gradin
d'or . . . je vois"), by the probable drug-suggestion in the
reference to foxglove, and by the marvellous subtlety of the
language:

D'un gradin d'or: a perspective for vision, also evidently a
structure of sound, emphasizing the play of vowels, nasals
and *d* and *r* consonants;

*parmi les cordons de soie, les gazes grises, les velours verts et les
disques de cristal qui noircissent comme du bronze au soleil:* a
setting, of both visual and linguistic sorts, the latter a

complex interweaving of vowels, nasals, alliteration on the letters *c, g, v, d, s,* as well as rhythmic patterning, in part through repetition of the article *"les"*;

je vois la digitale . . . : an object of vision, conjured through the flow of the sentence, by virtue of the fact that almost every sound has been prepared in what has gone before—except the *j* of *"je,"* thus perhaps foregrounding the perspective of the speaker.

Far from imitating a natural object, then, this opening sentence creates one. However, we should not miss the fact that amid all the apparently unnatural allusions, the first paragraph involves a speaker who claims to *see* a quite normal flower, this vision having been prepared by a simile introducing the light and warmth of the sun, and indeed in a sentence that is filled with concrete and satisfying evocations of color, shape, texture, warmth, and temporal process in a natural setting: "qui noircissent comme du bronze au soleil." The artificial and the linguistic are therefore not separable from the sensuous and even from the natural. Without minimizing a certain potential for sterility, "Fleurs" vindicates the power of the mind and language to generate an extraordinary sensuous concreteness.

Paragraph two also ends by asserting a natural reality, another flower, and the vagueness of the formula "la rose d'eau," within the unfolding structure of the poem, again stresses the priority of language and mind, as well as their capacity to engender consciousness of the natural world. For the words "rose d'eau" very nearly contain the concluding paragraph, with its sudden evocation of the vast and energetic life of nature: "la mer et le ciel attirent aux terrasses de marbre la foule des jeunes et fortes roses." Here there is no difficulty in naming the natural realities

that we all know—sea, sky, roses. Whereas intricacy, artificiality, and the human perspective dominated earlier,
now the scope widens, nature seems animated by enormous
power ("attirent," "la foule des jeunes et fortes roses"), and
the human is integrated into the natural scene ("terrasses
de marbre"). And beyond the human and the natural and
the linguistic, a quasi-divinity emerges: "Tels qu'un dieu
aux énormes yeux bleus et aux formes de neige, la mer et
le ciel. . . ." The explicit simile speaks volumes, in relation to Abrams's argument about the impulse in post-Kantian poetry to re-establish in a *secular* way a quasi-divine
marriage between the mind and nature. Rimbaud's poem
asserts the primacy of mind and language (it is therefore
idealist); but through it an apprehension of nature is generated that endows our experience of the world with a very
nearly paradisal beauty (it is therefore realist, and realistically millenial).

So in "Fleurs" nature is evoked as part of a satisfying
dialectic of mind and world. But this dialectic, often a
solitary one in romantic lyric poetry, needs to be extended
in the direction of the social and the historical. Marx and
Engels showed that well in *The German Ideology*, arguing
for the self as constituted socially, and neatly relating that
point to *nature* by reminding us that the cherry tree, about
whose existence outside the mind the German philosophers
had exercised themselves, does not grow naturally in Germany, having been imported for commercial purposes.
That is, the self exists in dialogue with others, in the
context of a physical world that has been transformed by
human activity—of social and economic (and finally governmental and military) kinds.

Note that this argument is made by Marx and Engels in
the course of their description of the evolution of the *city*,
of the emergence and decline of the medieval city and the

growth of the capitalist economy centered in the great industrial metropolis—and of the division of labor, class struggle, and alienation of consciousness that that process created. Consciousness therefore, for Marx and Engels, is neither essentially solitary nor consciousness of nature alone; it is socially conditioned, and within it nature no longer exists as purely natural—rather the world has been modified by man's historical activity, with a characteristic stress on the economic and with an awareness of the historical evolution from agricultural capitalism to urban industry.[3]

This link between consciousness, nature, and society finds an echo in Rimbaud, in "Ce qu'on dit au poète à propos de fleurs," and also in "Après le déluge." The first of these is rich in satirical and comic effects concerning the role of poetry in revealing the natural world. But the natural turns out to be related to a number of other factors: poetic convention and form, traditions of exoticism and theories of imitation, diffusion for a public, an acute sense of science, modernity, and history. Thus Rimbaud attacks traditional verse form—"l'Art n'est plus . . . de permettre / A l'Eucalyptus étonnant / Des constrictors d'un hexamètre" (Art no longer consists in permitting the astonishing Eucalyptus constrictors a hexameter long). The vigorous exoticism of this formula contrasts with the timid conventions of mimesis, nature, and imaginative voyage that the French poetic tradition had saddled itself with (three-dot ellipsis is Rimbaud's; others mine):

> De vos forêts et de vos prés,
> O très paisibles photographes!
> La Flore est diverse à peu près
> Comme des bouchons de carafes!
> ....

O blanc Chasseur, qui cours sans bas
A travers le Pâtis panique,
Ne peux-tu pas, ne dois-tu pas
Connaître un peu ta botanique?
....
Tu torcherais des floraisons
Dignes d'Oises extravagantes! . . .

  (*"Ce qu'on dit au poète à propos de fleurs"*)

In your forests and meadows,
O most peaceful photographers!
The Flora is about as diverse
As stoppers on carafes!
....
O white Hunter, who runs without socks
Through the panic Pasture,
Can't you, don't you have to
Know a bit of botany?
....
You'd knock off growths
Worthy of extravagant Oises! . . .

  The passivity of the photographer recalls Baudelaire's antimimetic justification of art in the *Salon de 1859,* while the humorous sockless poet implies a kind of literature out of contact with the reality of nature, a charge that Rimbaud might have leveled about that time against his own "Bateau ivre"—witness these lines from "Ce qu'on dit":

    Tu ferais succéder, je crains,
    Aux Grillons roux les Cantharides,
    L'or des Rios au bleu des Rhins,—
    Bref, aux Norwèges les Florides.

You'd make, I fear, Cantharides
Follow upon red Crickets,
The gold of Rios upon the blue of Rhines,—
In short, Floridas on Norways.

Indeed, such imagery and information could be found just
as well in illustrated books and magazines as in poetry—or
so Rimbaud researchers later discovered.[4] Rimbaud gives
that game away himself in "Ce qu'on dit," by his references to Grandville, Figuier, Hachette, implying a tradition of writing for a public desirous of a tame and ready-
made exoticism.

"Ce qu on dit" is an attack against that literature and an
affront to its public. By a series of references to excremen-
tal and other viscous substances, Rimbaud reasserts the
existence of organic nature. Lilies as "ecstasy enemas," the
Parnassian poet/addressee Banville's armpits and bath together with "filthy forget-me-nots," nymphs's spit, bellies
of basset hounds, butterflies shitting on daisies, droolings
and pommades and syrups—all lead to the basic question:

> —En somme, une Fleur, Romarin
> Ou Lys, vive ou morte, vaut-elle
> Un excrément d'oiseau marin?

> —In sum, is a Flower, Rosemary
> Or Lily, alive or dead, worth
> A sea-bird's excrement?

In "Rêve parisien" Baudelaire eliminated "le végétal"
from his strangely metallic dream world, thus reversing a
symbolic valorization of the vegetal over the mineral that
goes back at least as far as the seventh of Rousseau's

Rêveries. But "Ce qu'on dit" one-ups Baudelaire, and all of Parnassian poetry, and the Mallarmé of "Toast funèbre," and ultimately Rousseau too, in asserting, against the floral and the mineral, the underlying reality of the animal and the organic. That is, it encourages in poetry a much less conventional, a more fully sensuous and unrepressed contact with the physical reality of nature.

But, in parallel with Marxist notions of consciousness, "Ce qu'on dit" is not only about poetry and nature but also very much about the historical—societal, economic, even military—aspects of the interaction between the two. Toward the end a series of references (nickel spoons, sodium, rubber, the refraction of light, electric butterflies, the telegraph) creates a fantastic analogy between poetic activity and the scientific discoveries and technical inventions that have transformed the natural. Commerce and colonialism are also explicitly evoked (three-dot ellipsis is Rimbaud's, others mine):

> A notre époque de sagous
> Quand les Plantes sont travailleuses,
> ....
> Là! . . . Comme si les Acajous
> Ne servaient, même en nos Guyanes,
> Qu'aux cascades des sapajous
> ....
> Dis, non les pampas printaniers
> Noirs d'épouvantables révoltes,
> Mais les tabacs, les cotonniers!
> Dis les exotiques récoltes!
>
> Dis, front blanc que Phébus tanna,
> De combien de dollars se rente
> Pedro Velasquez, Habana;
> ....

Trouve, Ô Chasseur, nous le voulons,
Quelques garances parfumées
Que la Nature en pantalons
Fasse éclore!—pour nos Armées!

In our age of sagos
When Plants work,

....

There! . . . As if Mahoganies
Served, even in our Guianas,
Only for cascading monkeys

....

Tell, not the spring pampas
Black with fearsome revolts,
But tobaccos, cotton plants!
Tell of exotic crops!

Tell, white brow that Phoebus tanned,
How many dollars are earned by
Pedro Velasquez of Havana;

....

Find, O Hunter, we desire it,
Perfumed madders
That Nature may cause to bloom
As trousers!—for our Armies!

These lines are tongue-in-cheek and serious at the same time in describing "notre époque de sagous" ("sagous"—a starch-producing palm). They put poetry in close contact with the scientific modification of man's relation with nature, the exploitation of nature for nutriment, clothing, shelter, and profit. They substitute economic questions for conventionally exotic themes, and do so through a lovely conjunction of racial and poetico-mythological motifs ("front blanc que Phébus tanna"). The issue of colonialism, not pushed very hard, is nonetheless nicely there ("*nos*

Guyanes"), and in the last stanza quoted here flowers marvellously produce not poetry but the red pants of the
French army. We cannot forget that the text is dated July
14, 1871, two months after the defeat of the revolutionary
Commune to which Rimbaud was so devoted. When he
closes by calling the poet "Commerçant! colon! médium!"
there is a large potential for bitter irony and deception, as
well as a dangerous ambivalence. Poetry as an imaginative
form of the capitalist activities of selling and colonizing?
Rimbaud's own later life comes to mind. But even without
taking the poem that far, we still carry away its enlargement of the natural in poetry. Flowers and poems—impossible, says Rimbaud, without history, commerce, science,
colonies, armies. Again, consciousness, nature, history,
and poetry are drawn together.

That convergence appears again in the opening text of
the *Illuminations*, "Après le déluge." We earlier viewed
that poem as a myth of childhood and growth and loss and
poetry, themes that we can now integrate into the problematic of history, nature, city, and consciousness. A poem of
consciousness it is, beginning with "l'idée du Déluge,"
with the *notion* of purification and innocence. Immediately
after that idea recedes, comes the phase of nature—represented through innocent animals, biblical echoes, a sacred
view of the natural world: "Un lièvre s'arrêta . . . et dit sa
prière à l'arc-en-ciel à travers la toile de l'araignée" (A hare
stopped . . . and said its prayer to the rainbow through
the spider's web). Critics have commented on the motifs of
liquid continuity that integrate this vision and that recall
the romantic nature writers.[5] But this is a nonhuman or
prehuman world, and the flowers and precious stones that
hide do so because of the imminence of the human, which
bursts on the scene as, precisely, the city, with all its
extensions in trade, slaughter, sexual strife, organized reli-

gion, and finally systematic exploitation of the entire globe:

> Dans la grande rue sale les étals se dressèrent, et l'on
> tira les barques vers la mer . . .
> Le sang coula, chez Barbe-Bleue,—aux abattoirs,—
> dans les cirques, où le sceau de Dieu blêmit les fenêtres.
> ....
> Madame *** établit un piano dans les Alpes. La messe
> et les premières communions se célébrèrent aux cent
> mille autels de la cathédrale.
> Les caravanes partirent. Et le Splendide-Hôtel fut bâti
> dans le chaos de glaces et de nuit du pôle.

> In the dirty main street the stalls arose, and barks
> were dragged toward the sea . . .
> Blood flowed, at Bluebeard's,—in the slaughter-
> houses,—in the circuses, where the seal of God whit-
> ened the windows.
> ....
> Madame *** set up a piano in the Alps. Mass and
> first communions were celebrated at the hundred thou-
> sand altars of the cathedral.
> The caravans left. And the Splendid-Hotel was built in
> the chaos of ice and night of the pole.

This poem is like a condensed and supremely surreal version of Marx and Engels. The idea of innocence and natural existence hardly exists in human consciousness and history before the city appears. And the urban carries with it economic and sexual struggle for man, intimately connected with the fact of religion, and filth, slaughter, and subjugation for nature. The worldwide structure of city, commerce, and religion, in a system which in "Soir historique" and "Démocratie" Rimbaud explicitly recognized as that of bourgeois democracy, could not be clearer.

In this context the personal consciousness of the poet figure emerges, which, within the Marxist argument, is historically and inevitably accurate:

Depuis lors, la Lune entendit les chacals piaulant par les déserts de thym,—et les églogues en sabots grognant dans le verger. Puis, dans la futaie violette, bourgeon-nante, Eucharis me dit que c'était le printemps.

Since then, the Moon heard the jackals whining through the deserts of thyme,—and the eglogues in wooden shoes grumbling in the orchard. Then, in the violet, burgeon-ing forest, Eucharis told me that it was spring.

Personal, seasonal, mythic, and historical temporalities are evoked here—the cycle of the year and the myths of nymph and pastoral that have structured man's responses to nature *after,* in the wake of, the primal phenomenon of urbanization. So the flood that is desired at the end is heavy with meaning—protest against the social order, and perhaps against all ordered and exploiting structurings of experience; but desire also for transcendence of the *mediated* perception of the natural world, which is all that city-creating mankind can have; desire for an absolute purity of natural existence (the flood), which at the same time might be a victory over the limits of the natural world as it is now available to us (the witch).

"Après le déluge" thus synthesizes the themes addressed thus far in this chapter. It is a poem of history, about nature, city, and socioeconomic reality (seen intensely as surreality); it is also a poem about consciousness, myth, imagination, and human satisfaction. In Rimbaud, and I fancy in many other writers, it is crucial to see how these elements cohere. To understand him right, we must have them all—not make him on the one hand only a "reflection" of history, or on the other hand a creator of merely formalist, perfectly self-contained poetic pieces. At certain points, he approached one or the other of these extremes, but to read him only in one way is to trivialize his enormous importance. We must have both, both visions and habitations—the imaginative interactions of consciousness and language with natural and man-made reality; or poetry, nature, the city, and society.

The Attractions of Nature

We nonetheless need, within this unity, to isolate certain features for discussion—even amid the vast extent of writing about nature in the literature preceding Rimbaud. "Après le déluge" points us toward fruitful paths of investigation for it involves individual personal and poetic consciousness in the face of a natural world that has been transformed and mediated by human history. And, as we have suggested, its conclusion implies the desire to penetrate to an absolute, unmediated contact with the natural. But the unwilling witch insinuates also a metaphor of sexual conflict to describe the interactions of man and world, which may be finally unsatisfactory. Similar motifs and problems are encountered in romantic writing about nature and can be pursued there as well as later throughout Rimbaud's work.

Thus, in keeping with the *je* who suddenly emerges in "Après le déluge" and with the epistemological-poetic argument sketched earlier, we can first characterize nature in romantic literature, in its broadest application, as existing in counterpart with the self—as the mirror, foil, partner, antagonist of individual subjective existence. There are

melodramatic versions of this subject-nature motif, including great and not-so-great works of literature—think of
Werther, René, Lamartine's "L'Isolement," Hugo's "Tris-
tesse d'Olympio," melancholy and at times bathetic effu-
sions on the issues of isolation, libido, and mortality.

The theme also characterizes some of the most important works of romantic poetic sensibility—Rousseau's
Rêveries, with their movement through the natural scene,
their relative valorizing of natural objects and their culimi-
nation (in the fifth *promenade*) in a liquid absolutizing of
the self in nature; *Hyperion* and the great poems of
Hölderlin, which often picture the speaker alone amid the
roaring presence of wind, sun, rain, mountains, and volcanoes; the romantic lyrics of Coleridge and Wordsworth,
dramas of consciousness in the face of the world, of which
"Tintern Abbey" is the most famous example; indeed
Wordsworth throughout his work, from the fanciful movement in "I wandered lonely" from isolation to society in
nature ("Ten thousand saw I at a glance, / Tossing their
heads in sprightly dance"), to *The Prelude*'s narration of the
repeated encounters between child, older self, poet, and
the immensity and sublimity of the world—for such
poems Keats identified the Wordsworthian with the "ego-
tistical sublime."[6]

Consciousness, therefore, in dialectic with the elemental
presence and power of nature. Early in the romantic period,
in the fragment on nature (and later in "Die Metamorphose
der Pflanzen"), Goethe formulates the aspiration to fully
rediscover and value nature, seeing it as the inevitable context of all human activity, fascinating in its complexity,
escaping our control, capable of mighty generosity when
treated aright. This sounds like the fetishism of nature that
Lefebvre, following Marx, stresses. But the religious note,
the extension beyond the natural to the divine that marks so

much romantic poetry, cannot be minimized. In Hölderlin there is a rediscovery of myth that leads the poet to undertake the perilous prophetic mission of *naming* the holy, of leading the human community to a rediscovery of the sacred in the world. In "Der Rhein" Hölderlin interprets Rousseau as his predecessor in this undertaking, and Joseph Warren Beach enumerates how many strands of traditional religious thinking may have fed into Wordsworth's writing about the natural world. Lamartine's later poetry is a tissue of such conventions, and from the sacred horror of "A Albert Dürer" to the meditative poems of *Les Contemplations* Hugo, too, pursues this essentially religious interrogation of the universe.

How does Rimbaud relate to this poetry of the sublime? Some of his brief pieces appear like *objets d'art* in comparison with the mountain canvases of Hölderlin and Wordsworth. But we shall see later the continuing presence of the mythic and the mystical in his nature poetry, and we earlier encountered a version of the ecstatic-sublime in "Villes I" and "Barbare." This ecstatic dimension leads us to another strand of romantic poetry, which we may characterize as *sublimated* rather than sublime, and in which imagery of reflection, communion, and marriage implies a desire for a satisfying, ultimately erotic, bond between man and world.

Marcuse's blending of Marxist and radical Freudian perspectives throws light on this kind of writing in its historical context. He describes the poetic tradition as rebelling against societal and psychic repression, as involving a nonrepressive mode of sublimation in which nature is not exploited but becomes the theater of a joyful experience of self and world—in effect constructing a new, erotic sense of reality. The argument extends from Orpheus to Schiller and the surrealists, and within it we can integrate the positions of Blake and Nietzsche, the erotic and related imagery in Shelley's *Prometheus Unbound,* the sensuousness of Keats's verse, the explicit connections between nature and sexuality in Hugo's "invitation" poems (which Rimbaud would have read), and many elements as well in Rousseau, Wordsworth, and Hölderlin.

Indeed, links between nature, the erotic, and the creation of fiction are noted by Rousseau himself, and the fusion with nature in the fifth *promenade* is inescapably read at one level as a success of sublimated and solitary sexuality. Even in the supposedly asexual Wordsworth the libidinal element is clear—witness the violation of the grove in "Nutting," the bodily giving over to an eroticized nature in the intimate company of his sister in "Lines Written in Early Spring" and "To My Sister," the recurrent reflection and grove motifs in *The Prelude,* the intensity of the child's activity throughout that poem and elsewhere, even the sense of simple physical pleasure at the opening of the work:

> Oh there is a blessing in this gentle breeze
> That blows from the green fields and from the clouds
> And from the sky: it beats against my cheek,
> And seems half conscious of the joy it gives.
>
> *(I, 1–4, 1805–06 ed.)*

The deliberately plain (natural) language of this first version enhances the immediacy of the physical experience, accessible only outside the confines of the vast city. In other writers, in Keats and Hölderlin, for example, a more gorgeous kind of writing images a more variegated awareness of nature. Hölderlin, in fact, shows a range that in many ways comes close to Rimbaud's, from the isolated Hyperion, wanting to dissolve into the all of nature, in a realm where the motion of sea and field of grain are one, to his recurrent agricultural, alpine, polar and bacchantic imagery of profusion and power, reflection, echo, wine and flowers, communion and marriage.

But if Keats, Hölderlin, Rousseau, and Wordsworth give us versions of closeness to the world, constituting a bliss of perception and existence, they also recall a somber note that we encountered in chapter 1. Keats's "half in love with easeful Death" ("Ode to a Nightingale"), the suicidal symbolism of Hölderlin's Empedokles, Rousseau's absorption in the stasis of self and world, the dead Lucy and Boy of Winander all imply an involvement with nature that transcends the human, that if successful would be a kind of death. Lucy becomes the equivalent of natural objects:

> A violet by a mossy stone
>   Half hidden from the eye!
> —Fair as a star, when only one
>   Is shining in the sky.

Lucy is even so irradiated by nature as to be physically altered: "And beauty born of murmuring sound / Shall pass into her face." Ultimately she represents the human reduced to the level literally of the thing ("She seemed a thing that could not feel / The touch of earthly years"), participating fully in nature finally through the thingness of death:

> No motion has she now, no force;
>   She neither hears nor sees;
> Rolled round in earth's diurnal course,
>   With rocks, and stones, and trees.

This is what complete identification with the objects of nature would mean. So far indeed may go the effort to rediscover, to experience, and to inhabit the natural.

All these observations are relevant to Rimbaud's poetry. The self in the face of nature ("Après le déluge," "Larme"); the natural as elemental or mythic presence (from "Soleil et chair" to "Mémoire" and "Marine"); contact with the world as erotic satisfaction (many texts, from "Sensation" to the ecstasy poems discussed in chapter 2); the turning from the civilized in a pastoral movement toward pure nature ("Fêtes de la patience"); absorption, identification, death in nature (a number of the *Derniers Vers*); consciousness and language stretching for the substantiality of things ("Fleurs," "Mystique")—this list summarizes Rimbaud's writing on nature in relation to the romantic tradition, indicating the continuing import of the natural world in his poetry. Let us now discuss these ideas in some detail.

The eroticized contact with nature is quite prevalent in Rimbaud's writing, at times so specifically personal, at the same time so mythic. There is, for example, the early "Sensation," around which Frohock builds an argument about Rimbaud as the poet of simple felicity:[7]

Par les soirs bleus d'été, j'irai dans les sentiers,
Picoté par les blés, fouler l'herbe menue:
Rêveur, j'en sentirai la fraîcheur à mes pieds.
Je laisserai le vent baigner ma tête nue.

Je ne parlerai pas, je ne penserai rien:
Mais l'amour infini me montera dans l'âme,
Et j'irai loin, bien loin, comme un bohémien,
Par la Nature,—heureux comme avec une femme.

In the blue evenings of summer, I will go along the paths,
Pricked by the wheat, crushing the short grass:
Dreamer, I will feel its freshness on my feet.
I will let the wind bathe my bare head.

> I won't speak, I'll think of nothing:
> But infinite love will mount up in my soul,
> And I will go far, very far, like a gypsy,
> Through Nature,—happy as with a woman.

Much here is late romantic cliché: nature with a capital N, the generalized "soirs bleus d'été," the Hugolian "rêveur" and "amour infini" replacing prosaic modes of experience and expression, the gypsy, the explicit transferral to nature of the sexual. Already, however, Rimbaldian emphases are present—the reiterated projection toward the future, the bodily immediacy ("Picoté par les blés, fouler l'herbe menue"), an underlying sense of freshness and liquidity: "j'en sentirai la fraîcheur à mes pieds. / Je laisserai le vent baigner ma tête nue."

These elements feed off into many lines of Rimbaud's writing. Nature, concretely or fantastically, but always sensuously, is evoked as the setting of his adolescent sexual forays in "Roman" (ellipsis is Rimbaud's):

> Les tilleuls sentent bon dans les bons soirs de juin!
> L'air est parfois si doux, qu'on ferme la paupière;
> Le vent chargé de bruits,—la ville n'est pas loin,—
> A des parfums de vigne et des parfums de bière . . .

> The lindens smell good in the good June evenings!
> Sometimes the air is so sweet, that one closes one's lids;
> The wind laden with noises,—the city isn't far,—
> Has fragrances of the vine and fragrances of beer . . .

Similarly for the escapade in "Au Cabaret-Vert": a week on the road, the appeal of food, "la fille aux tétons énormes" (the girl with the huge tits), the presence in his drink of the nature he has just traversed—"la chope immense, avec sa mousse / Que dorait un rayon de soleil arriéré" (the immense mug,

with its foam gilded by a late ray of sun). And of course nature
is central to the poetic project in "Ma Bohème":

—Mes étoiles au ciel avaient un doux frou-frou

Et je les écoutais, assis au bord des routes,
Ces bons soirs de septembre où je sentais des gouttes
De rosée à mon front, comme un vin de vigueur.

—My stars in the sky had a soft rustling

And I listened to them, sitting on roadsides,
Those good September evenings when I felt drops
Of dew on my brow, like a wine of vigor.

The stars, the open road, the physical contact with the
freshness of the evening, the wine of communion—this
scene is depicted as an intimately felt, very original re-
enactment of romantic nature motifs.

Similar images continue to structure Rimbaud's evolving poetry of erotic quest, though the road is more and
more marked by obstacles and refusals. For example, "Les
Reparties de Nina" develops a Hugolian invitation for the
sexual in nature (ellipsis is Rimbaud's):

Hein? nous irions,
Ayant de l'air plein la narine,
Aux frais rayons

Du bon matin bleu, qui vous baigne
Du vin de jour? . . .

Well? we would go,
Nostrils filled with air,
In the cool rays

> Of the good blue morning, which bathes you
> With the wine of day? . . .

The liquid, Spring nature is quickly eroticized: "On sent dans les choses ouvertes / Frémir des chairs" (One feels in open things flesh quivering). The succeeding progression of motifs is all too evident: "mousse de champagne," "chair de fleur," "ravine," "grands bois," "petite morte," "ivre du sang" (champagne foam, flesh of flower, ravine, great woods, little dead girl, drunk with blood). This eroticism is followed not only by the imagined return, filled with farm realism, but also by Nina's curt refusal of the whole invitation: "*Et mon bureau?*"—a rejection of the natural and the erotic in favor of the prudent, and of the *commercial*. In other poems on figures of refusal and repression, "Accroupissements" and "Les Assis," the natural becomes obscene and sexually grotesque. Among other ungraceful notations we find "Aux contours du cul des bavures de lumière" and "leur membre s'agace à des barbes d'épis" (Along the contours of his ass droolings of light; their members grow excited against barbs of prickly straw). Moreover, as we noted in chapter 1, poems of constraint and imagination like "Les Poètes de sept ans," "Les Sœurs de charité," and "Le Bateau ivre" reach toward a sexualized experience of nature, but in a context of threat, despondency, death, and failure. So, throughout his writing, Rimbaud continues to make equivalences between the sexual and the natural; for example, the constitution of the female by elements of nature—and art—not only in "L'Etoile a pleuré rose" but later in "Fairy." At times nature is erotically transfigured ("Barbare"), at times that enterprise fails ("Being Beauteous"). The childlike, the natural, and the erotic are always at the base of consciousness, as in "Aube" and in the beautiful opening part of "Vies": "Je me souviens des heures d'argent et de soleil vers les fleuves, la main de la campagne sur mon épaule, et de nos caresses debout dans les plaines poivrées" (I remember the hours of silver and sun near the rivers, the hand of the country on my shoulder, and our caresses standing in the spice-scented plains). But often these elements are prelude to a sense of distance and loss: "Au réveil il était midi" (On waking, it was noon); "Je suis réellement d'outre-tombe, et pas de commissions" (I am really beyond the grave, and no commissions).

So, from "Roman," "Au Cabaret-Vert," and "Ma Bohème" to "Nina," "Les Poètes de sept ans," and some of the *Illuminations,* there is a convergence of the natural and the sexual in terms that interestingly recall Marcuse on repression, libido, and imagination. Our understanding of these features can now be extended by attention to the mythic, specifically the erotically mythic, in relation to nature and to history. As Bonnefoy and Eigeldinger indicate, from "Soleil et chair" to the *Derniers Vers* a motif of sensuous union links sky and earth.[8] In "Soleil et chair" it appears in a form that is as frankly literary as it is pagan:

> Le Soleil, le foyer de tendresse et de vie,
> Verse l'amour brûlant à la terre ravie,
> Et, quand on est couché sur la vallée, on sent
> Que la terre est nubile et déborde de sang.

> The Sun, source of tenderness and life,
> Pours burning love on the ravished earth,
> And, when one is lying in the valley, one feels
> That the earth is nubile and overflowing with blood.

But in the sombre "Les Premières Communions" the sensuous union is replaced by a realistic conflict between the priest and Rimbaud's acute, peasant sense of the maternal earth:

La pierre sent toujours la terre maternelle.
Vous verrez des monceaux de ces cailloux terreux
Dans la campagne en rut qui frémit solennelle,
Portant près des blés lourds, dans les sentiers ocreux,
Ces arbrisseaux brûlés où bleuit la prunelle,
Des nœuds de mûriers noirs et de rosiers fuireux.

Tous les cent ans on rend ces granges respectables
Par un badigeon d'eau bleue et de lait caillé:
Si des mysticités grotesques sont notables
Près de la Notre-Dame ou du Saint empaillé,
Des mouches sentant bon l'auberge et les étables
Se gorgent de cire au plancher ensoleillé.

The stone still smells of the maternal earth.
You will see heaps of those earth-clotted pebbles
In the countryside in heat that shudders solemnly,
Bearing near the heavy wheat, in the ocherous paths,
Burned shrubs where the wild plum grows blue,
Knots of black mulberry and rosebushes covered with cow
    droppings.

Every hundred years they make these barns respectable
With a whitewash of bluing and clabber:
If grotesque mysticities are notable
Near Our Lady or the stuffed saint,
Flies with the good smell of inn and stables
Gorge themselves with wax on the sunlit floor.

This is very fine poetry, in which literary myth is re-enacted in historical and social terms. Here appears a centuries-old kind of life ("Tous les cent ans"), an agricultural mode of existence by now nearly extinct in the West and already threatened in Rimbaud's period. There is a great concreteness—direct address to the reader, the evocation of objects, animals, and insects through sight and smell, also sound and implicitly touch (the buzzing flies on the warm and sunlit floor). Realistically "pastoral" poetry, in "ordinary" language more real (less purified) than that of the early Wordsworth. But the attack on Christianity is still there, as well as the sexual life of nature: "la campagne en rut qui frémit solennelle." Christ, of course, wins out, at least over the innocent girl in the poem.

We earlier described "Mémoire," from the *Derniers Vers*, as another poem of defeat, centering on the nostalgia for pure and immediate contact with the world. But within it occurs a sexual conflict as well, one that unfolds in human terms: "Madame se tient trop debout dans la prairie"; "Elle, toute / froide, et noire, court! après le départ de l'homme!" (Madame holds herself too upright in the prairie; She, all cold, and black, runs! after the departure of the man!). This conflict, however, also animates the landscape:

> Plus pure qu'un louis, jaune et chaude paupière
> le souci d'eau—ta foi conjugale, ô l'Epouse!—
> au midi prompt, de son terne miroir, jalouse
> au ciel gris de chaleur la Sphère rose et chère.
> ....
>
> . . . Hélas, Lui, comme
> mille anges blancs qui se séparent sur la route,
> s'éloigne par delà la montagne! . . .
> ....
>
> Regret des bras épais et jeunes d'herbe pure!
> Or des lunes d'avril au cœur du saint lit! Joie
> des chantiers riverains à l'abandon, en proie
> aux soirs d'août qui faisaient germer ces pourritures!

Purer than a louis, yellow and warm eyelid
the marsh marigold—your conjugal faith, O Spouse!—
at prompt noon, from its dim mirror, envies
in the sky gray with heat the rose and precious sphere.

....

. . . Alas, He, like
a thousand white angels separating on the road,
goes off behind the mountain! . . .

....

Longing of thick young arms of pure grass!
Gold of April moons in the heart of the holy bed! Joy
of abandoned river boatyards, in prey
to the August evenings that bred this rottenness!

The sexual mythology is still, though sadly, present. And there is something honest about a text that centers a personal and familial crisis in an appropriate natural setting.

Sexual strife and a decaying sense of nature abandoned by productive human activity converge at the end of "Mémoire" in moving lines about the failure of energy and insight:

Jouet de cet œil d'eau morne, je n'y puis prendre,
ô canot immobile! oh! bras trop courts! ni l'une
ni l'autre fleur: ni la jaune qui m'importune,
là; ni la bleue, amie à l'eau couleur de cendre.

Ah! la poudre des saules qu'une aile secoue!
Les roses des roseaux dès longtemps dévorées!
Mon canot, toujours fixe; et sa chaîne tirée
Au fond de cet œil d'eau sans bords,—à quelle boue?

Plaything of this mournful eye of water, I can pluck,
O immobile boat! oh! arms too short! neither the one
nor the other flower: neither the yellow one that importunes me,
there; nor the blue, friend of the ash-colored water.

Ah! the dust of the willows that a wing shakes!
The roses of reeds long ago devoured!
My boat, still stationary; and its chain drawn
In the depth of this rimless eye of water,—to what mud?

The drama of mind and world, set against the background of human work, and the awareness of the mythic force of reality in counterpoint with sexual conflict finally lead to this obscuring of immediacy and transparence. Again in original and troubling form, Rimbaud's poetry pursues the difficult interconnections between individual consciousness, family, myth, nature, and the transforming and passing history of human productivity.

These elements, the theme of memory, and the underlying water imagery make "Mémoire" a worthy successor to Wordsworth's and Rousseau's meditations on mind and nature, into which industry—city, factory, and railroad[9]—of course already intruded. The *Derniers Vers* as a group constitute a pristine reflection on nature and the ambivalent attractions that it exercises—immediacy, death, mystical participation in "la lumière *nature.*" Here we may recall the retrospective interrogation of the child in "Larme"; the water, diving, and drinking motifs that link the text to Rousseau and especially to Wordsworth; the gap between the child and even the peasant community: "mauvaise enseigne d'auberge" (bad sign for an inn); "Loin des oiseaux, des troupeaux, des villageoises" (Far from birds, from flocks, from village girls). That last formula, actually the opening line of the poem, distances the child in inverse order from his community: he is removed even from the birds, certainly from domesticated animals, and how much more from sexual contact with humans. The feminine form *villageoises* evokes Rimbaud's other poems of adolescent

sexuality and Marcuse's argument about the sublimation of
the erotic in nature. "Larme" initiates such a process of
sublimation, as the water lost on virgin sands at the end and
related imagery in "Fêtes de la patience" make clear, and
does so in a close, almost oppressive, nonetheless intimate
scene that typifies one of Rimbaud's versions of nature:

> Je buvais, accroupi dans quelque bruyère
> Entourée de tendres bois de noisetiers,
> Par un brouillard d'après-midi tiède et vert.
>
> Que pouvais-je boire dans cette jeune Oise,
> Ormeaux sans voix, gazon sans fleurs, ciel couvert.

> I drank, crouched in some heather
> Surrounded by tender hazel woods
> In a soft green afternoon fog.
>
> What could I have been drinking in that young Oise,
> Voiceless elms, flowerless grass, overcast sky.

In romantic writing there is sometimes an interaction
between a sun-filled, laughing nature and more elemental,
somber, sometimes fearsome or negative experiences. We
earlier discussed the myth and experience of sun and
warmth in Rimbaud; here we see another mode, intimate,
dense, enigmatic. It recalls the rough and immobile scene
at the end of Part IV of "Enfance": "Les sentiers sont
âpres. Les monticules se couvrent de genêts. L'air est immobile. Que les oiseaux et les sources sont loin!" (The
paths are rough. The knolls are covered with broom. The
air is immobile. How far away are the birds and the
springs!). It also recalls a comparable epiphany soured by
irony in one of the "Phrases":

Une matinée couverte, en Juillet. Un goût de cendres
vole dans l'air;—une odeur de bois suant dans l'âtre,—les
fleurs rouies,—le saccage des promenades,—la bruine des
canaux par les champs—pourquoi pas déjà les joujoux et
l'encens?

An overcast morning, in July. A taste of ashes flies in
the air;—a smell of wood sweating in the hearth,—the
retted flowers,—the devastation of the paths,—the
drizzle of canals in the fields—why not already toys and
incense?

Here language admirably evokes a particular kind of experience of nature, permeated by the rural activity of man:
time of day, season, weather, taste-contact with the air,
odor, vision, the touch of sodden ground and flowers—"les
fleurs rouies,—le saccage des promenades." This language
is remarkable for its sensuous immediacy, but the liquidity
encountered from "Sensation" on has become both more
realistic and more negative. In part this change is a factor
of weather, in part of the interaction of man and nature—
the fields and canals suggest agriculture and commerce,
and "rouies" is a technical term from the textile industry.
An opposite movement—the cold and cleansing wind in
the medievally religious and crow-filled "La Rivière de
Cassis" and "Les Corbeaux"—thus bespeaks a recurrent
need for purification, purification of the natural, elimina-
tion perhaps of the human.

From "Sensation" to "Après le déluge," by the interme-
diary of these other texts, emerges an intimate sense of the
natural scene, shadowed by man's community and economic activity, and an overriding desire for immediacy,
transparence, purity. "Comédie de la soif" and "Bannières
de mai," the first of the "Fêtes de la patience," pursue this

desire, illustrating its beauty and its menace. These sun-filled and death-filled poems reveal a more than pastoral urge, an impulse to transcend not only mankind but also nature and even life.

"Comédie de la soif" presents this impulse in supremely musical form and yet with another evocation of concrete, historical setting. The family in the opening part images again the rural mode of existence—in contact with the elements (moon, sun, water) and inhabiting and deriving sustenance from the natural:

> Nos vins secs avaient du cœur!
>
> ....
>
> Vois le courant du fossé
> Autour du château mouillé.
> Descendons en nos celliers;
> Après, le cidre et le lait.
>
> ....
>
> Tiens, prends
> Les liqueurs dans nos armoires;
> Le Thé, le Café, si rares,
> Frémissent dans les bouilloires.

> Our dry wines had heart!
>
> ....
>
> See the current in the moat
> Around the wet castle.
> Let's go down into our cellars;
> After, cider and milk.
>
> ....
>
> Here, take
> The liquors from our armoires;
> Tea, Coffee, so rare,
> Simmer in the kettles.

Part of the satisfaction, too, comes from a mode of life that sees itself as participating in the cycle of life and death: "—Vois les images, les fleurs. / Nous rentrons du cimetière" (See the holy cards, the flowers. We've just come back from the cemetery). Unquestionably such an existence, despite the naive arrogance of the speakers, is appealing; but the speaker of the poem is attracted only to that part of it that concerns death: "Mourir aux fleuves barbares"; "Aller où boivent les vaches"; "Ah! tarir toutes les urnes!" (Die in the barbarous rivers; Go where the cows drink; Ah! drain all the urns!).

In the three succeeding parts, this suicidal significance of the recurrent water imagery is developed in ways that are apt both for the autobiographical-historical and for the underlying spirituality of the poem. The second, "L'Esprit," evokes water as symbol of myth, imagination, literature; the third, "Les Amis," represents the attraction of actual drunkenness; the fourth, "Le Pauvre Songe," sets out the conventional parameters of a lifetime of effort and patience in our (and in particular the French) world:

> Peut-être un Soir m'attend
> Où je boirai tranquille
> En quelque vieille Ville,
>
> ....
>
> Si j'ai jamais quelque or,
> Choisirai-je le Nord
> Ou le Pays des Vignes?

> Perhaps an Evening awaits me
> When I will drink peacefully
> In some old City,
>
> ....

> If I ever have some gold,
> Will I choose the North
> Or the Region of Vines?

The life of the imagination, the attraction of inebriation, work and retirement are shown to be encoded in the
symbolism of drinking in human life, within a specifically
French geography; but such options are insufficient for the
absoluteness of Rimbaud's quest:

> Chansonnier, ta filleule
>   C'est ma soif si folle
> Hydre intime sans gueules
>   Qui mine et désole.
>
> ....
>
> J'aime autant, mieux, même,
> Pourrir dans l'étang,
> Sous l'affreuse crème,
> Près des bois flottants.
>
> ....
>
> —Ah! songer est indigne
>
> Puisque c'est pure perte!
> Et si je redeviens
> Le voyageur ancien,
> Jamais l'auberge verte
> Ne peut bien m'être ouverte.

> Songster, your goddaughter
>   Is my thirst so wild
> Intimate mawless hydra
>   That mines and desolates.
>
> ....
>
> I like as much, more, even,
> To rot in the pond,

Under the horrible cream,
Near the floating woods.

. . . .

—Ah! to dream is shameful

Since it's pure loss!
And if I become again
The ancient voyager,
Never will the green inn
Be able to be open to me.

The all-devouring, intimate thirst shrivels everything before it; no adequate object for it is found in all the universe
of human imagination, companionship, work, or shelter.
Only death remains, figured as identification with nature,
at first horribly physical and concrete ("Pourrir dans
l'étang, / Sous l'affreuse crème"), then in the "Conclusion"
ennobled as community and utter immersion in the natural
(ellipsis is Rimbaud's):

Les pigeons qui tremblent dans la prairie,
Le gibier, qui court et qui voit la nuit,
Les bêtes des eaux, la bête asservie,
Les derniers papillons! . . . ont soif aussi.

Mais fondre où fond ce nuage sans guide,
—Oh! favorisé de ce qui est frais!
Expirer en ces violettes humides
Dont les aurores chargent ces forêts?

The pigeons that tremble in the prairie,
The game, which runs and which sees at night,
The water animals, the animal enslaved,
The last butterflies! . . . are thirsty too.

> But to melt where this guideless cloud melts,
> —Oh! favored by what is cool!
> Expire in these damp violets
> Left by dawn in these forests?

Animal nature in fear of, enslaved by mankind in the rural setting; then, beyond the animal, the insect and vegetal world, melting finally in the directly felt liquidity of reality. Frohock is right to link such writing to the elusive Shakespearean songs, the best of German and English romanticism, and the subtle nature poetry of Emily Dickinson. The connection with the Rousseau of the *Rêveries* and Wordsworth's Lucy ("A violet by a mossy stone / Half hidden from the eye!") could also be stressed. This is superb late romantic nature poetry carried to its extreme limit within a sharply noted context of human society and nature.

The symbolism of thirst and hunger is pursued in others of the *Derniers Vers*—with overtones of sacrificial death in the conclusion of "Le loup criait," and earlier in that poem and throughout "Fêtes de la faim" with the intention of directly consuming the animal, vegetable, and inanimate world:

> Le loup criait sous les feuilles
> En crachant les belles plumes
> De son repas de volailles:
> Comme lui je me consume.
>
> Les salades, les fruits
> N'attendent que la cueillette;
> Mais l'araignée de la haie
> Ne mange que des violettes.
>
> ("*Le loup criait*")

The wolf cried out under the leaves
Spitting the beautiful feathers
Of his meal of fowl:
Like him I am consuming myself.

Lettuce, fruit
Await only to be picked;
But the spider in the hedge
Eats only violets.

Si j'ai du *goût,* ce n'est guères
Que pour la terre et les pierres.
Dinn! dinn! dinn! dinn! Mangeons l'air,
Le roc, les charbons, le fer.

....
Mangez
            Les cailloux qu'un pauvre brise,
            Les vieilles pierres d'église,
            Les galets, fils des déluges,
            Pains couchés aux vallées grises!

If I have any *taste,* it is hardly
For anything but earth and stones.
Dinn! dinn! dinn! dinn! Let's eat air,
Rock, coal, iron.

....
Eat
            The stones a poor man breaks,
            The old stones of churches,
            Shingle stones, sons of the floods,
            Loaves lying in the gray valleys!

("*Fêtes de la faim*")

Even here Rimbaud cannot prevent himself from suggesting a context of myth, religion, nourishment, work, and

poverty. "Après le déluge" and other politically pointed texts are in the background. But the major impulse is beyond the human and societal to the natural—and that in the most extreme way. *Eating the natural,* not in the human terms of the family in "Soif," but uncooked, unprepared; and eating it all, even the inanimate, the mineral, the geological (another evident sense of "déluges"). Wordsworth at least invented a character to represent this desire to become a thing like nature's rocks and stones and trees. Rimbaud speaks more extremely, in the first person, of the desire to extinguish human existence and to merge entirely with the ageless processes of the natural.

The aspiration to nature in "Bannières de mai," the first of the "Fêtes de la patience," is less brutal but just as troubling:

> Aux branches claires des tilleuls
> Meurt un maladif hallali.
> Mais des chansons spirituelles
> Voltigent parmi les groseilles.
> Que notre sang rie en nos veines,
> Voici s'enchevêtrer les vignes.
> Le ciel est joli comme un ange.
> L'azur et l'onde communient.
> Je sors. Si un rayon me blesse
> Je succomberai sur la mousse.
>
> Qu'on patiente et qu'on s'ennuie
> C'est trop simple. Fi de mes peines.
> Je veux que l'été dramatique
> Me lie à son char de fortune.
> Que par toi beaucoup, ô Nature,
> —Ah moins seul et moins nul!—je meure.
> Au lieu que les Bergers, c'est drôle,
> Meurent à peu près par le monde.

Je veux bien que les saisons m'usent.
A toi, Nature, je me rends;
Et ma faim et toute ma soif.
Et, s'il te plaît, nourris, abreuve.
Rien de rien ne m'illusionne;
C'est rire aux parents, qu'au soleil,
Mais moi je ne veux rire à rien;
Et libre soit cette infortune.

In the clear branches of the lindens
Dies a sickly hunting call.
But spiritual songs
Flutter among the currants.
Let our blood laugh in our veins,
Here the vines entangle themselves.
The sky is pretty as an angel.
The azure and the wave commune.
I go out. If a ray wounds me
I'll succumb on the moss.

That one is patient and that one is bored
Is too simple. Fie on my cares.
I want dramatic summer
To bind me to its chariot of fortune.
May through you alone, O Nature,
—Ah less alone and less worthless!—I die.
Whereas Shepherds, it's odd,
Die more or less in the world.

I am completely willing for the seasons to consume me.
To you, Nature, I give myself;
And my hunger and all my thirst.
And, if you will, nourish, give drink.
Nothing at all gives me illusions;
It's laughing at parents, as at the sun,
But me I wish to laugh at nothing;
And may this misfortune be free.

Sun-filled and somber indeed. The poem opens with the death of the human influence, the suppression of the last romantic convention of man in nature, the sound of the distant, and now "sickly," hunting horn. In the second stanza the pastoral, another literary metaphor for human contact with the natural, goes by the board, as Rimbaud musingly realizes that shepherds with a capital letter hardly represent, since the times of Virgil, much of a distancing from the human world. And in the last stanza the hearty relatives from "Comédie de la soif," still laughing in the sun, are again rejected.[10] No real or conventional image of man's life in the environment of the earth is to be retained.

Rimbaud, however, continues to portray nature as having many of the rich qualities attributed to it in religious and romantic tradition. Movement becomes spiritual sound ("des chansons spirituelles / Voltigent"); plant and human blood are joined in a relationship of consanguinity that re-enacts the blood, water, sap, and wine motifs so characteristic of Wordsworth and Hölderlin and present in Rimbaud as early as "Soleil et chair" and "Tête de faune." Even the syntax of simple juxtaposed parallelism and immediacy imitates this entanglement of inner and outer, nature and man: "Que notre sang rie en nos veines, / Voici s'enchevêtrer les vignes." And reflection, so extensively used in romantic literature as an image of unified nature, by an extreme simplification here becomes communion: "L'azur et l'onde communient."

At this point the speaker calls attention to himself for the first time, by the simplest of actions of going outside into the natural scene: "Je sors. Si un rayon me blesse / Je succomberai sur la mousse." In this clear and light-filled text ("branches claires des tilleuls"), this May-poem, a touch of lightness and humor introduces the serious themes of vulnerability, wounding, and death. The second and third stanzas indicate how absolute is this vulnerability. The speaker gives himself up, effort and patience, hunger and thirst, activity and passivity, life and death, to the *perhaps* beneficient action of nature, and does so unconditionally: "Je veux que l'été dramatique / Me lie à son char de fortune"; "Je veux bien que les saisons m'usent. / A toi, Nature, je me rends"; "Et, s'il te plaît, nourris, abreuve. / Rien de rien ne m'illusionne"; "Et libre soit cette infortune." Note the verb *rends,* which implies a myth of separation from nature, the human as alienated from the universe, and the wish to transcend that alienation. And again we encounter a death wish born of a solitude for which human society offers no assuagement: "Que par toi beaucoup, ô Nature, / —Ah moins seul et moins nul!—je meure."

In the succeeding poems of the cycle ordinary nature is transcended ("Chanson de la plus haute tour"), and a purified essence of the natural is *re*discovered:

> Elle est retrouvée.
> Quoi?—L'Eternité.
> C'est la mer allée
> Avec le soleil.
>
> *("L'Eternité")*

> It is rediscovered.
> What?—Eternity.
> It is the sea gone
> With the sun.

Here the reflection motif becomes a symbol for eternity. This mysticism, which we discussed in chapter 2, involves a radically simplified, communal, and paradisal relationship with nature: "Ce n'est qu'onde, flore, / Et c'est ta famille!"; "De quel Age es-tu, / Nature princière?" ("Age d'or": It's only wave, flora, and it's your family!; Of what Age are you, princely Nature?). For the moment the sense of solitude has been overcome and the threat of death has receded.

But, in "Entends comme brame," the mystic impulse is shown not to have escaped the conditions of mortality.[11] There, in another oppressive Spring landscape, we are told that in the rows of pea-plants we discover the saints still straining toward the heavens (ellipses are Rimbaud's):

Entends comme brame
près des acacias
en avril la rame
viride du pois!

Dans sa vapeur nette,
vers Phœbé! tu vois
s'agiter la tête
de saints d'autrefois . . .

Loin des claires meules
des caps, des beaux toits,
ces chers Anciens veulent
ce philtre sournois . . .

Or ni fériale
ni astrale! n'est
la brume qu'exhale
ce nocturne effet.

Néanmoins ils restent,
—Sicile, Allemagne,
dans ce brouillard triste
et blêmi, justement!

Hear how the green
sticks of peas
bellow in April
near the acacias!

In their sharp vapor,
toward Phoebe! you see
the heads of saints of old
moving about . . .

Far from bright haystacks
on capes, from lovely roofs,
these dear Ancients want
this sly philter . . .

Now neither ferial
nor astral! is
the mist exhaled
by this nocturnal effect.

Nonetheless they remain,
—Sicily, Germany,
in this sad and pale
fog, precisely!

The saints of old (Italian and German religious and mystical traditions) no longer exist in the sunlit landscape inhabited by mankind; they have not achieved erotic union with
the world ("philtre sournois"); their orthodox and occult
methods ("ni fériale / ni astrale") have not led to spiritual
transcendence or fusion with "la lumière *nature*." They are
simply, quite literally ("justement") dead, and the cover-
ing, foggy landscape closes in with utter finality.

    The *Derniers Vers* and a few related texts thus represent a
kind of superpastoral poetry, moving from the human-
historical-societal setting toward identification with the es-

sence of the natural, the natural for humans finally being identified with death. We now need to relate this impulse to existence in the natural with the questions of consciousness, vision, and language raised earlier. Paul De Man observes a tendency, expressed in Hölderlin's "Brod und Wein," for poetic language to aspire to the condition of a natural thing, not invented to represent something but possessing being in its own right.[12] As an image of this aspiration, to Hölderlin's words arising like flowers and Coleridge's fusion of vision and language in the preface to "Kubla Khan," we might add Wordsworth's Lucy, in death attaining "the calm / Of mute insensate things." Can consciousness, or language, ever attain such a natural state? Perhaps this question is another way of asking whether post-structuralist criticism is justified in its almost exclusively nonrepresentational approach to literature. Our earlier discussion of "Fleurs" broached this question; now we may carry the discussion further by studying two poems in the *Illuminations,* "Marine" and "Mystique." These poems emphasize the artificial and the natural aspects of the universe in which we live. For this reason it is important to see them together:

Marine

Les chars d'argent et de cuivre—
Les proues d'acier et d'argent—
Battent l'écume,—
Soulèvent les souches des ronces.
Les courants de la lande,
Et les ornières immenses du reflux,
Filent circulairement vers l'est,
Vers les piliers de la forêt,—
Vers les fûts de la jetée,
Dont l'angle est heurté par des tourbillons de lumière.

Seascape

The chariots of silver and copper—
The prows of steel and silver—
Beat the foam,—
Uproot the stumps of bramble.
The currents of the heath,
And the immense ruts of the ebb tide,
Move off circularly toward the east,
Toward the pillars of the forest,—
Toward the shafts of the pier,
Whose angle is struck by whirlwinds of light.

Mystique

Sur la pente du talus les anges tournent leurs robes de
laine dans les herbages d'acier et d'émeraude.

Des prés de flammes bondissent jusqu'au sommet du
mamelon. A gauche le terreau de l'arête est piétiné par
tous les homicides et toutes les batailles, et tous les
bruits désastreux filent leur courbe. Derrière l'arête de
droite la ligne des orients, des progrès.

Et tandis que la bande en haut du tableau est formée
de la rumeur tournante et bondissante des conques des
mers et des nuits humaines,

La douceur fleurie des étoiles et du ciel et du reste
descend en face du talus, comme un panier,—contre
notre face, et fait l'abîme fleurant et bleu là-dessous.

Mystic

On the slopes of the bank the angels turn their woolen
dresses in the steel and emerald pastures.

Meadows of flame leap up to the summit of the knoll.
On the left the earth of the ridge is trampled by all the
murderers and all the battles, and all the disastrous
sounds spin out their curve. Behind the ridge at the
right the line of orients, of progress.

And while the band at the top of the picture is formed
by the turning and bounding murmur of sea conches and
of human nights,
The flowering sweetness of the stars and of the sky and
of the rest comes down opposite the bank, like a
basket,—close against our face, and makes the abyss
flowering and blue below.

There are many rich resemblances and oppositions in
these two texts, much matter for reflection in the context
of romantic nature poetry. First, we know that in both we
are dealing with *poems,* with the artifice of poetic language.
Notwithstanding Wordsworth's early view of language as
derived from nature and his practice of writing nature poems
long after the actual experience,[13] whatever we derive from
these poems comes from our interaction with them
through a shared language, not from something that supposedly pre-existed them and that they imitate. Nonetheless, in their *convention* of describing some scene, they are
poems of vision, proposing a felicitous realm of imaginative perception rather than the phantasm of fusion with
nature that we have just discussed. To recognize the importance of such vision, we need to recall the appeal in
romantic poetry to a heightened acuteness of perception in
the reader, Rimbaud's lament on man's benighted condition in "Soleil et chair": "Misère! Maintenant il dit: Je sais
les choses, / Et va, les yeux fermés et les oreilles closes"
(Misery! Now he says: I comprehend things, and goes off,
his eyes closed and his ears closed), and his almost Wordsworthian conjunction of childhood, nature, and vision in
"Guerre": "Enfant, certains ciels ont affiné mon optique"
(As a child, certain skies sharpened my optic). To childhood, nature, and vision, we must also add *art,* for "ciels"
is an artist's word, normally describing skies as represented

in a painting. Can the highly artificial, the self-consciously crafted, make us *see,* see with something of the intensity of the child in nature? Yes, I would argue, on the evidence of "Marine" and "Mystique."

In "Marine," for example, in response to Rimbaud's language, we are able to imagine (Sartre's formula, "directed creation," is apt here) a vast natural scene: earth, sea, vegetation, moor, tide, horizon, forest, and—in a culmination of ascension, energy, and fusion—swirling clouds of pure light. Note some familiar and important elements of content here. This is a vision of nature; although man and his transforming activities are present, the vastness of nature dwarfs agriculture and commerce. In fact, the poem proposes a romantic, almost mystical apprehension of the immensity and elemental reality of the earth, animated by a single vast movement that combines the linear and the cyclical ("Filent circulairement vers l'est"), a movement which from the various elements and substances seems to produce at the end a simplified, ultimate world. We recall the romantic sense of the elemental liquid reality, Rimbaud's extensions of the reflection motif in "Fêtes de la patience," the vision of natural totality pursued by Rousseau in the *Rêveries* and by Hölderlin in *Hyperion* and represented by Wordsworth's child-man intuition of the oneness of all.

"Marine," therefore, partakes of the tradition of romantic poetry. But we must note as well its artistry, indeed its artificiality. We imagine a scene such as I described because the text names objects and features of a landscape and because it directs our eye, in imagination, eastward and upward. Much of this description, however, is unnatural by ordinary conventions. For example, "chars" does not normally describe farming equipment; the opening metallic imagery sounds a stylizing, uranian note; the

isolating synecdoche of "proues" contrasts with the fusion
of different objects and activities in the single expression
"Battent l'écume"; "courants," "ornières," "piliers," and
"fûts" leap out as unifying land and sea and also the
natural and man-made, until in that final, arbitrarily and
perfectly longer line everything dissolves in light. This is
not an ordinary natural description of the world or of
man's place in it. Instead a series of arbitrary tactics
coheres in an evocation that is elemental, unified,
mythic-mystical, and yet without any explicitly religious
overtones. In this sense "Marine" is a kind of desacralized
"thing" in its own right, a "concrete imaginary object,"
to use another of Sartre's phrases. And again, it is an
object that affords a special joy in the vision of the universe; through it we rediscover land and sea and sky and
the immense dynamism of all. To return to Abrams's
vocabulary, "Marine" is idealist, millenial, and realist all
at once.

I am arguing here for the integration of a post-Baudelairean, nonmimetic poetics into our life within the natural and
man-made world, for the discovery of nature through artifice. The argument holds as well for "Mystique," despite its
more unnatural convention. As in "Marine," this convention is abundantly perceptual, indeed visual, as the initially
impersonal speaker points to a number of spatially organized features that we are supposed to see: the slopes, the
angels, the pastures, the knoll, and so forth. According to
the speaker we are thus looking at something, but this
something is more clearly transnatural than the vista in
"Marine." Already the first two paragraphs mix the natural
("herbages," "mamelon," "terreau"), a series of terms capable of evoking both natural and man-made structures
("pente," "talus," "arête"), the supernatural and symbolic
("anges," "des prés de flammes," "la ligne des orients, des

progrès"), and the frankly artificial ("herbages d'acier et d'émeraude").

The normal conventions of perception are thus subverted, as are simple representational notions, even for the reader who gratefully seizes upon "tableau" at the beginning of the third paragraph. One could view the first two paragraphs as describing a painting, but according to paragraph three the band at the top of the picture is formed by "la rumeur tournante et bondissante des conques des mers et des nuits humaines"—not by a visible frame but by an extremely evocative and beautiful conflation of sound, movement, and human emotion.

This subversion of the visual is accompanied by a syntactic change. The short, simple, denotative, and locating structures of the first two paragraphs are followed by a single complex sentence that overflows from the third to the fourth paragraph and gives the scene a more markedly vertical movement, a sense of simultaneity and reciprocal dynamism, and a strongly human and personal presence:

> Et tandis que la bande en haut du tableau est formée de la rumeur tournante et bondissante des conques des mers et des nuits humaines,
> La douceur fleurie des étoiles et du ciel et du reste descend en face du talus, comme un panier,—contre notre face, et fait l'abîme fleurant et bleu là-dessous.

Here the unity of structure seems to be guaranteed by the reappearance of "talus," by the verb *bondir,* and by the closing spatial indication ("là-dessous"). But the artificial, supernatural, geometric, and abstract emphases of the opening paragraphs are relegated to the background ("et du reste"!), replaced by a sense of cosmic yet intimate and natural sweetness: "la douceur fleurie des étoiles et du ciel." We recognize an age-old religious and poetic topos, the parallelism of stars and flowers, which has miraculously precipitated out of the complications of the opening of the poem. It has been brought down to our level, literally, put right before our eyes, like an object of everyday domestic use ("descend en face du talus, comme un panier,—contre notre face"). And something equally miraculous occurs as a result in the speaker's estimate—and also ours (the plural "notre")—of the human condition below. It is an "abîme," but one that has been made "fleurant." Truly mystic wisdom, formulated initially in artificial terms, irradiating subsequently the human experience of the universe. The self-conscious poetic artifact, subverting the conventions of mimesis, constituting itself as a transnatural (concrete and imaginative) object, rivaling the things of nature, in the end is humanized, re-enacting the essential function of nature poetry in the religious and romantic tradition. Quite simply, "Mystique" opens our imaginations to the mystery and intimacy and beauty of the world.

The Senses of the City

So the most self-conscious artistry revalorizes our perception of nature. The dialectic of consciousness and world, the erotic transactions of the individual and the forces of nature, the natural as immediacy and death—in the end these are gathered up, transcended, redeemed by a poem. Throughout Rimbaud's work, however, we see an inevitable counterpointing of this mythic-spiritual-poetic quest with an acute sense of the organization of human family, society, and productivity. In "Marine" this transforming activity appears in a distanced and stylized perspective; in

"Mystique" the human is schematized into the abstract lines of disaster and progress. But the economic and social are unavoidably linked to issues of nature and imagination. Agriculture, the village, rural industry, and commerce were on the fringes of consciousness throughout our reading of this nature poetry. Now we must confront, as Rimbaud did, the reality of the industrial city.

That city is overwhelmingly present in his work, in its splendor and energy, its evil and oppression, as it was in the past, as it is now, and apparently as it will continue in ever-more gigantic forms. In "Après le déluge," we know, it is virtually identified with the human and the historical. And appropriately so, since the city always represents both economic realities (commerce, industry, capital, colonialism) and also spiritual aspirations (divinity, utopia, art and architecture in museum and monument). The city—classical, medieval, or modern—is an image of the society that engenders it. Thus, the city is a social and historical museum; the urban is marked by recurrent impulses and therefore by decipherable forms: the accumulation of population, goods, means of production, and also of consciousness, memory, creativity; the interaction of the artificial and the natural, with the latter progressively transformed; monumentality, gigantism, horizontal and vertical concentration in a form of totality that is ever in danger of disintegration. The city as history and form of human existence exercises a continuing fascination.[14] And not least—as theme, structure, history—in a mind-boggling series of *Illuminations*.

Let us rapidly trace these elements before exploring the meanings of Rimbaud's city poems in relation to romantic literature. The range of historical and geographic reference to the urban in the prose poems is extremely wide, as is well known. We earlier noted the oppressive industrial city in "Ouvriers," and there are similar glimpses in the cynical "Ville" and in the sinister smoke of "Métropolitain." But, in accord with the urban's typical temporal and spatial magnifications, when we are in one city in a Rimbaud poem, we are in many others as well. If the seas of Ossian at the opening of "Métropolitain" suggest the geography of the British Isles, the fantasmagoric vision of that text quickly has us in the Holy Land ("Samarie") and finally at the pole. The shanties on the bridges in "Les Ponts" have caused literal-minded critics to leap back in time, to an eighteenth-century or earlier London, and the cathedral near the Alps in "Après le déluge" similarly suggests Milan—which is not inappropriate, since Milan was one of the first urban agglomerations to exceed the limits of the medieval city, attaining a population of 200,000 by 1288. "Promontoire" alludes to Greece, Japan, Asia, Italy, and America; mentions Carthage, Venice, Scarborough, and Brooklyn; and references to Etnas and parks with Japanese trees suggest Syracuse and Tokyo as well. This poem looks like a compendium of the city throughout world history, and accordingly emphasizes leading urban themes: the subversion of the natural by the architectural (the promontory being equated with villa, hotel, city), the coexistence of past and present, and the paradoxical but accurate copresence of religion and war: "Des fanums qu'éclaire la rentrée des théories, d'immenses vues de la défense des côtes modernes" (Temples lighted by the return of processions, immense views of the defense of modern coasts).

"Villes I" and "Villes II" carry forward this poetic accumulation and concentration of the urban, again with attention to typical themes and structures. We earlier discussed the transformations of space-time in the first of these. As an ecstatic city text it exemplifies the tendency to commu-

nity, to festival, to *love;* and its bacchantic allusions remind us that Greek ecstatic religions were in part a protest
against the restrictions of the urban, an effort to return to
a more intense mode of existence. But in Rimbaud's poem
that antiurban movement becomes a pretext to redefine the
city as integration with the natural, so that people, mountains, volcanoes, cities, and the most artificial forms of
human creativity all cohere within the energy of the real.
Within this dynamism the primary dimension is that of
the vertical: "Sur les plates-formes au milieu des gouffres
les Rolands sonnent leur bravoure. Sur les passerelles de
l'abîme" (On the platforms in the middle of the chasms
the Rolands sound their bravura. On the footbridges over
the abyss). But those Rolands and the earlier "Alleghanys"
and "Libans" and, later, Bagdad, invoke the city throughout geographic space and historical time as well. Among
medieval accents, I am especially intrigued by the "corporations de chanteurs géants" (guilds of giant singers), a
communal note surrealistically recalling the associative
quality of the medieval city, with its guilds and its corresponding social and economic productiveness.

While "Villes I" is generally more archaic than modern,
"Villes II" moves toward the future, in a massive extension
of oppressively modern structures. To locate the future
city, it sketches a history of the urban: allusions to acropo-
lises, buildings in London and Paris, the Bible, northern
Europe, India. It represents the postmodern city as a barbarous degradation of earlier architecture: "L'Acropole officielle outre les conceptions de la barbarie moderne les plus
colossales. . . . On a reproduit dans un goût d'énormité
singulier toutes les merveilles classiques de l'architecture"
(The official Acropolis exceeds the most colossal conceptions of modern barbarity. All the classical marvels of architecture have been reproduced with a singular taste for

enormity). Here the gigantism inherent in the urban is out of control, and in ways that are historically resonant. The emphasis on power, authority, bureaucracy, ostentation, the magnificence of the state that characterizes baroque-modern city planning, finds an echo in formulations like "L'Acropole officielle," "l'éclat impérial des bâtisses" (the imperial splendor of the buildings), "Un Nabuchodonosor norwégien a fait construire les escaliers des ministères" (A Norwegian Nebuchadnezzar had the staircases of the ministries built). Indeed, "Villes II" begins with the official quarter, the seat of governmental power, whose cold magnificence produces a reaction of fear: "les subalternes que j'ai pu voir sont déjà plus fiers que des ***, et j'ai tremblé à l'aspect des gardiens de colosses et officiers de constructions" (the subordinates I was able to see are already haughtier than ***, and I trembled at the appearance of the guards of colossi and building officials).

In other historically apt ways "Villes II" implies an urban mode of grotesque proportions. First, there is the subordination of nature: "Les parcs représentent la nature primitive travaillée par un art superbe" (The parks represent primitive nature worked over by a superb art). There is also something like the expulsion of the working classes to the periphery of cities, such as occurred in Paris in the nineteenth century: "Par le groupement des bâtiments en squares, cours et terrasses fermées, on a évincé les cochers" (By the grouping of buildings in squares, courts, and closed terraces, they have ousted the cab-drivers). Such elements recur at the end of the poem, with surreal, artificial, and disoriented notes. For in the strangely elegant suburb, we finally encounter the radically reduced "élément démocratique" (only several hundred souls!—these cities are almost uninhabited) in a futuristic re-enactment of the tension between city and nature:

Là encore les maisons ne se suivent pas; le faubourg se
perd bizarrement dans la campagne, le "Comté" qui rem-
plit l'occident éternel des forêts et des plantations prodi-
gieuses où les gentilshommes sauvages chassent leurs
chroniques sous la lumière qu'on a créée.

There too the houses do not follow each other; the suburb loses itself strangely in the country, the "County"
that fills the eternal occident of forests and prodigious
plantations where the savage gentlemen hunt their chron-
icles under the light that has been created.

This conclusion, like "Après le déluge," suggests the fron-
tier of the worldwide exploitation and urbanization of nature: immense forests still exist but are invaded by prodigious plantations; a pioneer nobility tries to overcome its
savagery, to discover or create an appropriate genealogy
("chassent leurs chroniques"); but artificiality and technol-
ogy ("la lumière qu'on a créée") predominate.

Note as well the reiterated sense of puzzlement and disorientation: "Là encore les maisons ne se suivent pas; le
faubourg se perd bizarrement dans la campagne." Throughout, in fact, the speaker attempts to give a systematic account of these cities, following typical urban structure (areas
and quarters, horizontal and vertical axes):

Sur quelques points des passerelles . . . j'ai cru pouvoir
juger la profondeur de la ville!
[On some points of the footbridges I thought I could
estimate the city's depth!]

. . .

quels sont les niveaux des autres quartiers sur ou sous
l'acropole?
[what are the levels of the other quarters above or below
the acropolis?]

. . .

Le quartier commerçant. . . . l'idée de chercher des
théâtres
[The commercial district. . . . the idea of looking for
theaters]

But he is unable finally to penetrate and comprehend all
that he sees:

C'est le prodige dont je n'ai pu me rendre compte.
[That's the marvel I couldn't figure out.]

. . .

Pour l'étranger de notre temps la reconnaissance est impossible.
[For the foreigner of our time, recognition is impossible.]

. . .

la loi doit être tellement étrange, que je renonce à me
faire une idée des aventuriers d'ici
[the law must be so strange, that I renounce the idea of
imagining what adventurers are like here]

Later I will suggest a different purpose for this uncomprehending speaker. But on one level, at least, he implies an
urban form in which the human is lost.

Remember that Greek and medieval cities remained
small, and up through the Renaissance, with its vertically
dominated city plans, city dwellers attempted to attain a
perspective from which the urban would appear as the
meaningful totality of human existence. Such views from
above, we shall see, persist in nineteenth-century literature. More and more, however—as in "Villes II"—, the
vast, suprahuman sprawl of the modern city destroys the
perspective, and the importance, of the human. "Villes II"
thus seems to be a homology of the human situation in the
modern city; and in its attention to horizontal and vertical
dimensions, as in its enumeration of quarters and areas,
the poem itself embodies a kind of urban literary form.

"Métropolitain," too, leads us through a sequence of natural environment, city, suburb, and countryside before exploding off toward the pole. And if its title refers in part to a subway system, the poem also imitates the characteristic movement within the three-dimensional modern urban space—with its subways, elevators, and other means of transportation. Such movement, then, is another way in which Rimbaud's art in the *Illuminations* astonishingly evokes the phenomenon of the urban—its history, forms, and implications for human existence.

So the city is amply inscribed in Rimbaud's prose poems. We must now consider what kinds of meanings he specifically develops and their relation to the city in other nineteenth-century poetry. Here it is useful to recall that the city has always figured man's society (the social, the political, the economic), religion (divinity, communal aspirations, the mystic, ecstatic, and utopian), and art (the ability to reform and transcend the natural). Under the impact of the industrial city these three themes become enormously magnified in literature.

Under the heading of "society" (understood in its most elemental sense of the quality and significance of human existence in the natural and man-made world), we can evoke in somewhat greater detail the sustained and negative confrontation between literature and the industrial city. Rousseau, Blake, Wordsworth, Lamartine, Vigny in "La Maison du berger," Hugo in numerous texts but most powerfully perhaps in "Melancholia," and Baudelaire in many of the "Tableaux parisiens" and some of the *Spleen de Paris:* all testify to an experience of the urban as suffering, oppression, and the destruction of essential human values—childhood, innocence, freedom, creativity. They emphasize the city's oppressive physical environment, its suppression of the natural, its exploitation and corruption of spontaneity.

Recall here Rousseau and Emile contemplating Paris, Hugo's and Blake's orphans and chimney sweeps, Baudelaire's swan, the "lovely Boy" corrupted by London in Book VII of Wordsworth's *Prelude*. Baudelaire's "A une passante" and Wordsworth's description of the St. Bartholomew Day Fair depict the destruction of human relationship and community, and Baudelaire's "Mademoiselle Bistouri" and "Les Petites Vieilles" portray the reduction of the human to the grotesque. In their work, as in Marx's and Engels's, the modern city emerges as a social system in which money, power, church, and state are implicated, and in which enormous numbers of human beings encounter psychic disintegration, the dissolution of the family, vice, dehumanizing labor, terrible deprivation. Think of Wordsworth's glimpse of the sickly child and his working father—the "Artificer"—amid the roar of London (*Prelude,* VII, 594 ff.). Other powerful examples include Hugo's indignation in "Melancholia" against injustice and exploitation, starvation, child labor, and prostitution; Blake's enumeration in "London" of chartered commerce, psychic oppression, prostitution, and the disintegration of the family and political and religious responsibility; Baudelaire's encounter with vice and the struggle for existence in "Le Crépuscule du soir," a struggle not unconnected with the bourgeois world of the "gens d'affaire" (business people) which this text explicitly evokes, and in which thousands live a barely human existence: "Encore la plupart n'ont-ils jamais connu / La douceur du foyer et n'ont jamais vécu!" (Even more, most have never known the pleasure of a home and have never lived!).[15]

Although the city is a site of confrontation, nineteenth-century poets and novelists also desire to comprehend, dominate, even celebrate the city—an ambivalent mixture of revulsion and magnification that exploits familiar structures, dimensions, and themes. They move through the city, distance themselves from it, rise above it in imagination or by mounting one of its monumental edifices. These tactics are inherent in the urban form and inevitably concern vision, comprehension, and collectivity.

For example, Hölderlin in "Der Archipelagus" gives an intensely negative picture of modern man, alienated in his mechanical labor. There and elsewhere, on the contrary, his vision of the Greek city stresses community, interaction, and the fruitful interpenetration of man, nature, and the divine. Two other poems, "Heidelberg" and "Stutgard," celebrate German cities, the latter through the lateral movement of the speaker, who gathers up into the city experience the life of nature, the productivity of agriculture, and personal, family, and national history. The bridge in the first poem combines the horizontal and the vertical, to effect an intuition of the divine:

Wie von Göttern gesandt, fesselt' ein Zauber einst
    Auf die Brüke mich an, da ich vorüber gieng,
        Und herein in die Berge
            Mir die reizende Ferne schien,

Und der Jüngling, der Strom, fort in die Ebne zog.

As though sent by Gods, a spell once transfixed me
    On the bridge, as I was crossing over,
        And into the hills
            The alluring distance shone for me,

And the youth, the river, traveled off into the plain.

This epiphany of the mythic and the natural occurs in the city, amid the echoing movement of men and wagons, precisely at the point where the bridge, through reflection and related imagery, unites the commercial and collective aspects of the city with the natural. Hölderlin here celebrates a preindustrial city, an image of satisfying cooperation between mankind and a natural world experienced as divine. But this celebration is opposed to the drive of history toward the industrial. Thus the image of the speaker alone at evening in the market place in "Brod und Wein," like the scattered references to the ruins of Greek cities from the end of the first volume of *Hyperion* to "Lebensalter," more fittingly describes the solitude of the poet and the alienation of the divine from the modern urban setting.

Related movements and issues, of imaginative, social, and religious kinds, are visible throughout nineteenth-century poetry, especially in Blake, Vigny, Hugo, and Baudelaire. For example, Vigny and Hugo both contribute to the celebration of the city, to what Citron calls the "mythe de Paris." Texts like "Paris, élévation," "Bièvre," "Fonction du poète," and "Soleils couchants" involve a movement between nature and city, a dialectic of revulsion and celebration. They also depict an attempt to dominate the urban, to rise above it, to evaluate it in historical and symbolic terms. Finally, they express the desire to see Paris as the center of a productive and magnificent civilization, an ambivalent prospect, as a text like "Melancholia," with its movement *within* the city and its evils, reveals. Engels also employed such a technique, of passage through every portion of the city to make it demonstrate the social system it embodies, in the chapter "The Great Towns" in *The Condition of the Working-Class in England*. Long before that, Blake used the device to describe London:

I wander thro' each charter'd street,
Near where the charter'd Thames does flow,
And mark in every face I meet
Marks of weakness, marks of woe.

Similarly, Baudelaire later rises above Paris in "Paysage," but remains conscious of the "atelier" (workshop) below. In other texts he descends into the city, walks through it, encounters by chance or systematically pursues the figures of suffering that he so movingly depicts ("Le Cygne," "Les Sept Vieillards," "Les Aveugles," "Les Petites Vieilles"). In "Danse macabre" an imaginative elevation allows a traditionally apocalyptic condemnation of the city, but more often his peregrinations through Paris produce a sense of human community in suffering—"Le Cygne," the "Crépuscules," and especially "Les Petites Vieilles": "moi qui de loin tendrement vous surveille"; "Ruines! ma famille! ô cerveaux congénères!" (I who from afar tenderly keep watch over you; Ruins! my family! O minds of my own race!).

Here confrontation with the city fuses realistic social awareness, literary and mythic consciousness, religious feeling ("Eves octogénaires, / Sur qui pèse la griffe effroyable de Dieu"—Octogenarian Eves, on whom weighs the fearful talon of God) and the need for love: "aimons-les! ce sont encor des âmes!" (let us love them! they are still souls). In texts that are very different from Rimbaud's, Baudelaire's imagination confronts the infernal modern city and still discovers community and love.[16]

The works already mentioned indicate how closely social awareness is connected with themes of art and religion. This age-old convergence is reaccentuated in the nineteenth century, in which the city often figures the realms of art and visionary experience. The second of these has a long pedigree in apocalyptic tradition; for the first, while there are certainly earlier examples, in the nineteenth century there is a considerable enlargement, corresponding to the elaboration of a theory of the esthetic as disengaged from the conditions of the real. That last formula indicates the importance of both strands of city symbolism for Rimbaud, who is part of a tradition stretching from Blake to Yeats. At the end of the tradition we indeed see Yeats voyaging to the "holy city of Byzantium" in order to get "out of nature." Earlier Gautier made Notre Dame and the effort of climbing its towers represent the victory of art over the vile reality of the city, Hugo glimpsed fantastic constructions in the sky, and in Baudelaire's "Paysage" the city became the site and symbol of a self-willed and self-sufficient imagination, superior to nature and the human world.

The view of art as a form of internal transcendence of the oppressive conditions of reality is strong in Vigny, Gautier, Baudelaire, Mallarmé, and to a certain extent in Yeats. This esthetic transcendence is elaborated in counterpoint to the consciousness of the real conditions in the city. If Mallarmé's desire to transcend the real is matched by the rarity of his allusions to the city, in Vigny and Gautier the jewellike world of art exists in the face of an immediately felt urban reality. And, of course, Baudelaire is characterized by his aspiration to the self-sufficient world of imagination precisely in the midst of the city into which at any moment he can (and does) descend.[17]

The city as symbol of art is thus complexly related to the city as embodiment of the world of social experience. In chapter 2 we discussed another aspect of that symbol, the mystical and visionary movement toward a beyond not fully explainable in esthetic terms, but more mysterious, tempting, and fraught with spiritual dangers. The fantastic cities of Hugo's early poetry are not unrelated to the visionary impulse of his later work nor to orthodox and occult versions of an apocalyptic Jerusalem. "Melancholia" closes with a threatening glimpse of the eternal, as does Baudelaire's "Danse macabre." And Blake, capable of confronting the industrial metropolis so resolutely in "London," is sure that there is another, greater reality, a world of illumination that he represents largely in terms of the city of Golgonooza, known to men as "Art & Manufacture" but revealed by Blake's creative epistemology to be the "spiritual Four-fold London eternal" in which the apocalypse of the true Jerusalem is being prepared.

Earlier we noted as well the Dionysian and related imagery that gives this meaning of the city its transforming and ecstatic quality. We also discussed the ephemeralness of the ecstatic state, its loss and failure in such texts as Hölderlin's "Patmos," Coleridge's "Kubla Khan," and Rimbaud's "Villes I." Baudelaire and Gautier, too, emphasize the danger of transcendent imagination, sometimes in relation to the city symbol. Baudelaire's "Rêve parisien" uses fantastic city imagery to describe a (perhaps drug-induced) dream, frighteningly unnatural and leading the poet to a horrible reawakening to his real life. And in *Mademoiselle de Maupin* Gautier expresses the elusiveness of the ideal, experienced as erotic desire that tends inevitably to the hermaphroditic, by fantastic city imagery, symbolic of an imaginative vision that is brutally denied by reality. Rare are the writers who, like Blake, can avoid such failure; rare as well is Blake's ability to maintain contact between the visionary realm and historical sociopolitical reality. Through his symbolic system, Blake consistently perceives the latter as essentially urban:

The Wine-press on the Rhine groans loud, but all its central
  beams
Act more terrific in the central Cities of the Nations
Where Human Thought is crush'd beneath the iron hand of
  Power:
There Los puts all into the Press, the Opressor & the Opressed
Together, ripe for the Harvest & Vintage & ready for the
  Loom.

(Milton, *I, plate 25, 11.3–7)*

Revulsion against urban oppression; valorization or fetishism of the natural; celebration of the city in its preindustrial and industrial phases; interactions and conflicts of
historical reality, visionary perspective, and esthetic autonomy; and the difficulty of integrating the political and the
esthetic in a satisfactory ethical stance: all these themes
appear in nineteenth-century city poetry and are *exacerbated*
in Rimbaud's work. Situated historically later than Blake,
Hugo, and Baudelaire, Rimbaud records an even more
negative confrontation with the political, economic, esthetic, and human threat of the modern city. On the
whole his sense of urban evil is as acute as theirs. However, Rimbaud's poetic response to that evil is neither the
indignation of Blake and Hugo nor the compassion of
Baudelaire, but rather a decentered, alienated, fantastic
production of surreal city visions that we must interpret
within their historical and political context.

Prior to the *Illuminations,* the bulk of Rimbaud's production is located in nature. But the city, in the highly
politicized atmosphere surrounding the events of the Commune, the short-lived workers' government formed after
the French defeat by the Germans and crushed by *French*
reactionary forces in May 1871, nonetheless plays its role.

"Chant de guerre parisien," described in the *lettre du voyant*
as a psalm of contemporary events, attacks the right-wing
resistance to the Commune; a bit later, "L'Orgie parisienne" expresses the disgust of the young poet at the
spectacle of the triumph of that resistance. This somewhat
derivative poem offers a description of urban corruption
that is reminiscent of Baudelaire ("la putain Paris"—the
whore Paris), though with Rimbaud's characteristic élan:
"Avalez, pour la Reine aux fesses cascadantes!" (Drink up,
for the Queen with the cascading buttocks!). The poem
leads to a justification of the city and an optimism for the
future that recalls Hugo's spirit:

> La rouge courtisane aux seins gros de batailles
> [The red courtesan, breasts heavy with battles]
>
>   . . .
>
> O cité douloureuse, ô cité quasi morte,
> La tête et les deux seins jetés vers l'Avenir
> [O suffering city, O city almost dead,
> Head and twin breasts thrust toward the future]
>
>   . . .
>
> ton souffle de Progrès
> [your breath of Progress]
>
>   . . .
>
> L'orage t'a sacrée suprême poésie;
> L'immense remuement des forces te secourt;
> Ton œuvre bout
> [The storm has consecrated you as supreme poetry;
> The immense stirring of forces aids you;
> Your work is boiling]

Thus we see Rimbaud blame familiar urban problems,
such as prostitution, drink, gambling, and the corruption
of the natural, on the repressive society that the Commune
wanted to overthrow. He asserts that his role as poet is to

assume and express the continued will to revolt of the repressed: "Le Poète prendra le sanglot des Infâmes, / La haine des Forçats, la clameur des Maudits" (The Poet will take the sob of the Outcasts, the hatred of Convicts, the clamor of the Cursed). Rebellion is romanticized here, and this is not mitigated by the poet's sexist corrective for prostitution: "ses rayons d'amour flagelleront les Femmes" (his rays of love will scourge Women). Moreover, if after the defeat of the revolutionary struggle, the sinister and obscene life of the city begins again ("Société, tout est rétabli"—Society, all is re-established), why should the poet earlier in the poem assert: "Et ce n'est pas mauvais" (And it is not bad)? For all his intensity and involvement in the events of his time, the young Rimbaud here does not seem fully able to meaningfully apply poetic and historical insight to the theme of the urban.

This difficulty is even more apparent by the time of the *Saison,* written two years later, in which Rimbaud is much more lucid—and much more negative. His analysis of French society in "Mauvais Sang" is bitter and hopeless, and elsewhere in *Saison* he viciously criticizes his political and poetic enthusiasms and debunks his *voyance.* He is also sardonic about his feelings of fraternity for the oppressed (especially in "Délires II" and "Nuit de l'enfer") and deeply ambivalent, even despairing, about the city. True, the idea of a communal movement, "la marche des peuples," emerges in "Matin," and in "Adieu" Rimbaud looks forward to entering some vaguely conceived "splendides villes." But "Adieu" contains a violent attack on others and a revindication of absolute solitude. Note how it accords well with Rimbaud's earlier evocation of his own frightful experience of poverty, suffering, and alienation from others in the city, which he calls "le port de la misère, la cité énorme au ciel taché de feu et de boue" (the port of wretchedness, the enormous city with its sky stained with fire and mud). He says (ellipses are Rimbaud's):

Ah! les haillons pourris, le pain trempé de pluie, l'ivresse, les mille amours qui m'ont crucifié! Elle ne finira donc point cette goule reine de millions d'âmes et de corps morts *et qui seront jugés!* Je me revois la peau rongée par la boue et la peste, des vers plein les cheveux et les aisselles et encore de plus gros vers dans le cœur, étendu parmi les inconnus sans âge, sans sentiment . . . J'aurais pu y mourir . . . L'affreuse évocation! J'exècre la misère.

Ah! the rotten rags, the bread soaked in rain, the drunkenness, the thousand loves that crucified me! She will not stop at all then, this ghoul queen of millions of dead souls and bodies *that will be judged!* I see myself again, skin eaten by mud and plague, hair and armpits full of worms and even bigger worms in my heart, stretched out among strangers without age, without feeling . . . I could have died there . . . Horrible memory! I abhor poverty.

In these lines personal misfortune and the sufferings engendered by the socioeconomic system converge, and noticeably without the characteristic romantic reactions of social indignation or compassion. Psychic distress ("encore de plus gros vers dans le cœur"), motifs of religious punishment colored by personal bitterness ("cette goule reine . . . millions d'âmes et de corps . . . *qui seront jugés!*"), the stupor and poverty and dehumanization of the lowest group of city dwellers, drunks and vagrants—all characterize both the suffering of the poet and the quality of life in the late nineteenth-century city. Quite nakedly,

Rimbaud confronts that "port de la misère, la cité énorme au ciel taché de feu et de boue."

How different this version is from an earlier view of another city, "Bruxelles," one of the *Derniers Vers* generally thought to have been written in July 1872, that is, before the breakdown of Rimbaud's relationship with Verlaine and the collapse of the poetic project of *voyance*. Preceded by the notations *"Juillet,"* and *"Boulevard du Régent,"* it is a later companion to "Au Cabaret-Vert," a poem of escape situated in the city, with references to palaces, public gardens, houses, railroad stations, boulevards. The emotional tone is extremely happy: "Quelles / Troupes d'oiseaux, ô ia io, ia io!"; "C'est trop beau! trop! Gardons notre silence" (What flocks of birds, O ah oh, ah oh!; It's too beautiful! too! Let's keep our silence). Doubtless this happiness reflects Rimbaud's personal feelings at the moment, but the city lends itself to his happy vision, which includes elements of divinity and of mythic and sexualized nature:

> l'agréable palais de Jupiter
> [the delightful palace of Jupiter]
>
> · · ·
>
> c'est Toi qui, dans ces lieux,
> Mêles ton Bleu presque de Sahara!
> [it's You who, in these places,
> Mingle your almost Sahara blue!]
>
> · · ·
>
> Après les fesses des rosiers, balcon
> Ombreux et très bas de la Juliette.
> [After the cheeks of the rose bushes,
> Shaded and very low balcony of Juliet.]

The city is depicted as coexisting peacefully with the natural world ("Au cœur d'un mont, comme au fond d'un verger"—in the heart of a mountain, as in the depth of an orchard). And it is presented as a noncommercial place, a calm environment for esthetic and mythic awareness, corresponding to the German cities in Hölderlin or to Wordsworth's "Composed Upon Westminster Bridge," a celebration of sleeping London, at dawn, before the activity of the metropolis begins. The city is emptied of its characteristics of sound, movement, and economic activity, and it becomes a spectacle of infinite possibilities:

> —Boulevard sans mouvement ni commerce,
> Muet, tout drame et toute comédie,
> Réunion des scènes infinie,
> Je te connais et t'admire en silence.

> —Boulevard without movement or commerce,
> Mute, all drama and theater,
> Infinite joining of scenes,
> I know you and admire you in silence.

Here we glimpse Rimbaud's use of the urban as locus and symbol of imaginative vision. We should, however, note the firmly centered *je* who contemplates this world of theatrical enlargement. "Bruxelles" shows us a significant stage of poetic interaction with the city: a preindustrial, protovisionary experience within the tradition of the personal recounting self.

Thus many important features are apparent in these works: the interaction of city and nature, the idealization and criticism of a violent historical process centered in the city, a corresponding dichotomy of celebration of and revulsion against the urban poetic experience, the problematic of self and vision in relation to the city. Rimbaud's nature poems, "L'Orgie parisienne," "Bruxelles," and the

Saison trace an archetypal itinerary that leads toward the *Illuminations*. The prose poems must be seen in the context of these complex tensions among social evil, celebration, political struggle, Rimbaud's evolving poetics of self and vision, and a sense of deception that *at every point* threatens both the possibilities of human solidarity and the poetic enterprise.

Two of the prose poems correspond to this bleak outlook in their disturbing depiction of urban suffering and isolation, seemingly unrelieved by the promises of revolution or poetry. In "Ouvriers" we learn of a worker and his wife, poor and miserable, pursued by the smoke of a city even into the ravaged countryside around it. The style concisely reveals, as well as anything in Blake, Dickens, or Zola, the impact of the industrial city: "Nous faisions un tour dans la banlieue. Le temps était couvert, et ce vent du Sud excitait toutes les vilaines odeurs des jardins ravagés et des prés desséchés" (We were taking a walk in the suburb. It was overcast, and that wind from the South stirred up all the vile smells of the ravaged gardens and parched fields); "La ville, avec sa fumée et ses bruits de métiers, nous suivait très loin dans les chemins" (The city, with its smoke and its noise of trades, followed us very far in the paths). Wholly different from "Bruxelles," in this industrial city an atmosphere of helplessness prevails, as the narrator speaks of the "horrible quantité de force et de science que le sort a toujours éloignée de moi" (the horrible quantity of strength and knowledge that fate has always kept away from me).

In "Ville" a solitary speaker sardonically describes the evils of the modern city, its smoke, crime, vulgarity, its reduction of human life to monotony. Like Marx and Engels and other observers, he analyzes the city's subordination of the esthetic, the religious, the ethical, the communal, and indeed the human to the abstract rationality of industrial planning and production:

> tout goût connu a été éludé dans les ameublements et l'extérieur des maisons aussi bien que dans le plan de la ville. Ici vous ne signaleriez les traces d'aucun monument de superstition. La morale et la langue sont réduites à leur plus simple expression, enfin! Ces millions de gens qui n'ont pas besoin de se connaître amènent si pareillement l'éducation, le métier et la vieillesse, que ce cours de vie doit être plusieurs fois moins long que ce qu'une statistique folle trouve pour les peuples du continent.

> all known taste has been avoided in the furnishings and the exterior of the houses as well as in the plan of the city. Here you would note the traces of no monument of superstition whatsoever. Morality and language are reduced to their simplest expression, finally! These millions of people who have no need to know one another conduct education, occupation, and old age so similarly, that this course of life must be several times less long than what a mad statistic finds for the peoples of the continent.

The immense anonymous crowds of the modern city; personal existence reduced to the sequence *éducation, métier, vieillesse;* the human as demographic and economic statistic—thus this narrator, isolated in his cottage, sees the city. Like the worker in "Ouvriers," he cries out against it in the name of the values of nature and innocence: "O l'autre monde, l'habitation bénie par le ciel et les ombrages!"; "notre ombre des bois, notre nuit d'été!" (O the other world, the habitation blessed by the sky and the shadows!; our shadow of the woods, our summer night!).

So, like his predecessors, but without the satisfaction afforded by prophetic indignation or universal communion, Rimbaud records the horror of the industrial city, to which the human is utterly subordinated. Indeed, these dramatizations are pervaded by impotence and alienation. But if we recall the romantic tradition's dialectic of penetration, distancing, domination, celebration, and transcendence, we notice as well those techniques through which the city assumes a positive, even glorious, significance in other *Illuminations*. Among these techniques are narrative perspective (point of view, tone, rhetorical strategy), allusion (historical, geographic, legendary), and myth. Further, these techniques elucidate the issues of the poetic self and the relationship between reality and imaginative vision.[18]

We can begin to grasp these issues by reconsidering "Ouvriers" and "Ville" in terms of narrative perspective. The first of these poems is remarkable in the *Illuminations* for its convention of realism, for its description of the city (inhabitants, surroundings, weather) in terms that could apply directly to an actual city. The narrator of the poem, too, is a realistic and rather fully characterized personage— he is a worker, is poor and unhappy, had an unhappy childhood, is married to a woman whose name we learn, whose clothes are described, whose personality is suggested. For example: "Henrika avait une jupe de coton à carreau blanc et brun" (Henrika had on a white-and-brown checked cotton skirt); "Cela ne devait pas fatiguer ma femme au même point que moi. Dans une flache laissée par l'inondation du mois précédant à un sentier assez haut, elle me fit remarquer de très petits poissons" (That must not have tired my wife to the same extent as me. In a puddle left by the inundation of the previous month on a rather high path, she pointed out to me some very small fish).

It is important to understand the relationship between

the realistically characterized narrator and the realistic vision of the city. The narrator sees the city as real, evokes it on its own terms, as it were, precisely because he *is* a worker, inhabiting the city, submitting to its conditions—recall that in the *voyant* letters and the *Saison* work symbolizes precisely the subordination to an oppressive reality. The realistic convention and the perspective of the worker in "Ouvriers" are thus aspects of the same theme, that of the submission to the real, characteristically embodied in the city. So the worker's despair ("l'horrible quantité de force et de science que le sort a toujours éloignée de moi") at least in part concerns the struggle between reality and Rimbaud's transfiguring imagination.

A degree of transformation is already visible in "Ville," where the distancing tendency so characteristic of nineteenth-century city poetry begins to come into play, again with reference particularly to the narrator. He is not described in realistic detail; he is a simple *je* who does not describe relations with other people nor any activities in the city. Alone in his cottage, above the city and somewhat separated from it, he assumes the stance of an alienated contemplator rather than of a participant in its life. This stance is well expressed in his style, in which scorn for the absurdity of the city and superiority to its uncomprehending masses do not completely mask the speaker's bitter loneliness: "Je suis un éphémère et point trop mécontent citoyen d'une métropole crue moderne" (I am an ephemeral and not too discontented citizen of a metropolis thought to be modern).

The attitude of alienated scorn that is conveyed by these lines provokes a kind of transformation of the city, for to the narrator its evils are so intense that they take on an independent, even personalized existence. In the smoke he perceives "des Erinnyes nouvelles" (new Furies) and a frightful vision of "la Mort sans pleurs, notre active fille et servante, un Amour désespéré, et un joli Crime piaulant dans la boue de la rue" (Death without tears, our active daughter and servant, a desperate Love, and a pretty Crime whining in the mud of the street). Hallucinatory in intensity, these representations of the city in the mind of a suffering and solitary individual attain a mythic status, almost independent of particular persons or actions. Though products of alienation, they constitute the beginnings of a transcendence.

This transcendence is in part a function of the modulations of the speaking subject in these texts. From the realistic worker of "Ouvriers" to the almost depersonalized speaker of "Ville," we confront a progressive alienation from the modern city and also stages toward the deconstruction of the poetic self. "Ornières" corresponds to this proposition, for its transcendence (at least half-successful) involves both distance from the heart of the city and the suppression of a visible narrator or speaker:

> A droite l'aube d'été éveille les feuilles et les vapeurs et les bruits de ce coin du parc, et les talus de gauche tiennent dans leur ombre violette les mille rapides ornières de la route humide. Défilé de féeries. En effet: des chars chargés d'animaux de bois doré, de mâts et de toiles bariolées, au grand galop de vingt chevaux de cirque tachetés, et les enfants et les hommes sur leurs bêtes les plus étonnantes;—vingt véhicules, bossés, pavoisés et fleuris comme des carrosses anciens ou de contes, pleins d'enfants attifés pour une pastorale suburbaine.—Même des cercueils sous leur dais de nuit dressant les panaches d'ébène, filant au trot des grandes juments bleues et noires.

At the right the summer dawn awakens the leaves and the vapors and the noises of this park corner, and the banks at the left hold in their violet shadow the thousand rapid ruts of the wet road. Parade of enchantments. Indeed: chariots loaded with animals of gilded wood, with masts and with multicolored canvas cloths, to the full gallop of twenty mottled circus horses, and the children and the men on their most astonishing animals;—twenty vehicles, embossed, decked with flags and flowers like ancient or storybook coaches, full of children dressed up for a suburban pastoral.—Even coffins under their canopy of night raising the ebony plumes, filing past to the trot of the great blue-black mares.

This text exemplifies a number of the ideas discussed in this chapter. Read mimetically and thematically, it proposes a horizontal distancing from the city and a rediscovery of the natural: the dawn, summer, awakening, nature and park, the slope and road, light and liquidity, color and movement. It appears, moreover, that all this is perceived in a suburban park, into which a circus introduces a fantastic dynamism, the imaginative values of childhood, and a recrudescence of ancient fairy tale ("comme des carrosses anciens ou de contes, pleins d'enfants attifés pour une pastorale suburbaine"). Park and suburb have always represented the persistence of the natural in or near the city, a locus of utopia and myth, and they cohabit easily with the circus, embodiment of ancient values of joy, invention, freedom. The circus here seems a bit pathetic at first ("attifés pour une pastorale suburbaine"), but nonetheless it opposes the regimentation of the industrial city in a manner that recalls Dickens's *Hard Times,* Breton's *Nadja,* Aragon's *Le Paysan de Paris,* and many of Picasso's paintings of circus themes. Finally, too, the mythic sense of death and nature that

we found at the heart of romantic nature poetry re-
emerges, as the circus procession provokes a movement of
the dead underground—or such is my interpretation of
the sudden appearance of coffins, night, trees, and the
haunting figures of the horses of death, "filant au trot des
grandes juments bleues et noires."

The motif of the mythic in nature thus re-enters Rimbaud's poetry; even the participle "filant" recalls the cosmic nature experiences expressed by that verb in "Le Bateau ivre," "Marine," and "Mystique." But those last two
titles point to another feature of "Ornières," which like
them is a text of vision without a visible speaker, using
scenic indications and the suggestiveness of language to
tell us what we can, and therefore do, see. Hence we
encounter the right and left pictorial directions of "Mystique"; and the enumerative structure of the first sentence
of "Ornières," the demonstrative in "ce coin du parc," and
the naming power of words in fact cause a certain vision to
come suggestively "awake" in us. Hard upon this natural
scene comes the notation "Défilé de féeries," which in the
nonmimetic convention of Rimbaud's nature *Illuminations*
could make us imagine a good many things. Except that
the narrative voice brings us up short with the explicative
"En effet" followed by the description of the circus. Of
course, nothing obliges us to situate that description in the
realm of the real—an actual circus in an actual park—
except perhaps the element that has most influenced my
reading, within the perspective of the city: the note of the
"pastorale suburbaine." For the circus world, with its fantastic decor and magnified style of discourse (echoed in "les
enfants et les hommes sur leurs bêtes *les plus étonnantes*"), is
one precisely in which real people and objects enact fantasy
and pleasure, in which the separation between real and
imaginary is blurred.

Furthermore, at this point in the text the language insistently calls attention to itself through repetition, rhyme, assonance, and alliteration: "chars chargés," "bois doré," "toiles bariolées," "grand galop," and "chevaux de cirque tachetés" accentuate an autonomous linguistic generation of vision. And finally, even if we suppose ourselves brought back to the real, to the partially successful transcendence of the city wrought by the suburban circus, in the last sentence a more fundamental subversion of reality is enacted by the language. The categories of real and mythical, natural and supernatural, are confounded by the realistically cumulative "même," which seems to matter of factly continue the enumeration of events; by the correspondence with elements of an actual circus: "panaches," "trot des grandes juments"; and by the strangely deathlike imagery: "cercueils," "dais *de nuit*," "panaches *d'ébène*," "juments *bleues et noires.*" This concluding sentence thus affords us an illumination that transcends the normal parameters of both city and nature.

"Métropolitain" illustrates an extreme version of the transformation of the city through distancing, speakerless or speaker-transformed perspective, myth, and the intrusiveness of language. We earlier noted how this text imitates movement through and about the urban space, from nature, to city, to surrounding country and beyond. The next-to-last paragraph first describes recognizable suburban architecture: "Des routes bordées de grilles et de murs, contenant à peine leurs bosquets, et les atroces fleurs" (Roads bordered with gates and walls, barely containing their thickets, and the atrocious flowers). Outward movement then transports us to a global context: "possessions de féeriques aristocraties ultra-Rhénanes, Japonaises, Guaranies" (possessions of fantastic aristocracies from beyond the Rhine, Japanese, Guaranies). The language again begins to take off with its own momentum: "Damas damnant de longueur" (Damascus damning with dullness)—a phrase that has pretty well defied explanation. And we encounter familiar visionary themes, though negatively colored: "propres encore à recevoir la musique des anciens" (still fit to receive the music of the ancients); "des auberges qui pour toujours n'ouvrent déjà plus" (inns that for always are already no longer open); and "si tu n'es pas trop accablé, l'étude des astres—le ciel" (if you are not too overwhelmed, the study of the stars—the sky).

In the last quotation an unidentifiable person is evoked, perhaps the speaker himself, in which case the subject of the text indeed seems decentered or multiplied, explaining something he already knows to himself and, in the final paragraph, appearing ecstatically magnified: "Le matin où avec Elle, vous vous débattîtes parmi les éclats de neige, ces lèvres vertes, les glaces, les drapeaux noirs et les rayons bleus, et les parfums pourpres du soleil des pôles,—ta force" (The morning when with Her, you struggled among the bursts of snow, those green lips, the ice, the black flags and the blue rays, and the purple perfumes of the polar sun,—your strength). These lines open the paradigm of the city toward the globally visionary in terms recalling the polar, erotic, and city symbolism of "Barbare," "Génie," "Being Beauteous," "Dévotion," "Villes I," and "Villes II." But though suggesting a persistence of what in chapter 2 we called ecstatic memory, they nonetheless fix the experience definitively in the past. The poem ends on a note of loss that augments the initial sense of uneasiness.

Indeed, the strangely exalted opening paragraphs interest me most as illustration of the poetic transformation of the city in "Métropolitain":

Du détroit d'indigo aux mers d'Ossian, sur le sable
rose et orange qu'a lavé le ciel vineux, viennent de
monter et de se croiser des boulevards de cristal habités
incontinent par de jeunes familles pauvres qui s'ali-
mentent chez les fruitiers. Rien de riche.—La ville!

Du désert de bitume fuient droit en déroute avec les
nappes de brumes échelonnées en bandes affreuses au ciel
qui se recourbe, se recule et descend, formé de la plus
sinistre fumée noire que puisse faire l'Océan en deuil, les
casques, les roues, les barques, les croupes.—La bataille!

Lève la tête: ce pont de bois, arqué; les derniers potagers
de Samarie; ces masques enluminés sous la lanterne fouettée
par la nuit froide; l'ondine niaise à la robe bruyante, au bas
de la rivière; ces crânes lumineux dans les plans de pois—et
les autres fantasmagories—la campagne.

From the indigo strait to the seas of Ossian, on the
rose and orange sand washed by the winy sky, have just
arisen and intersected crystal boulevards inhabited immediately by poor young families who get their food at the
fruit dealers. Nothing rich.—The city!

From the asphalt desert there flee straight in rout with
the sheets of fog echeloned in frightful bands in the sky
that bends, recoils and sinks, formed of the most sinister
black smoke that the mourning Ocean can make, the hel-
mets, the wheels, the boats, the rumps.—The battle!

Raise your head: this wooden bridge, arched; the last
vegetable gardens of Samaria; these illuminated masks
under the lantern whipped by the cold night; the silly
water nymph in her rustling dress, at the bottom of the
river; those luminous skulls in the rows of peas—and the
other phantasmagories—the country.

This is far from "Ouvriers" and romantic confrontations
with the urban. The smoke, poverty, and strife of the city

no longer evoke human anguish. Rather they undergo a wonderful metamorphosis; the city has achieved a virtually self-sufficient status. Thus the potential for the phantasmagoric, always present in the suburban re-enactment of nature myths, is bizarrely exaggerated in the third paragraph, and an imperative implies that someone can perceive such phantasmagories. But already in the opening two paragraphs the detachment of this city from the real is clear. Note the brilliant colors, the way in which the city springs up almost magically ("viennent de," "incontinent"), the reduction of its boulevards to a crystalline pattern of lines ("monter et . . . se croiser des boulevards de cristal"), the allusions to Ossian and the mourning Ocean. The last of these makes the city seem the product of some universal upheaval, a mythic event rather than a human creation. This effect is fostered by the stylized conclusion of each paragraph ("La ville!", "La bataille!", "la campagne," "le ciel," "ta force") and by the syntax, especially in the second paragraph, in which the regular patterns of the city's smoke are paralleled by the obtrusive repetition of verbs and nouns and by the placement of the compound subject at the end of the sentence. By a mythological, decentered, verbally self-sufficient presentation of a fantastic city, "Métropolitain" proffers an independent urban entity, an autonomous and glorious realm of vision.

What is the path that leads from the oppressive city of "Ouvriers" to the vision of "Métropolitain"? To the devices already mentioned we can add a particular perspective, that of the observer-spectator-discoverer, which involves an almost progressive transformation of the city into a self-sufficient realm.

In "Les Ponts" this perspective appears as an advanced version of the distancing tendency noted in nineteenth-century poetry and present already in "Ville" and

"Ornières." The unidentified speaker is at a considerable remove from the urban scene that he appears to describe:

> Des ciels gris de cristal. Un bizarre dessin de ponts, ceux-ci droits, ceux-là bombés, d'autres descendant ou obliquant en angles sur les premiers, et ces figures se renouvelant dans les autres circuits éclairés du canal, mais tous tellement longs et légers que les rives, chargées de dômes, s'abaissent et s'amoindrissent. Quelques-uns de ces ponts sont encore chargés de masures. D'autres soutiennent des mâts, des signaux, de frêles parapets. Des accords mineurs se croisent et filent, des cordes montent des berges. On distingue une veste rouge, peut-être d'autres costumes et des instruments de musique. Sont-ce des airs populaires, des bouts de concerts seigneuriaux, des restants d'hymnes publics? L'eau est grise et bleue, large comme un bras de mer.—Un rayon blanc, tombant du haut du ciel, anéantit cette comédie.

> Crystal gray skies. A bizarre design of bridges, some straight, some arched, others descending or obliquing at angles to the first ones, and these figures renewed in the other lighted circuits of the canal, but all so long and light that the banks, laden with domes, sink and diminish. Some of these bridges are still encumbered with hovels. Others support masts, signals, frail parapets. Minor chords criss-cross and flow away, ropes rise from the banks. One makes out a red jacket, perhaps other costumes and musical instruments. Are these popular airs, scraps of manorial concerts, remnants of public hymns? The water is gray and blue, wide as an arm of the sea.— A white ray, falling from the top of the sky, annihilates this comedy.

The strategy of this text is comparable, in the realm of the urban, to that of "Fleurs" and "Mystique" for the natural. That is, the convention is one of notation of visual details (color of sky, bridges and buildings, persons and objects on the bridges), and it creates the impression of a person attempting to report accurately what he is viewing. This effect is accentuated by expressions such as "on distingue" and "peut-être," as the speaker wonders about the significance of objects and activities that he glimpses but cannot completely make out. By these touches, Rimbaud creates a speaker who seems honest, reporting faithfully what he sees and also indicating the limits of his vision. This convention creates an expectation of fidelity to the scene that is supposedly being described. But the scene is described from a distance, which complicates this expectation and affords the imagination an opportunity for a kind of transcendence. For the scene turns out to be neither stable nor substantial. References to painting, drawing, and music ("ciels," "dessin," "accords mineurs") endow it with the quality of a work of art and not only of visual art. Or if it is a real city, the peculiar light makes it seem artificial, and the bridges appear as a complicated pattern of lines that the narrator describes, but which the reader strives unsuccessfully to visualize.

Menaced by unsubstantiality from the beginning, the scene suddenly dissolves when "un rayon blanc, tombant du haut du ciel, anéantit cette comédie." The deliberate confusion of real and esthetic references in the narrative convention makes the reader imagine the scene, yet what he has been led to imagine is rapidly dissolved. The effect is to insinuate a disquieting instability into a world that seemed real and at the same time to place the imaginary scene, the "comédie," on an equal footing with it. The distanced observer thus seems to neutralize for a moment the opposition between real and imaginary, an opposition so insistently related to the city in nineteenth-century poetry, and the technique opens up the possibility of going beyond this opposition.

In "Les Ponts" the city is the setting for a momentary transcendence of this sort, emerging briefly and quickly dissolved. Earlier we looked at "Villes II" as magnifying all the city's qualities, especially the oppressive ones; but now we can view it in another way, as using that very magnification to effect a transcendence that seems definitive. For the cities in this poem are a permanently constituted world, flagrantly contradicting the ordinary norms of reality yet impervious to them. Their fantastic quality is emphasized by the enormity of their bizarre architecture and unbelievable proportions—buildings twenty times larger than Hampton Court, stairways built by a "Nabuchodonosor norvégien," a Sainte-Chapelle with a steel dome approximately 15,000 feet in diameter. This last detail, in particular, is an incredible dimension, yet it is given with the specification that it is only approximate, as if to suggest that this city, though beyond the realm of our normal experience, is really present, could even be measured.

The accumulation and mixing of fantastic and contradictory historical and geographical allusions (the Norwegian Nebuchadnezzar, polar drinks and diamond diligences, the Indian rupee, the architecture of Athens, Paris, London) perform the same function of suggesting a realm that goes beyond the normal categories of the real. Independent of these categories, this city seems in no way menaced by them. Comparison with our experience only seems to emphasize how much beyond our ideas and capacities this realm is: "L'acropole officielle outre les conceptions de la barbarie moderne les plus colossales. Impossible d'exprimer le jour mat produit par ce ciel" (The official Acropolis exceeds the most colossal conceptions of modern barbarity. Impossible to express the dull light produced by this sky).

All these touches are part of a rhetorical structure that

again depends on the narrator or speaker. The narrative strategy does not involve the speaker's distancing himself from a city like the real ones that we know; rather he represents himself as having arrived in a new city. Despite its flamboyant contradictions, he insists that it is present before his eyes, and like a guide he gives us a well-organized description of its quarters, official buildings, parks, suburbs, and countryside. Undoubtedly the power of the poem to evoke this world is also related to the speaker's status as a discoverer, "l'étranger de notre temps," who describes for us a strange world that he has come upon and does not yet fully comprehend:

> Sur quelques points des passerelles de cuivre, des plates-formes, des escaliers qui contournent les halles et les piliers, j'ai cru juger la profondeur de la ville! C'est le prodige dont je n'ai pu me rendre compte: quels sont les niveaux des autres quartiers sur ou sous l'acropole? Pour l'étranger de notre temps la reconnaissance est impossible. . . . Je pense qu'il y a une police. Mais la loi doit être tellement étrange, que je renonce à me faire une idée des aventuriers d'ici.

> On some points of the copper footbridges, the platforms, the stairways that circle the markets and the pillars, I thought I could estimate the depth of the city! That's the marvel I couldn't figure out: what are the levels of the other quarters above or below the acropolis? For the foreigner of our time recognition is impossible. . . . I think there is a police force. But the law must be so strange, that I renounce the idea of imagining what adventurers are like here.

The tone here is one of wonder, of excited curiosity. The narrator is amazed at this strange city, feels that he has penetrated some of its mystery, but admits that much is beyond his comprehension. The rhetorical effect insinuates the presence of what he describes—the fantastic city, though it contradicts our norms of reality, is accorded a literal acceptance, indeed a status more important than that of the real. As in "Les Ponts," this tactic involves the reader in a particularly self-conscious activity of imagining a realm independent of the conditions of reality. Although in less overt ways, all art is transnatural in the sense of never in fact giving the illusion of representing actual things. But Rimbaud's narrative technique flagrantly emphasizes this autonomy, revealing a power of pure imagination, of vision without object, that is seemingly unmotivated by reality, indeed superior to reality, pushing it to the side and imposing itself in its place. More than do the works of other nineteenth-century poets, "Villes II" and "Les Ponts" make the reader *experience* how the imagination is capable of creating a sense of surmounting the limits of the real. The poem as substantial object, victorious over nature, which we glimpsed in texts like "Fleurs" and "Mystique"—consciousness and language as self-generating and self-sustaining—finds its appropriate expression in a fantastic and transcendent city poem.

This sense of transcendence is primarily a property of art. We noted earlier, in Gautier, Baudelaire, and Yeats, the use of city symbolism—often accompanied by motifs of dream, voyage, diamond, metallic, and other nonvegetal imagery—to represent the inner world of imagination as well as its products, the works that through effort and will the artist fabricates and that seem to exist in a special dimension. Rimbaud develops somewhat similar aspects of the world of imagination and art in "Promontoire." As we saw earlier, the city plays an important, though subsidiary, role in this poem, which we need to re-examine in the context of the present argument.

As the title indicates, the central motif is that of the promontory, although not an ordinary one. It is encountered during a dream voyage and transcends the categories of the real by its monstrous size (as large as Epirus, the Peloponnesus, the large island of Japan, Arabia) and its fusion of different times and places (ancient religious rites and modern military defenses, the architecture of Italy, America, and Asia). And it does not remain only a promontory, but is in addition called a villa, a hotel, and a palace. It is also a city, because it contains railways and parks, canals and embankments like those of Carthage and Venice, and hotels. Promontory-Hotel-City, it is an imaginative realm with its own dimensions and substantiality, partaking of the qualities of both natural and artificial things, seeming indeed to belong to another world.

Many touches in the poem indicate that this world is that of the esthetic imagination and of the work of art. The objective tone is appropriate for describing an experience that is purely esthetic rather than personal. The narrator, unlike those in preceding works, minimizes his own importance, remaining simply "en face"—in the position of an observer—throughout the poem and allowing the promontory to absorb the reader's attention. Even more clearly, the natural world is not simply fused with the artificial; rather nature seems enfeebled ("de molles éruptions d'Etnas"—mild eruptions of Etnas) and gives way before the force of artifice: "des dunes illustrées de chaudes fleurs et de bacchanales" (dunes illustrated with hot flowers and bacchanales). The submission of nature to art is especially noticeable in the conclusion, which describes the promontory as a colossal hotel,

> dont les fenêtres et les terrasses à présent pleines
> d'éclairages, de boissons et de brises riches, sont ouvertes à

l'esprit des voyageurs et des nobles—qui permettent, aux
heures du jour, à toutes les tarentelles des côtes,—et même
aux ritournelles des vallées illustres de l'art, de décorer
merveilleusement les façades du Palais-Promontoire.

whose windows and terraces, presently filled with lights,
drinks, and rich breezes, are open to the spirit of travelers and nobles—who allow the hours of the day, all
the tarantellas of the coasts,—and even the ritornellos of
the illustrious valleys of art, to decorate marvellously the
facades of the Promontory-Palace.

Despite the syntactical complexity of these lines, the
esthetic domain is clearly emphasized. There are direct
allusions to forms of art, music, and dance, as well as to
art itself. The balance between nature and artifice seems
redressed somewhat, for the hotel is open to all influences,
including those of the natural world; and the reference to
ritournelles, instrumental refrains in a choral work, may
suggest that art is a kind of refrain to the world of nature.
But the relationship is really not equal, for the concluding
relative clause ("qui permettent") insists on the submission
of everything, natural world and creative faculties, in contributing to the work of art. In this context the voyagers
and nobles through whose intervention this process seems
to occur must be viewed as manifestations of the esthetic
impulse. Sensing themselves superior to the conditions of
the real, they journey to the world of art, in which nature
is transformed, becoming a marvellously decorated palace.

Despite the predominance of the esthetic in "Promontoire," to understand the city and its related architectural
forms as symbols of art does not exhaust the meanings of
the motif. The modulation of alienated, distanced, decentered, fragmented, wholly impersonal, and observing-
discovering perspectives to produce a realm of autonomous

vision, in which the poem seems to exist as self-sufficient
object, is one aspect of city poetry and an impulse in
romantic literature that is achieved by Rimbaud. But we
must not forget the tragically insistent, visionary-ecstatic
meaning of the city symbol, which perpetuates age-old
religious tendencies that are not reducible to the esthetic.
This meaning—expressed in texts from Blake, Hölderlin,
Novalis, and Nerval to Yeats—culminates, it might be
argued, in Rimbaud's remarkable city poem "Villes I."

I am not going to repeat what I have said about that
text in chapter 2, except to point out that it belies Leo
Bersani's view that Rimbaud's most characteristic work
does not express a nostalgia for a lost visionary experience.
Indeed, at the end, a (now quite ordinary) "subject" is
precipitated out of the ecstatic region of the poem into the
conditions of (precisely, urban) reality, from which he feels
completely alienated:

> Et une heure je suis descendu dans le mouvement d'un
> boulevard de Bagdad où des compagnies ont chanté la
> joie du travail nouveau, sous une brise épaisse, circulant
> sans pouvoir éluder les fabuleux fantômes des monts où
> l'on a dû se retrouver.
>
> Quels bons bras, quelle belle heure me rendront cette
> région d'où viennent mes sommeils et mes moindres
> mouvements?

> And one hour I went down into the movement of a bou-
> levard of Bagdad where groups of companions sang the
> joy of the new work, under a heavy breeze, circulating
> without being able to avoid the fabulous phantoms of the
> mountains where one must have met again.
>
> What good arms, what fine hour will render back to
> me that region from which come my slumbers and my
> slightest movements?

If this isn't nostalgia for lost visionary experience, then nothing is. Beyond that, note the inherent connection between that theme of loss and the city setting. Many familiar urban features reappear, in an apparently favorable light: the dynamism of an exotic, nonindustrial city, and the song and joy of collective and idealized work, even the immediate contact of nature. But there is a sharp discrepancy between that attractive world and the listless disinterest of the speaker, a discrepancy much more violently apparent, as we saw at the end of chapter 2, in "Angoisse." Recall Rimbaud's assertion there of the inability of sociopolitical activity ("des mouvements de fraternité sociale") to effect the "restitution progressive de la franchise première" (progressive restitution of the first franchise).

In fact, we encounter similar discontinuity at the term of every strand of Rimbaud's writing: in the gap between the masses and the abstracted activity of the child-youth-poet at the end of "Jeunesse," in the visionary descent of "Villes I," and in the frustration of Rimbaud's political enthusiasm and his furious rejection of others at the end of the *Saison*. An archetypally compelling poet of the beauties of childhood, ecstasy, nature, and city, Rimbaud intrigues us tragically as well by insinuating a contradiction at the basis of them all—and not least in the relation between the urban and poetic vision. Let us recall the disconcerting end of "Villes I," the continuing interest in the ecstatic in that text, and the persisting values of child and nature in the other works of Rimbaud.

These considerations suggest that the victory of pure imaginative vision, deconstructed and absolute, in some of the city poems, is tinged by the failure of a larger, more human and visionary, undertaking. The autonomous, fantastic realms of "Les Ponts," "Villes II," and "Promontoire" thus represent, at least on one level, *alienations* of the human. For the movement that produces them begins in the oppression of the industrial city ("Ouvriers," "Ville"), or at best in a city emptied of economic activity ("Bruxelles"), or in a distancing from the urban ("Ornières"). And if "Villes II" can be read, as I suggest, as both the triumphant autonomy of imaginative experience and also as the magnification of all that is oppressive in the supermodern city, then indeed the world of the deconstructed self, the successful strategies of liberated vision, are the ambivalent product of a flight from intolerable human conditions.

This proposition is borne out by a revealing paragraph near the end of the *Saison,* at a point when Rimbaud has rejected both his impulse to *voyance* and European society, while still having great trouble accepting the real:

Ma vie est usée. Allons! feignons, fainéantons, ô pitié! Et nous existerons en nous amusant, en rêvant amours monstres et univers fantastiques, en nous plaignant et en querellant les apparences du monde, saltimbanque, mendiant, artiste, bandit,—prêtre!

   ("L'Eclair")

My life is used up. Let's go! let's fake, let's loaf and shirk, O pity! And we will exist by amusing ourselves, dreaming monstrous loves and fantastic universes, complaining and questioning the appearances of the world, clown, beggar, artist, bandit,—priest!

This passage precedes by only two pages the evocation of suffering in the city in "Adieu," and it points to some of the city poems ("Les Ponts" and "Villes II" come to mind) as wholly imaginary, sterile quarrelings with the appearances of the world—correctly seen by Rimbaud to represent an extension of traditional alienated roles of the artist. The fantastic *Illuminations* as finally *priestly,* Freud and Marx would make hay with that, and it seems legitimate indeed to keep in our minds the links between those strange creations and the depressing social and political context from which they emerged. "Nous existerons en nous amusant"; "amours monstres et univers fantastiques"; "nous plaignant et . . . querellant les apparences du monde": these formulas and the roles of mountebank, beggar, artist, bandit, and priest indicate the ways in which Rimbaud anticipates many features of our contemporary literature—Genêt and Robbe-Grillet and the erotic metaphor of the inner-directed, nonmimetic text—and some of the critical theories that accompany it. Fortunately, though, Rimbaud's work also looks back to and gathers up some of the best in romantic poetry. The connection between the two directions, and their relationship to Rimbaud's historical context, must not be lost; especially here, the link between visions and habitations, between perception, creation, and nature, on the one hand, and social experience on the other, must be grasped.[19]

History and the Life of the Poet

This comparative and contextual emphasis is the keynote of this study of Rimbaud. As I have argued from the outset, the work of a great writer must be viewed within both its literary tradition and its contemporary historical and intellectual context. In Rimbaud's work, historical and political reference is so frequent that to ignore it would amount to falsification. From the beginning *and through to the end of his production,* the sociohistorical concern is remarkable, despite the disembodied estheticism of some of the city texts and the violently noncollective, antihuman sentiments he often expressed. Even "A la musique," an early poem of adolescent sexuality, is set within a fiercely cynical social context. The lawns in Charleville (note the precise indication, "Place de la Gare, à Charleville") are paltry; and the young poet also shows us "bourgeois poussifs," "rentiers à lorgnons," "gros bureaux bouffis" (wheezing bourgeois, the propertied in pince-nez, fat bloated businessmen), "clubs d'épiciers retraités" (clubs of retired grocerers) discussing treaties, and a bourgeois smoking contraband tobacco. The adolescent speaker is motivated by sexual desire, and so are the "pioupious" (soldiers); but their presence and that of the military orchestra are big with meaning, considering the political verse Rimbaud was also writing. These are the soldiers who turn up dead in "Le Dormeur du val," who are a surreal and violating presence in "Le Cœur volé." Thus the sexual theme is from the beginning embedded in an accurately noted social, economic, and political scene, as is the case in other adolescent texts of rebellion: "Les Douaniers," with its opening references to "Soldats, marins, débris d'Empire, retraités" (Soldiers, sailors, debris of Empire, pensioneers); "Les Premières Communions," with its allusion to the boys "destinés au chic des garnisons" (destined for the chic garrisons); and "Les Poètes de sept ans," with its rebellion against God and maternal repression and its attraction to the poor and working classes.

Similar themes—social injustice, oppression, poverty, war—run through the explicitly political verse of the early periods. "Le Forgeron," quite derivative from Hugo, reenacts a confrontation with Louis XVI and is interesting for its naive formulations concerning work and dignity. Its mythic blacksmith tries to communicate to the king the satisfactions of agricultural labor:

Or, n'est-ce pas joyeux de voir, au mois de juin,
Dans les granges entrer des voitures de foin
Enormes? De sentir l'odeur de ce qui pousse,
Des vergers quand il pleut un peu . . .

Isn't it joyful to see, in the month of June,
Enormous loads of hay enter the barns?
To smell the odor of things growing,
Of orchards when it rains a bit . . .

Here Rimbaud's peasant realism has a political significance. The blacksmith also idealizes the "splendides lueurs des forges" (splendid gleams of the forges), but admits that the people who are without work and dignity become "crapule" (scum). "Nous sommes Ouvriers, Sire! Ouvriers!" (We are Workers, Sire! Workers!). Such simple formulations, in an excessively mythic context, are nonetheless informed with realistic concerns, for example, war: "Que l'on arrive encor, quand ce serait la guerre, / Me prendre mon garçon comme cela, chez moi!" (That they should come again, even if there's a war, and take my boy like that, in my own home!). The text is also a provocative prelude for the poet who in the *Saison* would write more incisively of repressive societal forms while himself refusing all forms of work.

Other historically oriented texts, such as "Morts de Quatre-vingt-douze et de Quatre-vingt-treize," also recall Hugo and yet are similarly pointed for Rimbaud's own context: "Nous, courbés sous les rois comme sous une trique. / —Messieurs de Cassagnac nous reparlent de vous!" (Us, crouching under kings as under a bludgeon.— The Messieurs de Cassagnac talk to us again about you!).[20] Some, from "Rages de Césars" and "L'Eclatante Victoire de Sarrebruck" to "Chant de guerre parisien" and "L'Orgie

parisienne," closely follow the events of war, dissolution of
the Empire, the fortunes and destruction of the Commune.
Still others attack organized religion, not only as a psycho-
logically and sexually repressive force ("Les Premières
Communions") but also as implicated in the system of
oppression and war. Hence "Les Pauvres à l'église," and
especially "Le Mal" (first ellipsis is Rimbaud's):

Tandis que les crachats rouges de la mitraille
Sifflent tout le jour par l'infini du ciel bleu;
Qu'écarlates ou verts, près du Roi qui les raille,
Croulent les bataillons en masse dans le feu;

Tandis qu'une folie épouvantable, broie
Et fait de cent milliers d'hommes un tas fumant;
—Pauvres morts! dans l'été, dans l'herbe, dans ta joie,
Nature! ô toi qui fis ces hommes saintement! . . . —

—Il est un Dieu . . .

While the red spit of grapeshot
Whistles all day through the infinity of the blue sky;
While scarlet or green, near the King who mocks them,
Whole battalions collapse in the fire;

While a terrible madness crushes
And makes of a hundred thousand men a smoking heap;
—Poor dead! in summer, in the grass, in your joy,
Nature! O you who made these men in holiness! . . . —

—There is a God . . .

The romantic values are once more used in political protest; the link with Hugo is again clear. Indeed from Blake
to Prévost and Char emerges a community of left-wing

poetic concern for the values of life throughout the horrors of the historical process, a community to which Rimbaud belongs.

These kinds of concerns recur in Rimbaud's later work, though sentimentality is replaced by cynicism. We earlier discussed his vitriolic dissection in the *Saison* of an oppressive society in the wake of the failure of the Commune. "Faux nègres": merchant, magistrate, general, emperor. We also noted the ambivalent meanings of his desire to go to Africa, the colonial movement being similarly troubling in "Ce qu'on dit au poète à propos de fleurs." And in the *Saison* we observed a mixture of opposing views on relationship with others. Its conclusion is terribly solitary: "Damnés, si je me vengeais!" (Damned, if I avenged myself!); "Que parlais-je de main amie!" (What was I saying about a friendly hand?); "il me sera loisible de *posséder la vérité dans une âme et un corps*" ("it will be permissible for me to *possess truth in one soul and one body*). Yet its last chapters also show a nostalgia for collective solutions: "Le chant des cieux, la marche des peuples! Esclaves, ne maudissons pas la vie" (The song of the heavens, the movement of peoples! Slaves, let us not curse life); "Cependant, c'est la veille. Recevons tous les influx de vigueur et de tendresse réelle. Et à l'aurore, armés d'une ardente patience, nous entrerons aux splendides villes" (However, this is the vigil. Let us receive all the influxes of vigor and of real tenderness. And at dawn, armed with an ardent patience, we will enter the splendid cities). Significantly, the work ends without resolving these paradoxes of intense solitude and collective aspiration.

This last formula seems to illuminate the city poems, especially "Villes I." It might be argued that the literal content of that poem is archaic, politically uninvolved—

certainly this is the sense of the conclusion. But the form of the text is overwhelmingly communal, figuring an impossible collective joy to which the poet aspires. It is well to keep this in mind in considering the other, more alienated city texts in the *Illuminations.* We must not forget either that in some of the prose poems there are suggestions of unmitigatedly radical political insight. "Après le déluge" evokes nature as sacred and portrays human society as destructive of it, through city, commerce, sexual strife, slaughter of animals. The values are the same as in the early political verse, even if the vision is more poetic and sophisticated. Similarly, "Mouvement," acting out the commercial colonizing theme of "Après le déluge," sarcastically and fancifully shows us the diluvian explorations of modern "conquérants du monde / Cherchant la fortune chimique personnelle" (conquerors of the world searching for their personal chemical fortune). Only "un couple de jeunesse" (a couple retaining youth) seems to keep the threatened values of childhood and nature: "Est-ce ancienne sauvagerie qu'on pardonne?" (Is this ancient savagery that is pardoned?). Or, if specifically political writing is required to demonstrate the point, could anything be more persuasive than "Démocratie"?

"Le drapeau va au paysage immonde, et notre patois étouffe le tambour.

"Aux centres nous alimenterons la plus cynique prostitution. Nous massacrerons les révoltes logiques.

"Aux pays poivrés et détrempés!—au service des plus monstrueuses exploitations industrielles ou militaires.

"Au revoir ici, n'importe où. Conscrits du bon vouloir, nous aurons la philosophie féroce; ignorants pour la science, roués pour le confort; la crevaison pour le monde qui va. C'est la vraie marche. En avant, route!"

"The flag is off to the filthy countryside, and our patois stifles the drum.

"In the centers we will nourish the most cynical prostitution. We will massacre the logical revolts.

"To the spicy and sodden lands!—in the service of the most monstrous industrial or military exploitations.

"So long here, no matter where. Conscripts of the good will, we will have the ferocious philosophy; ignorant for science, crafty for comfort; croaking for the rest of the world. This is the real thing. Forward, march!"

Like "Mouvement," and "Soir historique," which we will examine in a moment, this is probably one of the last texts produced by Rimbaud.[21] The poet who in the *Saison* showed both the idealism and the exploitativeness of the aspiration to the non-European world, who himself enlisted in a colonial expedition, and who ended his life in commercial exploitation of overseas regions, here analyzes the ruthlessness of the European colonial thrust with as much lucidity as anywhere in his work. This is the only poem in *Illuminations* in which the entire discourse is placed within quotation marks, though a text like "Ouvriers" also represents the speech or thoughts of an imagined character. Presumably "Démocratie" embodies the ideas of the mercenary conscripts mentioned in the last paragraph, and perhaps the use of quotation marks emphasizes both the public bravado that they display and the set character of a speech that enunciates the policy of the European powers. The poem depicts European scorn for the other world ("paysage immonde"), for its culture and modes of expression ("notre patois étouffe le tambour"); the cynical use of any and all destructive and exploiting tactics (prostitution, massacre, monstrous industrial and military exploitation); and the irresponsible attitude of the mercenaries. The political acuity that we observed in the earliest erotic and nature pieces persists to the end, and it cannot be dissociated from the variegated and fantastic creations of the other *Illuminations*.

This proposition is further exemplified by "Soir historique," which we have to see in its entirety:

En quelque soir, par exemple, que se trouve le touriste naïf, retiré de nos horreurs économiques, la main d'un maître anime le clavecin des prés; on joue aux cartes au fond de l'étang, miroir évocateur des reines et des mignonnes; on a les saintes, les voiles, et les fils d'harmonie, et les chromatismes légendaires, sur le couchant.

Il frissonne au passage des chasses et des hordes. La comédie goutte sur les tréteaux de gazon. Et l'embarras des pauvres et des faibles sur ces plans stupides!

A sa vision esclave, l'Allemagne s'échafaude vers des lunes; les déserts tartares s'éclairent; les révoltes anciennes grouillent dans le centre du Céleste Empire; par les escaliers et les fauteuils de rocs, un petit monde blême et plat, Afrique et Occidents, va s'édifier. Puis un ballet de mers et de nuits connues, une chimie sans valeur, et des mélodies impossibles.

La même magie bourgeoise à tous les points où la malle nous déposera! Le plus élémentaire physicien sent qu'il n'est plus possible de se soumettre à cette atmosphère personnelle, brume de remords physiques, dont la constatation est déjà une affliction.

Non! Le moment de l'étuve, des mers enlevées, des embrasements souterrains, de la planète emportée, et des exterminations conséquentes, certitudes si peu malignement indiquées dans la Bible et par les Nornes et qu'il sera donné à l'être sérieux de surveiller.—Cependant ce ne sera point un effet de légende!

On whatever evening, for example, that the naive
tourist finds himself, withdrawn from our economic horrors, the hand of a master brings the harpsichord of the
fields to life; people are playing cards at the bottom of
the pond, evocative mirror of queens and mignonnes;
we've got the female saints, veils, threads of harmony,
and the legendary chromatisms, in the sunset.

He shivers at the passage of hunts and hordes. The
comedy drips on the stage of sod. And the confusion of
the poor and weak on these stupid plans!

Slave to its vision, Germany scaffolds itself toward
moons; the tartar deserts light up; the ancient revolts
swarm in the center of the Celestial Empire; from the
stairways and armchairs of rocks, a little pale and flat
world, Africa and Occidents, is going to be constructed.
Then a ballet of well-known seas and nights, a chemistry
without value, and impossible melodies.

The same bourgeois magic at all the points where the
mail train will put us down! The most elementary physi-
cist senses that it is no longer possible to submit to this
personal atmosphere, fog of physical remorse, the ascer-
tainment of which is already an affliction.

No! The moment of the cauldron, of seas swept away,
of subterranean conflagrations, of the planet carried off,
and of the consequent exterminations, certainties indicated with such little malice in the Bible and by the
Norns and which it will be given to the serious being to
oversee.—However this will not at all be an effect of
legend!

This text extraordinarily demonstrates my argument
about the inherent connection between the poetic act and
historical-political realities. In it history, economics, and
class are implicated in the forms, satisfying and unsatisfy-
ing, of imaginative vision, with an emphasis on the *substantial reality* that is desired for that vision. In particular,

Rimbaud extends his view of the significance of the colonial (in the *Saison* and "Ce qu'on dit au poète") to the fact of tourism. The first formulation of the theme is rigorously realistic, connecting history (the title); the subjective, almost anecdotal temporality of the individual ("en quelque soir, par exemple"); the naive expectations of the tourist; and the reality of the Western social and economic system ("le touriste naïf, retiré de nos horreurs économiques"). Here the poet sees the relationship between what he calls the bourgeois economic system, the possibility of global travel by significant numbers of Westerners, and the notion itself of tourism. But seeing the links between economics, leisure, and the commercialization of leisure travel is not enough—though it is extraordinary, given Rimbaud's period. In fact, all the materials treated here illustrate his remarkable historical prescience. Even more, as in "Après le déluge," Rimbaud also sees how these historical realities are related to perceptions of nature and of the imagination.

In the first two paragraphs of "Soir historique," a view of nature emerges that at first seems exciting, but that turns out to be a tissue of literary and cultural clichés. In this sense the poem is a worthy successor to "Ce qu'on dit au poète." The world seems to be animated by a masterful musician (a stock romantic motif of an ancient lineage); the familiar use of the reflection symbol to make nature an evocative mirror lamely reveals a cardgame in the depth of a lake; and the sun can be made to represent any number of banal sensations, feelings or themes: in the expression "*on a* les saintes, les voiles, et les fils d'harmonie, et les chromatismes *légendaires*" one can almost hear the fatigued voice of a tour guide. And in the second paragraph even the barbarous and surreal components of Rimbaud's own art are co-opted for the tourist, who has a satisfying shiver at the not very proximate passage of savage hordes, conveniently glimpses a Dali-like liquefication of nature and the theater, and seems embarrassed by a reflection filled with social prejudice in an overall context of stupidity.

If the first paragraphs seem not completely explicit, the next two paragraphs make it so. Characteristic motifs appear: the illusory mysticism of Germany (see "Age d'or" and "Entends comme brame"), Asiatic shamanism ("Délires I"), and the theme of rebellion in the context of an ancient and grandiose "Céleste Empire." These motifs contribute not to some visionary transformation but to the creation of a "petit monde blême et plat," which is all that the impoverished imagination can make of the meeting between Africa and the West. These all too familiar and impossible magics are then explicitly condemned as the products of bourgeois, subjective, guilt-ridden consciousness ("magie bourgeoise," "atmosphère personnelle," "brume de remords physiques"). This condemnation recalls the theory of *voyance* and Rimbaud's rebellion in ethics and religion; it also implies a convergence of elements close to the thinking of Blake, Marx, and Nietzsche. For the problem of this wholly unsatisfactory view of the world is related to economic and social class, to the predominance of remorse (so thick it becomes physical) that Nietzsche and Blake analyzed, to an excessive subjectivity that is attacked by Blake, Marx, and Nietzsche.

To what extent does this late and extremely penetrating formulation of a critique of socioeconomic *and* mental modes of existence and activity evidence a realization by Rimbaud that some of his poetic structurings possibly represent a form of alienation? The number of allusions to his own themes and motifs makes the suggestion an attractive one. Clearly, however, in the last paragraph Rimbaud is still aiming at some transforming act, apocalyptic and destructive, which he explicitly relates to traditional scriptures and myth, but in which he expects seriously to participate, and which will be neither subjective nor legendary but *entirely real.*

The character of this act is extraordinarily difficult to grasp. It is hardly to be a political transformation of any usual sort—the earlier, similar, verse poem "Qu'est-ce que pour nous, mon cœur" with its desire for the destruction of all of nature and of all political structures, seems to guarantee that. Neither will the act be mere mental activity, as we in our state of single vision understand that phrase. Rimbaud's later life shows clearly his own inability to realize the project, a fact that Ruff and Gascar relate to the deception of an entire generation in France,[22] and that we might relate to succeeding generations of Europeans and Americans, caught in what Blake early on saw as "mind-forg'd manacles" and economic, social, and political constraint.

But "Soir historique," one of Rimbaud's final and most comprehensive statements, continues to call to us. It exemplifies my argument about the intimate link between consciousness and the natural and socioeconomic world, visions and habitations. We began with nature, then confronted the city, and now face the global extension of the bourgeois economic and cultural system. The three stages, in reality summations of many complex factors, must be seen as interrelated, as Rimbaud saw them. Vision, nature, and economic reality are once again troublingly copresent in this third and worldwide phase. And the situation that emerges in that third state is already our own, so powerful was Rimbaud's *historical* vision, so illustrative was he of Blake's belief in the projective nature of the imagination. The questions the poem leaves are the questions we still have. The answers are not clear, but as this text suggests, they may perhaps be sought distantly in some deft combination of thinking that draws on Blake, Marx, Nietzsche, and Rimbaud himself.

Epilogue: King, Queen, and Charming Worker

"Bonne Pensée du matin," a slight, uncelebrated text, one of the *Derniers Vers,* dated on the manuscript May 1872, seems to surprisingly draw together much that I have argued throughout this book:

> A quatre heures du matin, l'été,
> Le sommeil d'amour dure encore.
> Sous les bosquets l'aube évapore
>   L'odeur du soir fêté.
>
> Mais là-bas dans l'immense chantier
> Vers le soleil des Hespérides,
> En bras de chemise, les charpentiers
>   Déjà s'agitent.
>
> Dans leur désert de mousse, tranquilles,
> Ils préparent les lambris précieux
> Où la richesse de la ville
>   Rira sous de faux cieux.
>
> Ah! pour ces Ouvriers charmants
> Sujets d'un roi de Babylone,
> Vénus! laisse un peu les Amants,
>   Dont l'âme est en couronne.
>
>   O Reine des Bergers!
> Porte aux travailleurs l'eau-de-vie,
> Pour que leurs forces soient en paix
> En attendant le bain dans la mer, à midi.

At four in the morning, in summer,
The sleep of love continues still.
Under the groves dawn evaporates
    The odor of festive evening.

But over there in the immense workyard
Toward the sun of the Hesperides,
In shirt sleeves, the carpenters
    Are already moving about.

In their desert of moss, tranquil,
They prepare the precious paneling
Where the riches of the city
    Will laugh under false skies.

Ah! for these charming Workers
Subjects of a king of Babylonia,
Venus! leave a little the Lovers,
    Whose souls are crowned.

    O Queen of Shepherds!
Bring brandy to the workers,
So that their strength may be at peace
While awaiting the bath in the sea, at noon.

Not a great deal of attention has been paid to this poem, although we can relate it to J.-P. Richard's use of the "Pamerde, Jumphe 72" letter to Delahaye as a springboard for his reading of Rimbaud's imagery. The biographical connection with the letter is apt—it underscores characteristic symbolism and situates the poet in mid-course of his itinerary: thirsty in the Paris heat, missing the rivers and caves of his native Ardennes, in a hiatus in his relationship with Verlaine, contemplating and creating in the city, alternating work and drunkenness. Richard's impressionist reading of sensations and substances is apt as well.[23] Both elements help us to see the poem as a parable—in quite clear succession—of all the themes we noted earlier: childlike spontaneity, nature, city, sexuality, work, oppression, and the mythic.

Thus the poem opens with essential romantic sensations and values: morning, summer, greenery, dawn, the immediacy of the evaporating freshness of the air. But, as throughout Rimbaud's work, these innocent motifs are seen in tension with a series of other themes—first of all the sexual, with its heavy odor of evening, feast, sleep, and love. This opposition is complicated in the succeeding two stanzas by evocations of the radically distanced realms of work ("là-bas . . . l'immense chantier") and of the city: "Dans leur désert de mousse," "les lambris précieux / Où la richesse de la ville," "sous de faux cieux." Stanzas four and five appeal to Venus to transcend these separations, to bring to the workers the satisfactions of sex (Venus herself), inebriation ("l'eau-de-vie"), and nature ("Reine des Bergers," "le bain dans la mer"). But their structure of desire and appeal only reaccentuates the oppositions. Innocence, nature, the erotic, work, and inebriation are therefore all involved, but so also are the city and the system of economic and political submission that it implies ("Ouvriers . . . / Sujets d'un roi de Babylone"). All are involved, yet also segregated; "Bonne Pensée" is like a poetic aside on the theme of the division of labor.

Hence the workers exist "là-bas," and are circumscribed as well by a mixture of realistic and mythological conventions through which their state is typically evoked in literature. The realistic "chantier," "en bras de chemise," "les charpentiers," "Ouvriers," "travailleurs" merge with the mythically immense, literary, natural, prettified suggestions of "immense chantier," "le soleil des Hespérides," "désert de mousse," "Ouvriers charmants." But the embellishment helps to underscore the exploitative relationships that such conventions embody, for workers and artists alike. For the artisans submissive to political authority are precisely those who have an explicit societal function:

> Dans leur désert de mousse, tranquilles,
> Ils préparent les lambris précieux
> Où la richesse de la ville
> Rira sous de faux cieux.

In these aptly simplifying formulas, poetic musicality manages to convey class separation ("Dans leur désert") and function ("Ils préparent"), as well as something of the links between the city, economic structure, and the theme of artificiality ("lambris précieux," "la richesse de la ville," "faux cieux"). Nicely, Rimbaud uses the standard plural for skies, but characterizes them as "faux"; whereas occasionally in the *Illuminations* the painter's word "ciels" seems to confuse the real and the imaginary. We observed the rich suggestiveness of that tactic in texts like "Les Ponts"; here the variety of skies insinuates instead the way in which art is related to another kind of riches, is caught in the constraints of the political-economic system.

If this is correct, if the "Ouvriers charmants" therefore figure both worker and artist, then "Bonne Pensée," written one year to the month after the defeat of the workers' Commune, records a conflation of the two realms that is unusual in Rimbaud's work. Think only of his attitude to work in the *voyant* letters and the opening of the *Saison,* or of the prose poem "Ouvriers." The end of the *Saison,* it is true, attempts to accept work, but only through a rejection of the effort toward visionary art and in connection with a frighteningly negative evocation of the city. In contrast, in "Bonne Pensée" city, political structure, work, and art all seem to coexist.

But of course that seemingly peaceful coexistence is explosively deceptive, as is signaled by the distances and divisions already mentioned and by the vocabulary of satisfaction (essentially libidinal) throughout the poem. The lovers' sleep, the festive evening, and the laughter of the rich hardly exist for the workers. The latter are depicted in an improbable and wholly uncharacteristic way, as "tranquilles" and "charmants." The exclamations in the last two stanzas imply a conflict between the realm of work and the sexual ("Vénus! laisse un peu les Amants"), and also between work and a conventional, pastoral view of nature ("O Reine des Bergers!"). This appeal evokes the erotic-ecstatic project, presided over by the figure of Venus from "Soleil et chair" to "Villes I" and "Barbare"; but here it in every way implies alienation, lack, unfulfilled desire.

We should note also the character of the satisfactions proposed for the workers in the last stanza. "L'eau-de-vie," suggestive of inebriation and reanimation, and the mythic-elemental contact with nature, that most romantic and Rimbaldian immersion, "le bain dans la mer, à midi," within the context of the poem have a significance that is, to say the least, suspect. Novelists from Balzac to Zola explore the function of drink for French workers in the nineteenth century; in Rimbaud's schematic vision of social and economic relationships, that function (indeed not far removed from keeping the workers' "forces . . . en paix") may perhaps be glimpsed behind the "poetic" evocations of "l'eau-de-vie." And the immersion at the end, the libidinal immersion in the sea, how can that represent truly Marcuse's "nonrepressive sublimation," when in fact it is procured at the cost of the psychic and sociopolitical divisions that the poem reveals? Here we glimpse a deprivation both personal and systematic that may go far to explain the lack of human compassion in Rimbaud's work, the dominant note of harsh anger and suffering. For the gaps and the distances, the separation from power, money, luxury, sexual satisfaction, are too apparent. "Bonne Pensée du matin" is a parable of the submission of the natural, the erotic, the productive, the artistic—a calm vision from which only rebellion can come. It is a poem that calls for the violence of the *Saison* and the *Illuminations*, in particular for the lucidly surreal and revolutionary stance of "Soir historique."

What is marvellous about this seemingly simple poem, finally, is its inclusive, analytical, and schematizing quality. All the themes that I have pursued, as well as the structure of my study ("separate," "thematic" sections aimed however at a contextual understanding of the full human significance of Rimbaud's entire production), are echoed in this poem. Childlike immediacy and immersion, the problems of erotic gratification attaining ecstasy ("l'âme . . . en couronne"), the implication of creation and work within the perceptual, political, and historical interaction of nature, city and society: all these are successively evoked in "Bonne Pensée du matin." That analytical successiveness, corresponding roughly to the structure of this book, reveals, as I want my study to reveal, the involvement of poetry in all these realms, as well as the alienations and oppositions by which these realms are ruled. Rimbaud has always had such an enormous impact, he remains of such major importance, because he speaks so violently and so magnificently to all these concerns—to our sense of our child and adult selves, to our insistent aspiration to entire satisfaction, to our perceiving and social existence in the man-made and increasingly vulnerable natural worlds. He animates the beauty of all these realms for us; and in his thoroughgoing dissatisfaction—stretching from family and sexuality to all known forms of community and to the outreach of colonial exploitation—he perhaps stirs in us a comparable and salutary movement of rebellion.

Notes

INTRODUCTION

1. See Jean-Louis Baudry, "Le Texte de Rimbaud," *Tel Quel*, no. 35 (Autumn 1968), pp. 46–63, and no. 36 (Winter 1969), pp. 33–53; Leo Bersani, *A Future for Astyanax: Character and Desire in Literature* (Boston: Little, Brown, 1976), pp. 5–6, 230–258; Atle Kittang, *Discours et jeu: Essai d'analyse des textes d'Arthur Rimbaud,* Contributions Norvégiennes aux Etudes Romanes, no. 5 (Bergen: Universitetsforlaget, 1975); Nathaniel Wing, *Present Appearances: Aspects of Poetic Structure in Rimbaud's "Illuminations,"* Romance Monographs, no. 9 (University, Miss.: Romance Monographs, 1974). An overview of Rimbaud criticism is provided by Kittang, pp. 13–34.

2. Aside from an occasional article or aside in books devoted to Rimbaud, there is indeed little comparative work on him. René Etiemble's *Le Mythe de Rimbaud,* 4 vols. (Paris: Gallimard, 1952–1961) concerns Rimbaud criticism, and the focus of Margherita Frankel's study, *Le Code Dantesque dans l'œuvre de Rimbaud* (Paris: A.-G. Nizet, 1975), is sufficiently indicated in its title. Notable comparative commentaries include Anna Balakian, *Literary Origins of Surrealism: A New Mysticism in French*

Poetry, 2d ed. (New York: New York University Press, 1965), especially pp. 77–89 on Rimbaud, and Kittang's *Discours et jeu,* which is generally comparative in relating Rimbaud's work to romantic literature as a whole, but in ways quite different from my approach and without sustained reference to any other writer.

3. Nick Osmond, ed., *Illuminations: Coloured Plates* (London: Athlone Press, 1976), p. 3.

ONE. *Childhood and the Origins of Poetry*

1. See Peter Coveney, *The Image of Childhood, the Individual and Society: A Study of the Theme in English Literature,* 2d ed., rev. (Baltimore: Penguin Books, 1967), pp. 29–32; Mark Spilka, *Dickens and Kafka* (Bloomington: Indiana University Press, 1963); C. G. Jung and C. Kerényi, *Essays on a Science of Mythology: The Myth of the Divine Child and the Mysteries of Eleusis,* tr. R. F. C. Hull, 2d ed., (Princeton: Princeton University Press, 1969); Gaston Bachelard, "Les Rêveries vers l'enfance," in *La Poétique de la rêverie* (Paris: Presses Universitaires de France, 1960), pp. 84–123. On Freud, see Norman O. Brown, *Life Against Death: The Psychoanalytical Meaning of History* (New York: Random House, 1961), especially pp. 30–33.

Among extensive critical writings on the child in Rimbaud, see especially Balakian, *Literary Origins;* Bersani, *Future for Astyanax;* Kittang, *Discours et jeu;* and Wing, *Present Appearances;* Robert Greer Cohn, *The Poetry of Rimbaud* (Princeton: Princeton University Press, 1973), especially pp. 3–28; C. A. Hackett, *Le Lyrisme de Rimbaud,* 2d ed. (Paris: Nizet et Bastard, 1938), *Rimbaud,* Studies in Modern European Literature and Thought (New York: Hillary House, 1957), *Rimbaud: A Critical Introduction* (Cambridge: Cambridge University Press, 1981); Wallace Fowlie, *Rimbaud* (Chicago: University of Chicago Press, 1965); Yves Bonnefoy, *Rimbaud par lui-même,* Ecrivains de Toujours (Paris: Editions du Seuil, 1961), especially pp. 5–30; René

Etiemble and Yassu Gauclère, *Rimbaud*, 2d ed., rev.,
Bibliothèque des Idées (Paris: Gallimard, 1950); Emilie Noulet,
*Le Premier Visage de Rimbaud: Huit Poèmes de jeunesse, Choix et
commentaire* (Brussels: Palais des Académies, 1953); Jean-Pierre
Richard, "Rimbaud ou la poésie du devenir," in *Poésie et profondeur* (Paris: Editions du Seuil, 1955), pp. 187–250. See also the
Freudian interpretations of Enid Rhodes Peschel, *Flux and Reflux: Ambivalence in the Poems of Arthur Rimbaud* (Geneva: Droz,
1977); the discussion of child, worker, and water in Marie-Jose-
phine Whitaker, *La Structure du monde imaginaire de Rimbaud*
(Paris: A.-G. Nizet, 1972), pp. 32–47, 81–96.

Among the biographies of Rimbaud I have most consulted
Henri Matarasso and Pierre Petitfils, *Vie d'Arthur Rimbaud*
(Paris: Hachette, 1962); Enid Starkie, *Rimbaud*, 3d ed. (New
York: New Directions, 1961); Suzanne Briet, *Madame Rimbaud:
Essai de biographie* (Paris: Minard, 1968); Ernest Delahaye, *Rimbaud: L'Artiste et l'être moral* (Paris: A. Messein, 1923) and *Souvenirs familiers à propos de Rimbaud, Verlaine, Germaine Nouveau*
(Paris: A. Messein, 1925). Unlike Philippe Ariès in *L'Enfant et
la vie familiale sous l'ancien régime* (Paris: Plon, 1960), I do not
find it especially pertinent, for Rimbaud, to insist on distinctions between childhood, youth, and adolescence. Finally,
throughout my discussion, "child poetry" refers to poetry about
childhood, rather than poetry by children.

2. See Bachelard, *Poétique de la rêverie*, pp. 92–93; and
Freud, *The Interpretation of Dreams*, "Screen Memories," and
Introductory Lectures on Psycho-analysis, lectures 7, 13, 23, *Beyond the Pleasure Principle*, chap. 3. "Screen memory" in Freud
designates a "memory" that apparently derives from the earliest phase of childhood but that, on analysis, proves to be a
later construction.

3. For the oceanic in Ferenczi and Wordsworth, see Freud,
Civilization and Its Discontents, chap. 1; Lionel Trilling, *The
Liberal Imagination: Essays on Literature and Society* (Garden City,
N.Y.: Doubleday, 1953), p. 143; and Norman O. Brown,
Love's Body (New York: Random House, 1968), pp. 88–89. For

water imagery, see Gaston Bachelard, *L'Eau et les rêves: Essai sur l'imagination de la matière* (Paris: J. Corti, 1960), and my article, "The Childlike Sensibility: A Study of Wordsworth and Rimbaud," *Revue de Littérature Comparée*, 42ᵉ année, no. 2 (April–June 1968), pp. 234–256, especially pp. 236–242.

4. See Henri Peyre's insightful reading of "Mémoire" in Stanley Burnshaw, ed., *The Poem Itself* (New York: Schocken Books, 1967), pp. 26–31.

5. For examples of the theme of the child's moral innocence, see Hölderlin, *Hyperion,* Book I, third letter to Bellarmin; also the final version of "Die Meinigen" and the opening of "Germanien"; Hugo, "A une jeune fille" (*Odes et ballades,* V, 17), "Lorsque l'enfant paraît," "La Prière pour tous" (*Les Feuilles d'automne,* XIX, XXXVII, as well as XV), "La Voix d'un enfant d'un an" (*La Légende des siècles,* XXXVI, "L'Idylle du vieillard"), "Fonction de l'enfant" (*La Légende des siècles,* LVII, iii), *Chansons des rues et des bois* (livre deuxième, II, ii and iv), "Le Poëme du Jardin des Plantes," "L'Immaculée Conception," and "Jeanne endormie" (*L'Art d'être grand-père,* parts IV, VII, XVII), and the passages on the "gamin de Paris" in *Les Misérables* (part III, book I, chaps. 1, 6); Dostoyevsky's Sonya in *Crime and Punishment* and Alyosha in *The Brothers Karamazov;* Jacques Prévert, "Maintenant j'ai grandi," "L'Enfant de mon vivant" (*La Pluie et le beau temps*), and "Les Enfants qui s'aiment" (*Spectacle*).

6. Freud, "On Narcissism: An Introduction." For this and the following paragraph, see also Hugo, *Toute la lyre,* III, ii, and *L'Art d'être grand-père,* I, iii, vi. For Yeats, see "To a Child Dancing in the Wind," "Sweet Dancer," and "A Crazed Girl"; *A Vision* (New York: Macmillan, 1961), pp. 82, 88; *The Autobiography of William Butler Yeats* (Garden City, N.Y.: Doubleday, 1958), pp. 128, 166, 193–194. Among many other passages and writers, see André Breton, *Manifestes du surréalisme,* Collection Idées (Paris: Gallimard, 1963), p. 55: "l'enfance où tout concourait . . . à la possession efficace, et sans aléas, de soi-même" (childhood, when everything contributed to the effective, risk-free possession of oneself).

7. See Brown, *Life Against Death*, pp. 30–32; Coveney, *Image of Childhood*, pp. 33–34, 291–302; Freud, *Three Essays on the Theory of Sexuality, Leonardo da Vinci and a Memory of His Childhood*, "Formulations on the Two Principles of Mental Functioning," and *Introductory Lectures on Psycho-analysis*, lectures 13, 20; Wordsworth, "Tintern Abbey," "Louisa," *Prelude*, I, 288–300, 425–463, and II, 24–40; Blake, *Visions of the Daughters of Albion*, plate 6.

8. Quotations from "Conte," "Being Beauteous," "Matinée d'ivresse," "Angoisse," "Génie." For the Freudian argument in the following paragraphs, with particular reference to "Les Poètes de sept ans" and "Les Sœurs de charité," see *Introductory Lectures on Psycho-analysis*, lecture 23; Cohn, *The Poetry of Rimbaud*, pp. 5–11, 97–106, 119–125.

9. See Coleridge in the *Athenaeum* of March 13, 1809, in Kathleen Coburn, ed., *Inquiring Spirit, A New Presentation of Coleridge From His Published and Unpublished Writings* (London: Routledge and Paul, 1951), p. 89. See also Hugo, *Les Feuilles d'automne*, XX; *L'art d'être grand-père*, XII; *Les Rayons et les ombres*, XXXI; *Les Contemplations*, III, xvii. Finally, see Blake, *The Book of Thel*, the little boy and girl lost and found and the chimney-sweep poems in *Songs of Innocence and Experience;* Wordsworth, "Ruth," "The Idiot Boy," "Lucy Gray, or Solitude," *Prelude*, VII, 288–381; and Hackett, *Le Lyrisme de Rimbaud*, pp. 76–96.

10. In addition to texts specifically mentioned in my discussion of religion and education, see Rousseau, *Emile*, especially Books I and II; Blake, "The School Boy" (*Songs of Innocence*); Coleridge, *Inquiring Spirit*, pp. 76–87. I also draw on Wordsworth, *Prelude*, III, IV, and V. See also Hugo, *Les Rayons et les ombres*, XIX; *L'Art d'être grand-père*, VIII; X; XI; XV, ii, vii; *L'Ane*, V; *Les Quatre Vents de l'esprit*, I, xxxi. Finally, see Yeats, "Among School Children"; Prévert, "Chasse à l'enfant," "Le Cancre," "Page d'écriture" (*Paroles*), "Le Beau Langage" (*La Pluie et le beau temps*), "L'Enfant abandonné," "La Belle Vie," "Les Olvidados," "L'Enseignement libre" (*Spectacle*).

11. Cited by Pierre Gascar, *Rimbaud et la Commune,* Collection Idées (Paris: Gallimard, 1971), p. 29.

12. The poem's buffoonish qualities include a singsong rhythm, heavy rhyme and alliteration, and grotesque diction ("Ithyphalliques et pioupiesques," "hoquets bachiques"). For critical references on this poem in the following paragraph, see Bonnefoy, *Rimbaud par lui-même,* p. 43; W. M. Frohock, *Rimbaud's Poetic Practice: Image and Theme in the Major Poems* (Cambridge, Mass.: Harvard University Press, 1963), especially p. 123; Colonel Godchot, *Arthur Rimbaud ne varietur,* 2 vols. (Nice: Chez l'auteur, 1936–1937), I, 176–180.

13. For my argument here and in the following paragraph, see Hölderlin, "Hyperions Schicksaalslied." Relevant texts by Hugo include *Les Rayons et les ombres,* XI; *Les Contemplations,* III, xiv, xv, xxiii; VI, viii; *Toute la Lyre,* III, xxii. See also Wordsworth, "The Sailor's Mother"; "Elegiac Verses in Memory of My Brother, John Wordsworth"; *Prelude,* V, 364–397, 426–459 and VII, 288–381; *The Excursion,* III, 990–991; *Itinerary Poems of 1833,* xvi, xvii. Among critics, see Geoffrey H. Hartman, *Wordsworth's Poetry, 1787–1814* (New Haven and London: Yale University Press, 1964), pp. 19–22, 231–233; David Ferry, *The Limits of Mortality: An Essay on Wordsworth's Major Poems* (Middletown, Conn.: Wesleyan University Press, 1959).

14. For the child in "Le Bateau ivre," see Bernard Weinberg, *The Limits of Symbolism, Studies of Five Modern French Poets* (Chicago: University of Chicago Press, 1966), pp. 89–126.

15. For this paragraph and the following materials on child, vision, and temporality, see Blake, letter to Dr. Trusler, 23 August, 1799, as well as "There is No Natural Religion," "All Religions are One," *The French Revolution, The Marriage of Heaven and Hell, America, A Prophecy, Songs of Experience* ("Introduction," "The Tyger," "To Tirzah"), *Europe, A Prophecy, Milton* (especially the preface and conclusion), "The Everlasting Gospel," and also the troubling text "The Mental Traveller"; Hugo, *Les Rayons et les ombres,* XXXV; Baudelaire, "Le Peintre

de la vie moderne," "Morale du joujou," "Exposition universelle" of 1855 (*Œuvres*, pp. 530–539, 682–683, 709, 885–891, 912–913); Wordsworth, *Prelude*, V, 341–346, 460–533; VII, 407–457; Hölderlin, "Da ich ein Knabe war," "Hälfte des Lebens," "Andenken," *Der Tod des Empedokles*, second version, I, iii, as well as "Lebensalter," "Mnemosyne," "Der Archipelagus," "Patmos"; Freud, "Creative Writers and Day-Dreaming," "Recollecting, Repeating and Working Through," *Beyond the Pleasure Principle*, chaps. 2, 4, and 5, *Introductory Lectures on Psycho-analysis*, lectures 7, 13, 23, "A Note upon the Mystic Writing-Pad"; Jacques Derrida, "Freud et la scène de l'écriture," in *L'Ecriture et la différence* (Paris: Editions du Seuil, 1967), especially pp. 300–307, 329–334; Brown, *Life Against Death*, pp. 95, 109, 162–163; Herbert Marcuse, *Eros and Civilization: A Philosophical Inquiry into Freud* (New York: Random House, 1961), p. 18.

16. See Herbert Lindenberger, *On Wordsworth's Prelude* (Ithaca: Cornell University Press, 1954); Brian Wilkie, *Romantic Poets and Epic Tradition* (Madison: University of Wisconsin Press, 1965); John Porter Houston, *The Design of Rimbaud's Poetry*, Yale Romanic Studies, Second Series, II (New Haven: Yale University Press, 1963), pp. 194–200.

17. Until recently scholars debated the relation between dates of composition of *Illuminations* and *Saison;* see Henri de Bouillane de Lacoste, *Rimbaud et le problème des "Illuminations"* (Paris: Mercure de France, 1949) and Charles Chadwick, *Etudes sur Rimbaud* (Paris: A.-G. Nizet, 1960). Now most scholars, myself included, believe that the prose poems were largely written after the *Saison* and that the prose poems themselves evidence considerable evolution. Osmond, *Illuminations*, persuasively argues these points on the basis of his analysis of the manuscripts, order of publication, and the poems themselves. Similarly, discussion of the *Saison* by Baudry ("Le Texte," pp. 33–53) and Kittang (*Discours et jeu*, pp. 136–159) dovetails with some of my arguments in presenting the work as a kind of last gasp of confessional, retrospective form, revelatory of an

ideologically stifling situation, prelude to the quite different, scenic mode of many of the *Illuminations*. My disagreements with Baudry and Kittang are visible in the following section; however, their ideological argument converges with some of my positions on poetry and society in chapter 3.

18. *Eros and Civilization*, pp. 146–156.

19. See Hölderlin, "Da ich ein Knabe war" and the last two stanzas of "Germanien," and Wordsworth, "It is a beauteous evening, calm and free" and "The world is too much with us."

20. For the archetypal resonances of such motifs and of the imagery in the fifth part of "Enfance," see Wordsworth, *Prelude*, IV, 354–460, XIII, 142 ff., "Resolution and Independence," "The Old Cumberland Beggar," "Animal Tranquillity and Decay," "The Solitary Reaper," "To a Highland Girl"; Hölderlin, "Mnemosyne"; Hugo, *Les Contemplations*, III, xxx, V, xvii, xxiii; Yeats, "The Three Hermits," "Shepherd and Goatherd," "The Fisherman," "Ego Dominus Tuus," "The Tower," "All Souls' Night," "Symbols," "Meru" (in "Supernatural Songs"); Baudelaire, "Rêve parisien"; Mallarmé, "Hérodiade."

21. Osmond (*Illuminations*, pp. 9–16, 30–38) argues that "Guerre" and "Jeunesse" are the most mature expressions of Rimbaud's child poetry. For the comparative context of "Guerre," see Wordsworth, "Three years she grew in sun and shower," *Prelude*, I, 357–400, II, 302–322; Blake, *The Marriage of Heaven and Hell*, virtually all the prophetic poems—especially the preface to *Milton*, and letters to Dr. Trusler and Thomas Butts, 23 August 1799 and 22 November 1802; Breton, *Manifestes du surréalisme*, opening pages of the *Second Manifeste*.

22. Perhaps this state resembles Yeats's unity of being; see semimystical texts like "All Souls' Night" and "Byzantium." See also Frank Kermode, *Romantic Image* (London: Routledge and Kegan Paul, 1957); and Rimbaud, "Phrases": "J'ai tendu des cordes de clocher à clocher; des guirlandes de fenêtre à fenêtre; des chaînes d'or d'étoile à étoile, et je danse" (I have stretched cords from steeple to steeple; garlands from window to

window; golden chains from star to star, and I dance). For the several senses of "raison" see the second *voyant* letter, "A une raison," and "Génie."

23. See the first *voyant* letter, "Soir historique," "Après le déluge," and "Guerre."

24. Bersani (*Future for Astyanax,* pp. 230–258) plausibly argues that in many cases it is not a matter of failure at all, but rather of an accession to decentered, scenic consciousness.

25. The sense of failure is accentuated by the use of *songer,* the verb that in the *Saison* and "Guerre" announces the poet's expectation of future action or vision.

TWO. *Ecstatic Realizations*

1. The term "altered states of consciousness" denotes multiple, sometimes contradictory, modifications of normal consciousness whose culminations can be called ecstatic or mystical. "Ecstatic" designates maximum excitation in a "deselved" state; "mystical" is closely allied, but often involves a supernal peace and always an experience of unmediated participation in the ultimate reality. In Rimbaud it is most productive to study the ecstatic (transformations of consciousness and unselvings that stress the body, excitation and intensity) and ambivalent transcendent and immanent impulses. See Roland Fischer, "Cartography of Inner Space," in *Altered States of Consciousness: Current Views and Research Problems* (Washington: Drug Abuse Council, 1975), pp. 1–57; *Encyclopaedia of Religion and Ethics,* ed. James Hastings, 13 vols. (New York: Scribner's Sons, 1928), I, 157–159; *New Catholic Encyclopedia,* 17 vols. (New York: McGraw-Hill, 1967), V, 86–88; Ben-Ami Scharfstein, *Mystical Experience* (Baltimore: Penguin Books, 1974), especially pp. 141–175.

Mystical, visionary, occult, alchemical, surreal, sexual, and ecstatic features of Rimbaud's work are variously treated by Balakian, Bonnefoy, Cohn, Etiemble and Gauclère, Frohock,

Houston, Osmond, Starkie, as well as by Gwendolyn Bays, *The Orphic Vision, Seer Poets from Novalis to Rimbaud* (Lincoln: University of Nebraska Press, 1964); Marc Eigeldinger, *Rimbaud et le mythe solaire* (Neuchâtel: A la Baconnière, 1964), and "La Voyance avant Rimbaud," in Gérald Schaeffer, ed., Arthur Rimbaud, *Lettres du voyant* (Geneva and Paris: Droz and Minard, 1975); Jacques Gengoux, *La Pensée poétique de Rimbaud* (Paris: A.-G. Nizet, 1950); Jean Richer, *L'Alchimie du verbe de Rimbaud, ou Les Jeux de Jean-Arthur* (Paris: Didier, 1972).

2. My condensation of Blake's work refers, in addition to passages explicitly mentioned, to the following: "The Human Abstract" and "A Poison Tree" from *Experience; The Marriage of Heaven and Hell;* "The Everlasting Gospel"; portions of Blake's shorter prophetic books—in particular, *The First Book of Urizen,* chap. vii, *The Song of Los,* plates 4, 7; *The Four Zoas,* especially IX, 728–855; *Milton,* especially I, plates 23, 27; and *Jerusalem.* My argument on the body in Blake agrees with Thomas R. Frosch, *The Awakening of Albion, The Renovation of the Body in the Poetry of William Blake* (Ithaca: Cornell University Press, 1974).

My discussion of Nietzsche is based on *The Birth of Tragedy, The Dawn, Thus Spoke Zarathustra, Beyond Good and Evil, Toward a Genealogy of Morals, Twilight of the Idols,* in particular the following passages from *Werke:* I, 12–13, 49, 1015; II, 300, 438, 617, 834, 1022–23, 1032. Translations and paraphrases of Nietzsche are mine, except for Zarathustra on the bodily self and the psychology of the orgiastic from the end of *Twilight of the Gods,* which I take from Walter Kaufmann, tr., *The Portable Nietzsche* (New York: Viking Press, 1968), pp. 146, 562.

3. Noulet, *Premier Visage,* p. 105; see also R[obert] F[aurisson], "A-t-on lu Rimbaud?," *Bizarre,* no. 21–22 (1961), 1–48.

4. For the link between these crucial, and late, texts, see Osmond, *Illuminations,* pp. 30–31, 163–166, 172–173. For a superb discussion of "Génie" in relation to Rimbaud's total œuvre, see James R. Lawler, *The Language of French Symbolism*

(Princeton: Princeton University Press, 1969), pp. 71–111. Balakian, *Literary Origins*, especially pp. 16, 39, 83, 85–86, is also relevant to my argument.

5. *Werke*, I, 38. For further references to Nietzsche in my discussion of "Génie" see I, 14; II, 416, 454–455, 463, 466, 556–557, 617, 1024–25, 1030–32.

6. "Trance" implies obliteration of consciousness, while "ecstasy," for which "frenzy" may be a preliminary or contributory stage, involves maximum psychic excitation—the three appearing in the African trance, Mongol or Scandinavian fury, and drug ecstasy of "Mauvais Sang," "Délires I," and "Nuit de l'enfer," respectively. "Dissociation" describes extensive loss of contact with the normal sense of reality, as at the conclusions of "Nuit de l'enfer" and of both "Délires," and in "O saisons, ô châteaux!" "Mystical" suggests dissolution of self and participation in some ultimate reality, in the *Saison* a purified and essential "lumière *nature*" ("Délires I," "Fêtes de la patience").

7. *Les Déserts de l'amour* evokes a similar phenomenon of hallucinatory dreams persisting into waking life, and adds: "Peut-être se rappellera-t-on le sommeil continu des Mahométans légendaires" (Perhaps the prolonged sleep of the legendary Mohammedans will be recalled), a reference to another recognizable mystic-ecstatic tradition. Louis Massignon, *Essai sur les origines du lexique technique de la mystique musulmane*, 2d ed., rev. (Paris: J. Vrin, 1968), discusses ecstatic states in Islamic mysticism, noting in particular an awareness of the danger of pursuing such experiences for themselves and the critique of degraded techniques, including the use of drugs (pp. 105–108). Significantly, in "L'Impossible" Rimbaud affirms: "Je n'avais pas en vue la sagesse bâtarde du Coran" (I did not have in mind the illegitimate wisdom of the Koran).

8. For beautiful commentary linking the *Derniers Vers* and the *Saison* to the spiritual experience and symbolism (dark night, castles, burning intensity) of Christian mystics, especially John of the Cross, Theresa of Avila, and Pascal, see Houston, *Design of*

Rimbaud's Poetry, pp. 126–136; and Starkie, *Arthur Rimbaud,* pp. 159–212. Starkie also emphasizes the alchemical component, while R. C. Zaehner, *Mysticism Sacred and Profane: An Inquiry into Some Varieties of Praeter-natural Experience* (Oxford: Clarendon Press, 1957), pp. 50–83, stresses Rimbaud's nature mysticism. Bonnefoy, *Rimbaud par lui-même,* pp. 63–72, evokes the religious nature of Rimbaud's quest in "Délires II," the *Derniers Vers,* and throughout the *Saison.* Note, however, Rimbaud's debunking of the mystical in "Entends comme brame" and my article "*Entends comme brame* and the Theme of Death in Nature in Rimbaud's Poetry," *French Review,* 43 (1970), 407–417. For my discussion in the next paragraph of the motifs of insect, light, excrement, see also my essay, "Rimbaud's *Images immondes,*" *French Review,* 40 (1967), 505–517.

9. Rimbaud's writing here is close to the elements William James felt most characteristic of the mystic: ineffability, noetic quality (the feeling of superior revelation), transiency, and passivity. See James, *The Varieties of Religious Experience: A Study in Human Nature* (New York and London: Collier Macmillan, 1977), pp. 299–300.

10. Blake, *Marriage of Heaven and Hell, Complete Writings,* p. 154; Nietzsche, *Dawn, Werke,* I, 1024. Despite Nietzsche's attack on ecstasy (*Ekstase*), frenzy or inebriation (*Rausch*), and madness (*Wahnsinn*) in *Dawn* (*Werke,* I, 1022–58), his work shows a persistently positive view of similar experiences as uniting animality, lucidity, and creativity. See *The Birth of Tragedy,* chaps. 1–8 and the introduction Nietzsche added to it in 1886, and the *Genealogy of Morals, The Twilight of the Idols,* and certain formulations in *Dawn* (*Werke,* I, 13, 1022–24, 1192–93; II, 785–788, 994–997, 1024–25, 1030–32).

My discussion to the end of this section also draws on N. Kershaw Chadwick, "Shamanism Among the Tatars of Central Asia," *Journal of the Royal Anthropological Institute of Great Britain and Ireland,* 66 (1936), 75–112, and *Poetry and Prophecy* (Cambridge: Cambridge University Press, 1952); Brown, *Life Against Death,* p. 158, following F. M. Cornford, *Principium Sapientiae,*

The Origins of Greek Philosophical Thought (Cambridge: Cambridge University Press, 1952), pp. 88–127; Mircea Eliade, *Shamanism: Archaic Techniques of Ecstasy,* tr. Willard R. Trask (Princeton: Princeton University Press, 1972); Aldous Huxley, *Moksha, Writings on Psychedelics and the Visionary Experience (1931–1963),* ed. Michael Horowitz and Cynthia Palmer (New York: Stonehill Publishing Co., 1977), especially pp. 22–25, 60, 90–91, 121, 124–128, 190–209; W. K. C. Guthrie, *The Greeks and Their Gods* (London: Methuen, 1950), pp. 145–182, arguing against the idealized presentation of Walter F. Otto, *Dionysus, Myth and Cult,* tr. Robert Palmer (Bloomington: Indiana University Press, 1965); Fischer, "Cartography of Inner Space," in *Altered States of Consciousness,* pp. 1–57.

11. My argument is in partial agreement with Bays, who overstates Rimbaud's "confusion of ways," linking him almost exclusively to a nocturnal Illuminist tradition that is viewed as masking the true, mystic way. See Bays, *Orphic Vision,* especially pp. 3–30, 221–229, 243–247.

12. Chapters 1–8, especially 5 and 6, are relevant to Rimbaud's letters. For my argument throughout this section, see *Werke,* I, 117, 133, 1090–93, 1179; II, 438, 579–581, 615–616, 645–647, 957–961, 1024–25. See also Blake, letter to Thomas Butts, 22 November 1802, as well as *Milton* and *Jerusalem;* Hölderlin, "Brod und Wein" and "Patmos"; Coleridge, *The Complete Poetical Works of Samuel Taylor Coleridge,* ed. E. H. Coleridge, 2 vols. (Oxford: Clarendon Press, 1912); *Coleridge's Shakespearean Criticism,* ed. Thomas Middleton Raysor (Cambridge, Mass.: Harvard University Press, 1930), 2 vols., I. 184–185, and II, 263; *The Notebooks of Samuel Taylor Coleridge,* ed. Kathleen Coburn (New York: Pantheon Books, 1957–1973), 3 vols., I, nos. 1421, 1554, 1575, 1770; II, no. 2086; *Coleridge's Miscellaneous Criticism,* ed. Thomas Middleton Raysor (London: Constable and Co., 1936), pp. 209–210, 387, 389; *Biographia Literaria,* ed. J. Shawcross (Oxford: Clarendon Press, 1907), 2 vols., chap. 13, also I, 77, 225; Table Talk, 23 June, 1834, in *The Complete Works of Samuel Taylor Coleridge,* ed. W.

G. T. Shedd (New York: Harper and Bros., 1854), 7 vols., VI, 517–518; *The Statesman's Manual,* Appendix C, in *Lay Sermons, The Collected Works of Samuel Taylor Coleridge,* ed. R. J. White (London and Princeton: Routledge and Kegan Paul, 1972), VI, 80; and my article, "Toward a Model of Ecstatic Poetry: Coleridge's 'Kubla Khan' and Rimbaud's 'Villes I' and 'Barbare,' " *Modern Language Studies,* 12 (1982), 42–58.

For Keats, see letter to George and Thomas Keats, December 1817, and "Sleep and Poetry," "Ode to a Nightingale," "Ode on a Grecian Urn," "The Fall of Hyperion," in *Selected Poems and Letters,* ed. Douglas Bush (Boston: Houghton Mifflin, 1951); Mallarmé, letter to Henri Cazalis, 14 May, 1867, *Correspondance,* ed. Henri Mondor, Jean-Pierre Richard, Lloyd J. Austin, 5 vols. (Paris: Gallimard, 1959–1981), I, 240–244; Yeats, "The Statues," "Byzantium," *A Vision;* Paul De Man, "Structure intentionelle de l'image romantique," *Revue Internationale de Philosophie,* 14 (1960), 68–84. See also the extensive list of possible sources or analogues cited by Bays, *Orphic Vision,* pp. 166–206, and Eigeldinger, "La Voyance avant Rimbaud," in Schaeffer, *Lettres du voyant,* pp. 9–107.

13. Fischer, "Cartography," p. 11. Although warnings about the unreliability of much "split-brain" argument—for example, Howard Gardner, "What We Know (and Don't Know) About the Two Halves of the Brain," *Harvard Magazine,* 80 (1978), 24–27—need to be kept in mind, Fischer derived his model from an extensive base of scientific experiment. See also Scharfstein, *Mystical Experience,* pp. 120–121; and Frankel, *Le Code Dantesque,* pp. 36–37, for succinct links between Dante, Rimbaud, and exalted states.

14. For the following discussion of ecstatic imagery, see Fischer, "Cartography," pp. 13–16, 18, 31–35, 37–39; Baudelaire, "Du Vin et du haschisch," *Œuvres complètes,* pp. 426–429; Frosch, *The Awakening of Albion,* pp. 136–150; Coleridge, *Notebooks,* I, 925, 1681; Huxley, *Moksha,* pp. 59, 61–66, 89, 91, 200–208, 278–281; Jean Houston, "Exploration and Uses of Altered States of Consciousness," *Altered States of Consciousness:*

Current Views and Research Problems, pp. 59–89; Scharfstein, *Mystical Experience,* pp. 118–121; Guthrie, *Greeks,* pp. 145–182; Otto, *Dionysus, Myth and Cult.*

15. See Nietzsche, *Werke,* I, 49–52; II, 996–997; Chadwick, *Poetry and Prophecy,* pp. 41–57; Eliade, *Shamanism,* pp. 236, 240–241, 252–253, 265, 314, 322, 510–511. Bersani (*Future for Astyanax,* pp. x, 5–7, 238 ff.) argues that the deconstructed, theatricalized self in the *Illuminations* is antivisionary and involves a "celebratory sense of the failure of idealistic vision." I disagree and argue that the visionary remains serious in Rimbaud ("Soir historique") and that nostalgia for a failed ecstatic project is not absent from the *Illuminations* ("Conte," "Villes I," "Vagabonds"); the texts I examine in the next section systematically pursue the ecstatic through structures that Bersani neglects.

16. Blake's *Milton* may be used to illustrate the contrast I am making. I do not wish to minimize the momentariness of Blake's deselved experience at the end of the work, nor the struggle to organize the narrative of the history of the universe, nor the illuminations which occur discontinuously, nor the redefinition of our experience of time and space. But *Milton* does build toward a reconstruction of the visionary apocalyptic reality and in this sense contrasts with Rimbaud's brief, deconstructed forms.

For the other authors in the following discussion of nineteenth- and twentieth-century ecstatic writing, see Charles Mauron, *Des Métaphores obsédantes au mythe personnel: Introduction à la psychocritique* (Paris: J. Corti, 1963), pp. 64–80, 148–156; Nerval, *Aurélia,* part 1, chap. 3, with its equation of visionary state and cataleptic trance; Fischer, "Cartography," pp. 10–12, 29, 43–44 on the "jammed computer states" of schizophrenia and catatonia in Nerval; Jean Laplanche, *Hölderlin et la question du père* (Paris: Presses Universitaires de France, 1961); Hölderlin, "Der Archipelagus," "Menons Klagen um Diotima," "Am Quel der Donau," "Germanien"; Yeats, "The Phases of the Moon"; Alethea Hayter, *Opium and the Romantic Imagination*

(Berkeley: University of California Press, 1968), especially pp. 191 ff., p. 363, n. 60; Patricia Adair, *The Waking Dream: A Study of Coleridge's Poetry* (New York: Barnes and Noble, 1968), pp. 108 ff.; R. C. Bald, "Coleridge and *The Ancient Mariner:* Addenda to *The Road to Xanadu,*" in *Nineteenth-Century Studies,* ed. Herbert Davis, William C. de Vane, R. C. Bald (Ithaca: Cornell University Press, 1940), pp. 1–45; John Beer, "Coleridge, the Wordsworths, and the State of Trance," *Wordsworth Circle,* 8 (1977), 121–138; Humphrey House, *Coleridge, The Clark Lectures 1951–52* (Philadelphia: Dufour, 1965), pp. 142–156; Charles I. Patterson, Jr., "The Daemonic in *Kubla Khan:* Toward Interpretation," *PMLA,* 89 (1974), 1033–42; Elisabeth Schneider, *Coleridge, Opium and "Kubla Khan"* (Chicago: University of Chicago Press, 1953); Maud Bodkin, *Archetypal Patterns in Poetry: Psychological Studies of Imagination* (London: Oxford University Press, 1971), pp. 90–114. See also "Kubla Khan," in *The Complete Poetical Works of Samuel Taylor Coleridge,* vol. 1; and my article, "Toward a Model of Ecstatic Poetry: Coleridge's 'Kubla Khan' and Rimbaud's 'Villes I' and 'Barbare.' "

In addition to the authors mentioned, a more complete survey would take note of Novalis: *Heinrich von Ofterdingen, Die Lehrlinge zu Sais, Hymnen an die Nacht, Geistliche Lieder,* many of the *Fragmente;* see especially the bodily-sexual-ecstatic element of pieces such as "Astralis" from *Heinrich* and the seventh of the *Geistliche Lieder,* in *Werke, Briefe, Dokumente,* ed. Ewald Wasmuth (Heidelberg: L. Schneider, 1953), 4 vols., I, 179–181, 425–426, 456–459. In Shelley we find Dionysian, uranian, city-jewel-architectural, and oceanic motifs throughout *Prometheus Unbound*—see II, iii; II, v; III, iii; IV, especially lines 280 ff., 332–337, 354–355. Relevant in Hugo's work are the concluding movements of *Les Contemplations,* the entirety of *La Légende des siècles,* in particular the pantheistic "Le Satyre." Among twentieth-century figures, André Breton is particularly relevant: the *Manifestes,* the poetry, *Nadja,* and especially the "entrée en transe" in the second of the "Ajours" in *Arcane 17,* Collection 10/18 (Paris, 1965), p. 148.

17. Concerning Rimbaud's knowledge of the *Haschischins* see *Œuvres*, pp. 495–496. On "Kubla Khan," see Bodkin, *Archetypal Patterns*, pp. 93–94.

18. Antoine Adam, "L'Enigme des *Illuminations*," *Revue des Sciences Humaines*, Nouvelle Série, fascicule 60 (1950), 221–245, reduces the text to a description of masturbation after excitement by an Oriental dancer.

19. See Osmond, *Illuminations*, pp. 157–159, as well as Albert Py, *Arthur Rimbaud: Illuminations* (Geneva: Droz, 1967), pp. 220–223. *Baou* means *puer* (to stink), contributing to the imagery of insects and odors (Bernard's note, *Œuvres*, p. 534).

20. Chadwick, *Poetry and Prophecy*, pp. 20–21. See also Brown, *Life Against Death*, p. 164 (quoted later in this paragraph) and pp. 175–176, as well as *Love's Body* and Marcuse's *Eros and Civilization*. For the polar imagery, see Coleridge's "Dejection" and "Ancient Mariner," and the end of "Génie." "Archetypal" assumes its full range of meaning here: historical (the literal connection between arctic landscape and shamanistic ecstasy), psychological (in the senses both of Fischer and Jung, as designating the symbolism accompanying exalted states and some elemental layer of the psyche), and literary (the recurrence of related imagery in Blake, Coleridge, Nietzsche, and Rimbaud).

21. See Fischer, "Cartography," pp. 13–14.

22. "Villes I" exemplifies what Osmond (*Illuminations*, p. 35) calls the *poème-fête* (poem-festival).

23. We observed a comparable phenomenon among child poems in "Aube." Note that the ecstatic part of "Villes I" is not without some reference to our normal world—for example, the expression "fleurs grandes comme nos armes et nos coupes" (flowers as big as our arms and goblets).

24. The relationship between ecstasy and debilitation has general relevance for Rimbaud, who repeatedly rebels against work and action (the first *voyant* letter, "Mauvais Sang,"

"Délires II," "L'Eclair." This theme illustrates Fischer's argument that the extremes of altered consciousness eliminate the will to motor activity in the real world ("Cartography," pp. 9–10, 35–40).

THREE. *Visions and Habitations: Nature, City, and Society*

1. This opening discussion of nature, city, and society draws on Lewis Mumford, *The City in History, Its Origins, Its Transformations, and Its Prospects* (New York: Harcourt, Brace and World, 1961); Henri Lefebvre, *La Révolution urbaine* (Paris: Gallimard, 1970); Raymond Williams, *The Country and the City* (New York: Oxford University Press, 1973); Pierre Citron, *La Poésie de Paris dans la littérature française de Rousseau à Baudelaire,* 2 vols. (Paris: Editions de Minuit, 1961); Friedrich Engels, *The Condition of the Working-Class in England, From Personal Observation and Authentic Sources,* in Karl Marx, Friedrich Engels, *Collected Works,* tr. R. Dixon et al., 15 vols. (New York: International Publishers, 1975—1980), IV, 295–596; Jacques Rougerie, *Paris libre 1871* (Paris: Editions du Seuil, 1971); Houston, *The Design of Rimbaud's Poetry,* pp. 21–24; Rousseau, *Emile* (the adieu to Paris at the end of book IV); Frohock, *Rimbaud's Poetic Practice,* p. 4. Materials of general interest on the city include David R. Weimer, *The City as Metaphor* (New York: Random House, 1966); the *Yale French Studies* issue "Paris in Literature," 32 (1964); and Burton Pike, *The Image of the City in Modern Literature* (Princeton: Princeton University Press, 1981).

2. For this and the following paragraph, see M. H. Abrams, *Natural Supernaturalism, Tradition and Revolution in Romantic Literature* (New York: Norton, 1973); E. A. Burtt, *The Metaphysical Foundations of Modern Science,* (Garden City, N.Y.: Doubleday, 1954); Alfred North Whitehead, *Science and the Modern World* (New York: Macmillan, 1944); Coleridge, *Biogra-*

phia Literaria, especially chap. 12; Etiemble and Gauclère, *Rimbaud;* François Ruchon, *Jean-Arthur Rimbaud, sa vie, son oeuvre, son influence* (Paris: H. Champion, 1929), especially p. 140; Sartre, *L'Etre et le néant, Essai d'ontologie phénoménologique* (Paris: Gallimard, 1943), "Faire et avoir," pp. 643–708; and previously cited works by Bachelard and J.-P. Richard.

3. *The German Ideology,* vol. I, *Critique of Modern German Philosophy According to its Representatives Feuerbach, B. Bauer and Stirner,* in Marx and Engels, *Collected Works,* vol. 5; Henri Lefebvre, *La Pensée marxiste et la ville* (Paris: Casterman, 1972), especially pp. 29–61; and on "Ce qu'on dit au poète," Kittang, *Discours et jeu,* pp. 79–80.

4. Henri de Bouillane de Lacoste, E. de Rougemont, and Georges Izambard, "Recherches sur les sources du *Bateau ivre* et de quelques autres poèmes de Rimbaud," *Mercure de France,* 15 August 1935, pp. 5–23.

5. Notably Richard in *Poésie et profondeur,* 209. See also Houston, *The Design of Rimbaud's Poetry,* p. 71.

6. Letter to Richard Woodhouse, 27 October 1818. For what follows on nature in writers other than Rimbaud, in addition to works explicitly mentioned, see Keats' odes, among them the "Ode to a Nightingale," quoted from *Selected Poems and Letters,* ed. Bush; Rousseau, seventh "promenade" of the *Rêveries* (for his relative valorizing of natural objects, to which he initially prefers the transcendent ecstasy of imaginative revery), book IX of the *Confessions;* Wordsworth, Preface to *Lyrical Ballads,* "She dwelt among the untrodden ways," "A slumber did my spirit seal," "Three years she grew in sun and shower"; Hölderlin, "Der Archipelagus," "Unter den Alpen gesungen," "Heimkunft," "Am Quel der Donau," "Die Wanderung," "Germanien," "Patmos," *Hyperion,* book I, second letter to Bellarmin; Lamartine, many of the poems in *Harmonies poétiques et religieuses;* Hugo, *Les Voix intérieures,* X, *Les Rayons et les ombres,* XXXIV, *Les Contemplations,* II, i, xiii, xxiii; Abrams, *Natural*

Supernaturalism; Joseph Warren Beach, *The Concept of Nature in Nineteenth-Century English Poetry* (New York: Pageant, 1956); Marcuse, *Eros and Civilization,* pp. 144–156. The phrases from Goethe's "Fragment über die Natur" used as an epigraph to this chapter come from Beach's translation, p. 277.

7. *Rimbaud's Poetic Practice,* pp. 10–15. On nature and the erotic in early Rimbaud lyrics, see Kittang, pp. 62–69.

8. Bonnefoy, *Rimbaud par lui-même;* Marc Eigeldinger, *Rimbaud et le mythe solaire.*

9. See not only the city in *The Prelude, Emile,* and the *Rêveries* but also Rousseau's comic description of coming upon a stocking factory amid sublime scenery (seventh "promenade" of the *Rêveries*) and Wordsworth's "On the projected Kendal and Windermere Railway," *Miscellaneous Sonnets,* III, xlv (the latter dating from quite late, 1844). For the contrast between laughing and somber landscapes, compare the passage in the seventh "promenade" with the fifth or with *Prelude,* VI, 489 ff.

10. Recall Rimbaud's angry and parodic version of similar motifs in letter to Ernest Delahaye, May 1873, during the composition of *Une Saison en enfer:* "O Nature! ô ma mere! . . . Je n'ai rien de plus à . . . dire, la contemplostate de la Nature m'absorculant tout entier. Je suis à toi, ô Nature, ô ma mère!" (O Nature! O my mother!; I have nothing more to say, the contemplostate of Nature absorbassing me completely. I am yours, O Nature, O my mother!). On the *Derniers Vers* see the excellent treatment by Bonnefoy, *Rimbaud par lui-meme,* pp. 61–87; Frohock, *Rimbaud's Poetic Practice,* pp. 132–161; Houston, *Design of Rimbaud's Poetry,* pp. 93–136.

11. See my *"Entends comme brame* and the Theme of Death in Nature in Rimbaud's Poetry," *French Review,* 43 (1970), 407–417.

12. "Structure intentionelle de l'image romantique," *Revue Internationale de Philosophie,* 14 (1960), 68–84.

13. Wordsworth, preface to *Lyrical Ballads* and the accompanying appendix. For the following argument on "Marine"

and "Mystique," see Sartre, *Qu'est-ce que la littérature?*, II (Paris: Gallimard, 1972), pp. 49–85; and Michael Polanyi, "What Is a Painting?," *The American Scholar*, 39 (1970), 655–669.

14. For my sketch in this paragraph and in the following pages of the presence of the city throughout the *Illuminations*, see again Lefebvre, *La Révolution urbaine;* Mumford, *The City in History*, especially p. 95 (quoted in this paragraph) and ff., 186, 202–203, 300, 344–430, 531–563.

15. In addition to texts mentioned in this summary of the oppressive city in the romantic tradition, see Rousseau, *Confessions*, book IV; *Emile*, book IV; the eighth "promenade" of the *Rêveries*. See also Blake, *Songs of Experience;* Wordsworth, *Prelude*, VII–VIII; Lamartine, "Les Preludes" (*Nouvelles Méditations poétiques*), "Bénédiction de Dieu" and "La Retraite" (*Harmonies poétiques et religieuses*), the septième vision of *La Chute d'un ange*, and the huitième époque of *Jocelyn;* Musset, "Lettre à M. de Lamartine" (*Poésies nouvelles*); Auguste Barbier, *Iambes et poèmes*. Hugo's treatment of the city is complex. Simple criticism of urban corruption and the desire to flee to nature are found from "Rêves," *Odes et ballades*, V, xxv, to banal versions of the same theme in *Chansons des rues et des bois* and *Dernière Gerbe*. This view is outweighed, however, by the continuing consciousness of Paris ("Bièvre," *Les Feuilles d'automne*, XXXIV) and the necessity of facing its moral and social significance ("Fonction du poète," *Les Rayons et les ombres*, I). Hugo celebrates Paris in *Les Chants du crépuscule*, I; *Les Voix intérieures*, IV; the self-parodic "Paris" written for the Exposition of 1867; and in his evocation of the siege and Commune of 1870–71 in *L'Année terrible*. But such celebration involves condemnation of the injustice embodied in the city: see *Les Chants du crépuscule*, VI; *Les Rayons et les ombres*, XXXI; *Les Contemplations*, III, ii; the description of poor children in Paris in *Les Misères* and *Les Misérables*. For the city in these and other writers, see Citron, *La Poésie de Paris dans la littérature française de Rousseau à Baudelaire*, and my article, "The Search for Community: The City in Hölderlin, Wordsworth, and Baudelaire," *Texas Studies in Literature and Language*, 13 (1971), 71–89.

16. Raymond Williams, *City and Country,* pp. 148–149, 232, discusses the varieties of movement within and above the city in Blake and Hardy. Among French novels, consider the movement by the characters throughout Paris, and their various dominating perspectives on the city, in Balzac's *Le Père Goriot* and Flaubert's *L'Education sentimentale,* as well as a pathetic version of the same motifs on Gervaise's wedding day in Zola's *L'Assommoir.*

17. For the material in the preceding two paragraphs, see Yeats, "Sailing to Byzantium"; Hugo, "Soleils couchants," II, III, V (*Les Feuilles d'automne,* XXXV), as well as *Les Orientales,* XXXVI; Gautier, "Notre-Dame," "Le Sommet de la tour," "Paris," in *Poésies complètes,* 2d ed., rev., ed. René Jasinski, 3 vols. (Paris: A.-G. Nizet, 1970). Note that even in the case of Mallarmé, study of "Les Fenêtres," "L'Azur," and "Quelle soie aux baumes de temps" indicates that the aspiration to the ideal is situated in an urban scene whose roles as human habitation, destroyer of nature, and political community are deftly evoked. For my argument in the following paragraph, see Blake, *Milton,* I, 6, 24 and 26, and II, 39; *The Four Zoas,* nights eighth and ninth; *Jerusalem,* I, especially 5, 10–16, and III, 53; see also Gautier, *Mademoiselle de Maupin,* preface and chaps. 2 and 11. We should also keep in mind the supernal and infernal city motifs in such visionary, postvisionary, or antivisionary works as Novalis' *Heinrich von Ofterdingen,* Nerval's *Aurélia* and *Voyage en Orient,* Lautréamont's *Les Chants de Maldoror* (chant deuxième), Breton's *Nadja,* Aragon's *Le Paysan de Paris,* Burroughs's *Naked Lunch,* and even perhaps Sartre's *La Nausée.*

18. For what follows the considerable body of excellent criticism on the city in Rimbaud is relevant. See Cohn, *Rimbaud;* Etiemble and Gauclère, *Rimbaud,* pp. 75, 141–142, 169–170, 188–195; Fowlie, *Rimbaud,* pp. 185–206; Gengoux, *Pensée poétique,* especially pp. 530–533; Kittang, *Discours et jeu,* pp. 96–97, 102–104, 232–245; Jacques Plessen, *Promenade et poésie, l'expérience de la marche et du mouvement dans l'œuvre de Rimbaud* (The Hague: Mouton, 1967), pp. 208–214; Whitaker, *Structure du monde imaginaire,* pp. 167–177; Wing, *Present Ap-*

pearances, pp. 95–111. See also Michael Riffaterre, "Sur la sémiotique de l'obscurité en poésie: 'Promontoire' de Rimbaud," *French Review,* 55 (1982), 625–632.

19. For my argument here, consider the *trompe-l'œil* urban descriptions in Robbe-Grillet's *Les Gommes* and *Dans le labyrinthe,* the fusion of sadosexual and urban motifs in *Projet pour une révolution à New York,* as well as Roland Barthes' championing of Robbe-Grillet in *Essais critiques* (Paris: Editions du Seuil, 1964) and his valuation of nonreferential, decentered forms of *écriture* in *S/Z* (Paris: Editions du Seuil, 1970), among other works. Kittang, *Discours et jeu,* pp. 160–180, 333–343, first valorizes positively the "Ma vie est usée!" passage that I discuss here, then later stresses the limitations and failures of Rimbaud's effort to deconstruct traditional forms of discourse.

20. The Cassagnac *père et fils* were bonapartist publicists, whose appeal to the memory of the soldiers of the *grande Révolution* infuriated the young but lucid Rimbaud. Despite sentimentalizing tendencies, this poem from the summer of 1870 is an impressive piece of poetic-political emotion.

21. For these late, politically pointed texts, see Osmond, *Illuminations,* pp. 151–152, 155–157; Baudry, "Le Texte de Rimbaud," *Tel Quel,* no. 36, pp. 46–53; Kittang, *Discours et jeu,* pp. 250–259, 322–329.

22. See Marcel-A. Ruff, *Rimbaud,* Connaissance des Lettres (Paris: Hatier, 1968), especially chaps. 3 and 4; Pierre Gascar, *Rimbaud et la Commune,* especially p. 45. One of the *Derniers Vers,* "Qu'est-ce pour nous" contains similar imagery to "Soir historique," without the sophistication of the later text nor its outrageous confidence. Indeed it ends on a plaintive statement of the speaker's utterly untransformed state: "Ce n'est rien! j'y suis! j'y suis toujours" (It's nothing! I'm here! I'm still here!).

23. See Richard, *Poésie et profondeur,* pp. 189–190; see also *Œuvres,* pp. 350–352. Richard has little to say about the political and ideological aspects of the poem nor does Cohn in his otherwise fine commentary on this text (*Rimbaud,* pp. 191–194).

Index

Designer: Janet Wood
Compositor: Huron Valley Graphics
Printer: Braun-Brumfield, Inc.
Binder: Braun-Brumfield, Inc.
Text: 12/14 Garamond
Display: Garamond